TH

First published in 1997 by
Sports Publishing, Inc.
804 N. Neil
Champaign, IL 61820

Cover layout by Kenny O'Brien
Front cover design by Christine Checinski
Front cover illustration by Greg Gaenzle
Photos by Bryant McMurray and LaDon George

The information in this book is true and complete to the best of our knowledge. All recommendations are made without any guarantees on the part of authors or the publisher, who disclaim any liability incurred in connection with the use of this data or specific details.

We recognize that some words, model names and designations, for example, mentioned herein are the property of the trademark holder. We use them for identification purposes only. This is not an official publication.

ISBN: 1-58261-317-6

Printed and bound in the United States of America.

Tim Bongard has been a Richard Petty fan since his Dad introduced him to stock car racing when he was a young boy. Always fascinated with racing and how things worked, Tim found hobbies such as photography, model building, and writing natural ways of understanding and appreciating more about racing. As a result, he has worked extensively in the photographic industry, written many how-to articles and features, and won numerous awards for his models.

Robert W. (Bill) Coulter has had a fascination with the automobile since he was a child. He is a dedicated Richard Petty fan, a collector of Petty paraphernalia and a self-proclaimed Petty historian. Coulter earned a bachelor of science degree in design from the University of Cincinnati. He worked in industry for the next 30 years for Mead Corporation, Eastman-Kodak and AM International as a creative staff professional. He has operated Complex Communications since 1990 specializing in creative writing, advertising, marketing, and corporate communications.

For 25 years, Bill Coulter has been a free-lance writer and photographer for several automotive publications. Coulter was introduced to Richard Petty during a trip to Daytona in 1972. He credits that meeting with opening up opportunities to exercise his skills as a writer and photographer in motorsports. Bill lives in Xenia, Ohio with Gail, his wife of 32 years.

Dedication

and Thanks

This book is lovingly dedicated to our wives, Maureen Bongard and Gail Coulter, whose endless support and love have made the long hours and hard work easier by their caring.

As in the fulfillment of any dream, ***The Cars of the King*** exists because of some wonderful people and their desire to see this book become a reality. The authors would like to thank each and every one of those who have helped us and aided our efforts for their help and support.

Thanks for all the staff at Petty Enterprises, especially Martha Jane Bonkmeyer, Barbara Davis, Ann Fogelman, Doris Gammons, Julia Groce, and Louise Loflin for their patience, hospitality and cooperation. Special thanks to Dale Inman for spending time with us and allowing us to pick his brain.

Kind thanks are owed to Kathy Thompson as well, for her encouragement and support and for working so well with us. Thanks also to Buddy Smith for his hospitality and friendship.

Our special thanks for Ken Schiess for his belief in the dream when it was first hatched and Rob Ehrgott for nurturing its development.

This project simply wouldn't have happened *at all* without the efforts of Jimmy Martin of Petty Enterprises and Curtis Rice of Realistic Racing Colors. They believed in what we were doing and made sure that the message was heard. ***The Cars of the King*** is a reality in no small measure due to their personal efforts on our behalf and they have our heartfelt thanks.

Not surprisingly, the biggest thank you goes to Richard Petty himself. Thanks for allowing us the privilege of telling the story of ***The Cars of the King.***

When all is said and done, there is one giver of dreams, one giver of the desire to try, one giver of grace when you fail, one who brings you safely across the finish line and one who always holds us all in the palm of his hand.

Soli Deo Gloria.

Tim Bongard and Bill Coulter

Over the years, I've had lots of folks ask us all sorts of questions about the cars I drove. People sometimes amaze me with what they remember about me and those cars, and real often they will ask questions about things that were forgotten about a long time ago. In racing, we are constantly working on our cars, finding ways to make them better. Changes most of the time come gradually — although I guess NASCAR does make enough of their own that can change things pretty quick. Even then, it's back to refining things and making those changes. What I'm saying is sometimes it's hard putting your finger on when or how some of these things happened. Somebody ought to write them all down.

Then there is the odd stuff that we tried for a while and didn't keep using. In '68 we tried running the car with the top painted black and everyone thought it was a vinyl top. Stranger still was the white top we used later that year. Most everybody has forgotten about that deal. I have a hard enough time remembering all the neat stuff that has happened to me, let alone all the neat stuff we've tried with the cars over the years.

I guess that's what makes a book like this so interesting. This isn't just another story about me. Lord knows we don't need another book on Richard Petty. This is a book about the race cars that have come out of the shops here at Petty Enterprises. There's stuff here that hasn't been seen by our fans for a long, long time. And there are some stories about those cars and the folks that put 'em together that ought to be told. That's what this book is all about.

This book is like a big photo album of all the cars we've run since Daddy's time, so if you're a race fan, you will really get a kick out of seeing how stock cars developed from cars driven right off the showroom floor to the fancy cars we run today.

If you're one of those folks who likes models of race cars, then this book is for you too. You won't find a better deal for learning to do it right. Back in the sixties, I used to come home from a hard day working on the race cars and actually build model cars as a way to relax after the kids were in bed. I worked on the big ones all day and then the little bitty ones at night. It's been a long time since I've actually built a model, but I can tell you I think it's a mighty fine hobby — and you ought to see some of the things these cats nowadays are building. We have a ton of models in the museum sent to us from folks all over the world and it looks like that deal is gonna be around for a right good while.

I've been very lucky in my life to be surrounded by some very dedicated people. Working with good people makes everything better. But the thing that has made it even easier is the love and dedication of our fans. This book is for you.

Richard Petty
Level Cross, NC

Table of Contents

INTRODUCTION

by Tim Bongard

Bill Coulter and I have been Richard Petty fans for more than 25 years, and we are constantly looking for illustrations and information about the cars he drove during his long career. Many books contain highlights of his career — bits and pieces actually — but no single volume showed us all the fascinating things either of us wanted to know. What were the first cars he drove? Was his number always 43? When did they start painting the cars Petty Blue? The list goes on and on. The more we researched, the more we realized that large portions of the King's career are obscure, a mystery to the legions of stock car racing fans and modelers who have discovered the sport in recent years.

Though topics such as Richard's 1964 championship season are well covered, information about his 1963 season is hard to come by. Richard drove a Barracuda drag car during the 1965 Chrysler boycott of NASCAR — but try finding out what he drove when the boycott ended. There are many photos of Richard leading the 1962 Daytona 500, but very little prior to that. When the Charger was phased out and the switch was made to the Dodge Magnum in 1978, what did Richard end up driving? Was there something wrong with the Magnum? In the years that followed, how did Petty Enterprises end up with Pontiac? For the diehard race fan or modeler — for the diehard Petty fan or modeler— these questions and gaps can be either exasperating or the source of an endless treasure hunt.

Filling in the gaps not only helps complete the picture for an amazing career of racing's most popular driver, or provide information for enthusiasts, but also helps trace the history of the great sport that has come to be known as stock car racing. By studying the careers of Lee and Richard, you automatically trace NASCAR's growth and see how the sport developed from the racing of showroom stock cars to the specialized supercars we have today. By following the race cars of the Pettys through history, you discover when window nets came into use, when quick-fill fuel couplings were first allowed, and when the first fuel cell was used. The Cars of the King will answer these questions and more.

There is something else you will find and see as you comb through these pages and all this history. You will discover, as we did, that it is impossible to separate the man from his machines, or vice-versa. Though this is very much a book about the cars of Petty Enterprises, it is still the story of how a man and his family have lived through the ups and downs, joys and sorrows, defeats and victories of life in their chosen profession. What makes Richard and the Pettys so special is that they in many ways are just everyday folks like you and me who struggle through difficulties like everyone else. Richard has had to make some tough decisions and go to work hurt. He's had some situations go completely awry and has had to work through them all. I think what makes Richard so special to so many folks is the unbounded poise, calm, and peace he seems to possess. In a day and age when other superstars are unapproachable, Richard still manages to stay available to the legions of fans, both young and old — even when he's having a really bad day.

I think you will come to agree with us on this — Richard's skill as a race car driver earned him a place in the record books, the title of "King of Stock Car Racing," and the admiration of legions of fans. However, it's the way he lives his life that has earned our continued devotion and respect. We all, drivers and fans, would do well to follow Richard's winning ways both on and off the track.

THE CARS OF
THE KING
RICHARD PETTY

Design/layout and production:
Christina Checinski

Production coordinator/consultant:
Ken Schiess

Cover illustration:
Greg Gaenzle

The Petty dynasty begins

The Lee Petty Years

Lee leads a group of cars past the photographers in the infield in a race from 1950. Petty's lightweight Plymouth didn't have the power of some of the other cars, but tended to be more durable.
Richard Petty Private Collection

Who could have dreamed that a middle-aged North Carolina truck driver would found one of the world's best-known racing dynasties? It's doubtful Lee Arnold Petty at age 35 had any idea his love of tinkering with mechanical things and an early interest in racing would lead to fame, fortune, and world-wide celebrity for the whole Petty clan.

Race cars weren't a common sight in the Southeast during the early years of the 20th century. If you wanted to see "real" race cars you needed to go to California, New York state, or the Midwest. And of course, many people thought "real" race cars didn't have fenders!

Before World War II, the Carolinas, Tennessee, and Kentucky were rural areas with little heavy industry, dependent primarily on agriculture. It was easy to raise a crop of corn "up the hollar," but it was a completely different proposition if you couldn't afford to get it to market. Home-brewing whiskey was the simplest way to "harvest" your corn crop, and transporting it in the trunks of souped-up cars became the quickest way to get the product to your customers. The stretch of two-lane highway from Harlan, Kentucky, to Bearden, Tennessee, was the early breeding ground for fearless drivers, top mechanics, and very fast cars, according to Alex Gabbard's *Return to Thunder Road.*

After the war the federal government cracked down on unauthorized production and sale of homemade whiskey. For the Feds, there was one overriding element missing from this basic, uncomplicated system of inter-state commerce — nobody was paying any taxes.

Lee Petty paces the 1959 Daytona 500 in his 1959 Oldsmobile. Hard tops lined up on the inside while the convertibles lined up on the outside.
Richard Petty Private Collection

The distillation and sales of illegal "moonshine" proved to be not only a lucrative business but also a seriously unhealthful one — high-speed chases while sometimes dodging hot lead. Rivalries developed among the moonshiners, and when the guys with the fast cars weren't "doin' business," they held midnight road races where a few thousand dollars could change hands as well. Others who knew how to make cars go fast often joined in the action. Lee Petty admits that when he wasn't operating the family trucking business, he participated in a few of

these late-night races — and won his share of the bounty.

Eventually these nocturnal events evolved into more organized free-for-alls in someone's cow pasture, complete with paying spectators, large fields of cars, and the typical shady promoters. Lee Petty and his brother Julie paid to watch a few of these early races and decided they could do at least as well or maybe even better than what they saw. After building a 1937 Plymouth with a Chrysler inline engine, Lee Petty won the first race he entered and finished well in a few others he competed in.

A transplanted northern promoter and sometime driver Bill France, Sr., and a few of his friends met about the same time in Daytona Beach, Florida, to lay the groundwork of a "strictly stock" racing series for brand-new American-built cars. They named the

Lee takes a break in his 1955 Chrysler. If you look carefully, you can see a very rudimentary roll bar and brace behind the front seat.
Richard Petty Private Collection

new series the "National Association for Stock Car Auto Racing" (NASCAR). It was the first sanctioning body to bring supervision and organization to the racing in the Southeast.

The Pettys realized their Plymouth coupe was not suited for the new series. Since Lee didn't have a new car to race, a family friend lent his new 1948 Buick Roadmaster to Petty, hearing promises of great fortunes to be made. Lee's pit crew consisted of his wife, Elizabeth, and sons Richard and Maurice. He loaded up the family in the borrowed car, threw in a few tools for good measure, and headed for Charlotte, North Carolina.

The first NASCAR race for Lee Petty and the big Buick was at the Charlotte Speedway (long since gone), June 19, 1948. Thirty-two cars of all makes, shapes, and sizes started

on the one-mile clay oval; the drivers included such legendary figures as Red Byron, Bob, Tim and Fonty Flock, Bill Blair, Buck Baker, Curtis Turner, Joe Weatherly, and of course Lee Petty.

Early in the race, as Petty moved his mammoth mount toward the lead position, the sway bar let go. The Buick swerved and barrel-rolled four times, spewing parts and pieces in all directions. When the pile of crumpled metal finally came to rest, Lee Petty emerged with only a minor cut. However, one look at the condition of the borrowed car and he felt really sick.

This inaugural experience taught the Pettys an important lesson — bigger (and powerful) isn't always better! The Buick was much too heavy for the rigors of dirt track racing. They decided on the spot to look for a much lighter and more nimble car. By 1949 Petty was racing a new six-cylinder, 97 horsepower Plymouth coupe. Though no powerhouse, the little coupe proved to be the right combination. Lee Petty established a kinship with Plymouth that became a trademark for much of his career and set a pattern for the family racing activities for many decades.

Lee didn't always drive white cars or blue cars. His red and white 1956 Dodge is shown here on Langhorne's unique circular track in April 1956.
Ray Masser

In 1955, Lee drove a Chrysler 300-B, shown here at Langhorne, Pennsylvania. Ray Masser

Lee stands next to his 1954 Chrysler on the beach at Daytona. Petty won the race on the 4.1-mile beach course in this car. Jack Cansler via the Richard Petty Private Collection

SIGNIFICATA

1949

- The first Strictly Stock race is held on a 3/4 mile Charlotte Speedway dirt track in Charlotte, NC. Jim Roper wins in a '49 Lincoln. Lee Petty finishes 17th after wrecking the Buick Roadmaster he was driving.

- Lincoln, Olds, and Plymouth all win their first Grand National races.

- Lee Petty's first win comes at the half-mile Heidelburg Speedway in Pittsburgh, PA on October 2, 1949. He finishes a full five laps ahead of the rest of the field in his lightweight Plymouth.

- The Strictly Stock Division will be renamed the Grand National Division by the end of the first season.

- Oldsmobile begins a horsepower race by fitting its biggest engine into its smallest car.

- Races are held at Martinsville and North Wilkesboro among other tracks.

- Driving an Olds 88, Red Byron wins the series Championship run in eight races. Lee Petty finishes second in points.

1950

- NASCAR's official rules were first published on a single sheet of paper and were shockingly brief. The rules included: Cars limited to the 1946 through 1950 model years and must have complete bodies, fenders, hood, etc.; headlights removed or covered with masking tape; muffler must be removed; rear seat cushions must be removed; front seat must be intact; doors must be strapped shut. While wheels, hubs, and some steering and parts were allowed to be reinforced, most other items had to be stock and unchanged.

- Darlington International Speedway opens to become the circuit's first super-speedway.

- Ford wins its first Grand National race.

- Driving an Olds 88, Bill Rexford wins the Grand National Championship over the course of 19 races. Lee Petty finishes third in points.

Lee Petty took to his new occupation of race driver as though born to it. His consistency was legendary. Lee Petty never finished lower in the points chase for the NASCAR Grand National (now Winston Cup) Championship title than fourth during the decade 1949 through 1959. He didn't fall from the top five in season's points until 1960. During that ten-year stretch, Lee Petty won the championship three times. His first title came in 1954. He added a second in 1958, and his third and final title in 1959.

Lee Petty's success came for the most part on the short tracks. The official records credit Petty with 54 career wins. In 1954 he won 12 times. That season he finished 34 times in the top five. In 1958 Petty won seven times, with 28 top fives and 43 top tens in 50 races. Again there was consistency in 1959. There were 11 wins, 27 top fives, and 32 top tens in 42 events. In 1960 Lee won only three times, but his season's earnings nearly matched the previous year's — an indication that the prize money per event was on the rise due to the construction of super speedways like Atlanta and Charlotte.

Victories at classic races like the Southern 500 won't be found on Lee Petty's résumé. But he will best be remembered for winning the inaugural Daytona 500 in 1959. After a near-dead-heat, three-car finish among Johnny Beauchamp, Petty, and Joe Weatherly at the start-finish line, NASCAR spent three days studying

Power sliding the cars through the dirt was all part of racing back then. Here Lee pursues the #87 1954 Olds 88 driven by Buck Baker. Ray Masser

Lee strikes a pose with his 1956 Dodge. Note the cracked windshield and the nifty hood securing device used then. Richard Petty Private Collection

finish-line photos and finally declared Petty the winner.

The year 1961 was pivotal in the life, times, and career of Lee Petty. The newly reskinned 1961 Plymouths didn't seem to handle well on the high banks in practice for the Daytona 500.

Lee poses with one of the 1960 Plymouths fielded by Petty Engineering. Jim Paschal usually piloted the #44 car that season. Richard Petty Private Collection

A young Richard poses with his driver father. Lee is sitting in one of the convertibles they raced in the convertible division NASCAR had in the late '50s and early '60s. NASCAR photo via the Richard Petty Private Collection

Lee's NASCAR Grand National career had a less than grand start. This Buick Roadmaster he was driving was the prized possession of a neighbor who had loaned him the car for the race. The Richard Petty Private Collection

Lee poses beside his 1959 Oldsmobile that won the inaugural Daytona 500. Note the use of a truck-style hood latch near Lee's left hand and the towing ball on the front bumper of the car.
Richard Petty Private Collection

NUGGETS

The Forgotten Side of Lee Petty

Most race fans nowadays don't remember the early years of stock car racing since we were either in diapers or not even born yet. Most of us can't remember a time when all other racers were measured against the stature of Richard Petty. But there was a time when even Richard was measured against another champion — Lee Petty.

Lee was one of the original big names in the sport during those early years and set some pretty high standards. In his years of competitive driving, Lee never finished lower than sixth in the points and won the championship three times — the first man to do so. He not only won 53 races in his career, but was voted the most popular driver by fans on numerous occasions. Yet the media has been hard on Lee over the years, preferring to let his son take the limelight. Perhaps Lee was the sport's first Dale Earnhardt — you either loved him or hated him, but God could he drive a racecar!

During the qualifying races, both Lee and son Richard "left the park," crashing through the guard rails and into the parking lot in different skirmishes. Richard Petty wasn't hurt, but his daddy didn't fare nearly as well.

Johnny Beauchamp and Lee Petty tangled going into a corner trying to avoid a spinning Banjo Matthews. The collision propelled Petty's number 42 Plymouth through the fence with a wide-open throttle at 150-plus mph. The flying race car finally landed in the parking lot, having shed its engine and virtually every piece of sheet metal that could be jarred loose.

Lee Petty somehow survived this near-fatal accident. He spent the next four months in the hospital after two surgeries to repair a punctured lung and a mangled left leg. For the most part Lee Petty's competitive career was at an end. Though he did drive a race car again in late 1961 and a few more times through mid-1964, he never again had the competitive drive and desire to "let it all hang out" that spurred him to success earlier in his racing career. Lee Petty's last ride was at Watkins Glen, July 19, 1964.

In a short but productive racing career, Lee Petty drove several makes of cars. After his first NASCAR race in a 1948 Buick we mentioned earlier, he spent 1949 through 1952 behind the wheel of Plymouth coupes. In 1953 Lee drove a hemi-powered Chrysler on the beach course at Daytona but then switched to a 1953 Dodge, lighter than the Chrysler but still hemi-powered.

Lee drove the newly designed 1955 Dodge for that season and continued with Dodge for the 1956 campaign. Oldsmobile made the Pettys a deal they couldn't refuse for the 1957 season, and they ran an 88 two-door hardtop for most of the season, along with a topless version for the convertible series events. Petty continued with the '57 Oldsmobiles through the 1958 season, even though Oldsmobile by this time wasn't providing as much assistance.

Lee and grandson Kyle at Riverside in 1981.
Bob Tronolone

LEE'S 1959 DAYTONA 500 WINNER — 1959 OLDSMOBILE

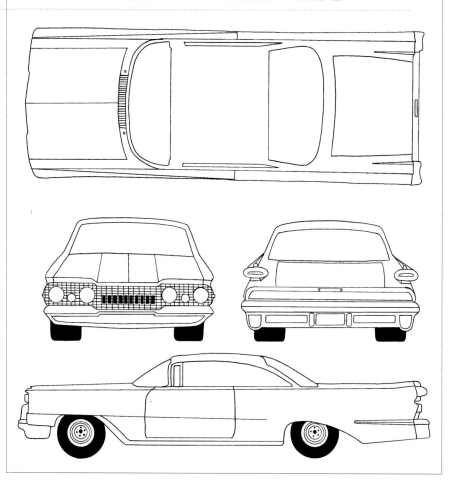

With Dodge's first V-8 engine, the '53 Dodge allowed Lee Petty to run with the bigger and more powerful cars on the circuit at the time. The Richard Petty Private Collection

SIGNIFICATA

1951

- Hudson, Nash, Studebaker, and Chrysler nameplates all win their first Grand National races.
- Chrysler introduces the Hemi-headed Firepower V-8.
- Driving a Hudson Hornet, Herb Thomas wins the Grand National Championship over the course of 41 races. Lee Petty finishes fourth in points.

1952

- Driving a Hudson Hornet, Tim Flock wins the Grand National Championship over the course of 34 races. Lee Petty finishes third in points.

1953

- Roll-over bars are recommended for competitors and required on cars without a center door pillar.
- When the headlight is removed, the hole must be covered over with sheet metal.
- Straight exhaust pipes exiting the rear of the car are recommended.
- Hudson introduces the 7X dual-carburetor engine at the request of NASCAR drivers. This is one of the first instances of direct factory support.
- Dodge wins its first Grand National race.
- Driving a Hudson Hornet, Herb Thomas wins his second Grand National Championship over the course of 37 races. Lee Petty finishes second in points.

1954

- Bungee cords and bolts are used to help hold hoods closed.
- Dodge, Ford, and Mercury receive their first overhead valve V-8 engines. The flathead becomes a dinosaur.
- Chrysler introduces the first 300hp regular production automobile, the Chrysler 300.
- Driving a Chrysler 300, Lee Petty wins the Grand National Championship over the course of 37 races.

The Lee Petty Years

After driving a new Olds 88 coupe in the 1959 Daytona 500, Lee Petty decided it was far too heavy and bulky a car for the shorter tracks. So once again Plymouth got the call from Petty Enterprises for the remainder of the 1959 season. Of course, by this time the team was running a two-car operation full-time, with eldest son Richard piloting the second car. The two Pettys alternated between a 1959 Plaza two-door post sedan and a Savoy two-door hardtop.

Lee Petty finished out his career driving Plymouths, in 1960 and 1961 at the wheel of a two-door hardtop Belvedere, and in 1962 in a Savoy two-door post sedan.

Lee Petty's final victory came on the road course at the Citrus 250 during Speed Weeks in 1961. Petty drove a blue four-door Plymouth Valiant, number 44, to the win, holding off a final lap charge by Glen "Fireball" Roberts in a four-cylinder Pontiac Tempest.

The success enjoyed by Lee Petty in his short but brilliant career laid the framework for the Petty Enterprises juggernaut just over the horizon. One can only ponder what Lee Petty might have accomplished with a few more years of racing. But his decision to go racing at 35 years of age dramatically changed the face of American motorsports forever.

SIGNIFICATA

1955

- Plymouth, Chevrolet, and Pontiac all receive their first overhead valve V-8 engines.
- Chevrolet wins its first Grand National race.
- Driving a Chrysler, Tim Flock wins his second Grand National Championship over the course of 45 races. Lee Petty finishes third in points.

1956

- Ford hires Pete De Paolo to organize a factory-backed racing effort.
- Martinsville Speedway is paved.
- Driving a Chrysler, Buck Baker wins the Grand National Championship over the course of 56 races. Lee Petty finishes fourth in points.

1957

- Ford introduces a supercharged version of their 312 cubic inch Y-block to counter Chevy's new fuel-injected 283 cubic inch small-block.
- GM President Red Curtice persuades the AMA to ban factory-backed racing programs.
- Holman and Moody is formed when De Paolo leaves Ford. Ford pulls out of racing shortly afterwards.
- NASCAR runs for the first time at the road course at Watkins Glen, NY.
- North Wilkesboro is paved between the first race and second races held there that year.
- After switching to a Chevrolet, Buck Baker wins the Grand National Championship over the course of 53 races. Lee Petty finishes fourth in points.

1958

- Goodyear enters NASCAR racing and a tire war with Firestone begins.
- Ford and Chevrolet both introduce their "big-block" engines.
- NASCAR runs for the first time at the road course at Riverside, California.
- Nashville is added to the Grand National circuit.
- Driving an Olds 88, Lee Petty wins his second Grand National Championship over the course of 51 races. Richard competes in nine races, has one top-ten finish, and places 36th on the points list.

A 1956 photo shows Lee posing with his crew in front of his Dodge. Richard sits on Lee's left while Maurice is on Lee's right. The Richard Petty Private Collection

Lee races past the camera in his 1957 Oldsmobile. The Richard Petty Private Collection

Lee sits in the cockpit of one of his later race cars. Note the Bell helmet and the modified dash panel. The Richard Petty Private Collection

The convertible division gives Richard his start

A Humble Beginning

For Richard Lee Petty, eldest son of Lee Arnold Petty, it wasn't so much if he would follow his father into the driver's seat of a NASCAR Grand National stock car but when he would try his hand at the occupation his father was so successful in. Richard Petty literally grew up as a part of the sights, sounds, and aurora of the birthing of what was to become America's most popular non-betting spectator sport.

Richard found a place in the family racing operation by performing all the gritty nuts-and-bolts jobs that any entry-level employee would be expected to do. He very naturally worked his way up through the family organization, acquiring basic working knowledge of the rudimentary aspects of tearing apart and rebuilding engines, transmissions, rear ends, pounding out the kinks and wrinkles from battle-damaged fenders and doors, and learning how to tune, set up, and prepare racing stock cars for competition. Understandably, he chased his share of parts and swept his allotment of shop floors along the way as well.

Richard Petty had the opportunity to see many parts of the United States by traveling often with his father to the Midwest, the West Coast, and up and down the Eastern seaboard, including New England, plus many treks into Canada. These were the infant days of NASCAR, the barnstorming days when rugged drivers

Richard stands in the cockpit of his 1957 Olds convertible. Note how the hood is held closed with hasps and a bungee cord. Richard Petty Private Collection

competed in 90 to 100 events a season and raced two, three, four, or more times a week — often with a great distance between one event and another and many times driving all night to get there!

Occasionally, young Richard Petty, traveling solo, would "deliver" a fresh race car to his father, sometimes pushing on for days to meet up with the family breadwinner in some far-off location. Afterward, Richard was alone again on the road, returning the "used" equipment to the reaper shed

race car shop and the friendly confines of the Petty compound in North Carolina. The task of driving a race car, thinly disguised as a street-driven machine, on the public highways across open country forced young Petty to call upon every resource he could muster. The prospect of suddenly being alone with all that responsibility must have forced Richard Petty to grow up quickly.

Shortly after getting his highway driver's license, Richard suggested to his father, Lee, that he might be

interested in trying his hand at the competitive driving side of the family business. Lee, who had not started his spectacular career until comparatively late in life, told his eldest son to wait until he was 21. He felt Richard needed a bit more seasoning and probably hoped he might have a different perspective on things by that time.

Not long after turning the legal age of 21, Richard again approached his dad with the same question about his future in racing. Young Petty had decided it was time for him to give it a go and find out if he too might be happier as a driver than as just his father's mechanic. This time the answer was different. Lee's indirect response was to simply motion toward a much-used '57 Oldsmobile convertible sitting idle in the corner of the shop, suggesting Richard could use it.

On July 12, 1958, only ten days after his 21st birthday, Richard Petty and his cousin Dale Inman towed the old convertible behind his '56 Dodge to Columbia, South Carolina, for a 100-miler on the half-mile dirt track. Thus began one of the most celebrated careers in all of motorsports. Richard drove a steady race, managing to stay out of trouble and finishing sixth that day. He won all of $200 in that first drive as he finished five laps behind eventual winner Bob Welborn. Maybe it wasn't a spectacular beginning, but the joy was all his since father Lee had allowed Richard to do it himself.

Lee wasn't there to see Richard Petty run his first race. Richard's younger brother Maurice had accompanied their father to Asheville, North Carolina, for a NASCAR sedan race. But Lee Petty has had the thrill of being present for many of the other triumphs in Richard Petty's career.

Lee Petty had his own career to be concerned about. The year 1958 would mark his second NASCAR Grand National title and his first since sweeping the 1954 series. Of the 50 NASCAR points-paying races the elder Petty competed in, he won seven times, with 28 top five and an unbelievable 44 top ten finishes to his credit. Consistency was always the hallmark of the Petty racing effort. Though Richard Petty was embarking on his own driving career, supporting his father's title contention remained the primary focus.

That first season Richard Petty competed in three convertible races and eight NASCAR Grand National sedan events. He finished 33rd in the final "open-top" points standings, with one top ten finish and $650 in prize money. Richard Petty finished in 36th position in the hardtop division for 1958, with two top five and three top ten finishes for the season. He took home a paltry $750 for his efforts in this division. One event in Salisbury, North Carolina, featured a mix of convertibles and hardtops. NASCAR referred to these races as "sweepstakes" events. It was a sure way of guaranteeing a full field of cars and attracting the best known drivers.

Race #1 for Richard Petty came in 1957 Oldsmobile convertible number 42 at Columbia, South Carolina, on July 12, when he finished sixth. Race #2 took place in Toronto, Canada, July 18 in the number 142 '57 Olds hardtop. Richard was involved in an accident and recorded his first DNF (did not finish). In a Buffalo, New York, July 19 sedan event, Richard Petty finished 11th in the Olds No. 42A. Then it was on to Belmar, New Jersey, for a hardtop race on July 26, when young Petty scored a ninth-place finish also in No. 42A.

Returning home to the Carolinas, Richard Petty competed in a hardtop race at Myrtle Beach, South Carolina, on August 23, recording a DNF in the No. 2 '57 Olds. Then it was on to Wilson, North Carolina, on September 7 for his second convertible race where he came home fifth racing the No. 42 again. On September 28 Richard raced at Hillsboro, North Carolina, in a sedan event, finishing 31st in car number 2. Race #8 of the 1958 season for Richard Petty came at Salisbury, North Carolina, where NASCAR filled out the field with con-

vertibles and hardtops. Richard finished fifth in the '57 Olds convertible number 2 on September 5.

Richard Petty's last two appearances of the 1958 season were at North Wilkesboro, North Carolina, on October 19 in a hardtop race where he finished 23rd in car number 2. His final race of the season was on the old one-mile dirt track in Atlanta, Georgia, on October 26. He placed 35th in the Oldsmobile number 42.

Amazing as it may seem, there is no record of Richard Petty driving a race car in 1958 using the number 43. Actually, Richard Petty made do many times with his father's number 42 already on the '57 Olds convertible. Of course, on many occasions Lee and Richard competed in different events. A few times Richard added the letter "A" or distinguished his race car from

1957 OLDSMOBILE CONVERTIBLE

Learning by doing

A lesson that we could all learn from Richard's start in auto racing is that success, fame, and all those things we associate with Richard all came about slowly. It took Richard a while to learn the craft of racing and even longer to learn the skill of winning. There was no doubt that young Richard had skill, but he was not an overnight success. It took time — as with anything of any worth — and a lot of hard work.

He didn't start off driving the number he is famous for. His cars weren't Petty Blue at first - that would come later. STP, cowboy hats, sunglasses, and cowboy boots would all come later on as time passed. Instead, Richard started with his dad's number, an old used race car, second hand gear and an understanding that things take time to grow. Perhaps growing up in farm country blesses you with the common sense to realize that nothing is born fully grown, success takes time, and the trick is to keep at it.

We all look at Richard now and see what the years of hard work and persistence have brought him and his team. Yet we somehow think of being a success — like Richard — has to come quickly. Nothing could be further from the truth. Keeping at it is what counts.

his father's by adding the number 1 to make 142. Occasionally Richard simply removed the number 4 from the 42 and ran as number 2.

In spite of an inauspicious beginning, Richard eventually overcame the learning curve in stock car racing, though he seems to have torn up his equipment more often than he cares to remember. Though these numbers may not look like a major league start to a record-setting career, Richard Petty gained valuable experience from coming to NASCAR racing when the early pillars of the sport were at their zenith. Drivers like the Flock brothers, Dick Rathmann, Marshall Teague, Curtis Turner, and Hershel McGriff had made their mark in the sport. NASCAR Grand National racing was

ready for a fresh face and the series was ripe for some new heros.

Richard Petty liked the exhilaration of competitive driving, the slammin' and bangin', the fender-to-fender rubbin' and bumping, the adrenalin rush of engine whinin', pedal-to-the-floor, no-holds-barred racing! He was hooked for good!

Anticipation was high at Petty Enterprises as the 1959 season promised to open up new opportunities for Richard Petty the race car driver. Many forthcoming events would fall into place and begin to define his public persona for the history books.

1958 marked the final year of racing for the famous 4.1 mile Daytona Beach race.

Something old, something new, something borrowed, something blue

The Birth of #43

Richard takes the checkered flag in his 1959 Plymouth. The darker number 43 was red while the car was white with pale blue trim.
The Richard Petty Private Collection

The Petty organization was again in transition in preparation for the 1959 NASCAR Grand National season. The Oldsmobile division of General Motors had come forward with a factory deal for Lee Petty in 1957, but the support dried up shortly thereafter due to the GM corporate-wide edict forbidding direct involvement in major league motorsports. Petty Engineering had soldiered on through 1957 and '58 using up what was left of Oldsmobile's goodwill and whatever parts and expertise had been made available.

With the opening of a brand-new 2.5 mile high-banked track at Daytona Beach, Florida, Lee Petty was convinced that a large, heavy, high-powered race car was the right choice for the inaugural 500-mile event that would kick off the 1959 series. Already with considerable experience racing an Oldsmobile, Lee had a clear choice: he would build a 1959 Oldsmobile 88 hardtop race car.

The racing budget at Petty Engineering was meager at best, so budding young driver Richard Petty was relegated to whipping his much-used and seasoned 1957 Oldsmobile

convertible into shape for his assault on the 1959 Grand National series.

Records show that the first use of number 43 by Richard Petty was at the 1959 Daytona 500. Much in the casual way his father picked 42 from the first two numbers on the license plate of his personal car, Richard chose number 43 for his race car mainly because it was the number following the one used by his father.

Both the convertible and Grand National (sedan) series continued to operate separate schedules for the 1959 season. However, NASCAR had developed the idea of having both

- Daytona International Speedway Opens.
- Holman and Moody build a fleet of 430 cubic inch powered Thunderbirds with a sticker price of $5,500. Ralph Moody runs the first hot laps at Daytona in one of these cars.
- Plymouth introduces its "big-block" at 361 cubic inches.
- After winning the Daytona 500 in an Olds, Lee Petty wins his third Grand National Championship over the course of 37 races using a '59 Plymouth. Richard starts in 21 races, has 6 top-five and 9 top-ten finishes. He comes in 15th on the championship list.

types of cars compete in common events called "Sweepstakes" races. The first Daytona 500 race was such an event. Thus the convertibles and sedans held separate 40-lap qualifying races and the results were combined to establish the starting field for the big 200-lap race. Richard Petty was surprisingly competitive in the convertible race. He finished a strong third behind Shorty Rollins and Marvin Panch. Lee didn't fare as well in the sedan qualifier. He wound up eighth, a lap down to race winner Bob Welborn in his '59 Chevy.

Lee Petty went on to win that first Daytona 500 in legendary fashion.

Richard Petty, in the "open air" Olds, dropped out after only eight laps due to engine failure. Richard Petty won a paltry $100 for his first Daytona 500, and though outqualifying his father and starting in sixth position, the younger Petty had to settle for a 57th-place finish in the 59-car field.

As the 1959 season proceeded, Lee Petty reverted to his well-used but trusty '57 Oldsmobiles. The new Olds was considered too big and cumbersome to maneuver well on the shorter tracks, where being quick and nimble was more desirable than simple, sheer, brute power.

After Daytona Richard Petty continued to concentrate on the convertible series, with an occasional foray into the Grand National ranks in a second '57 Olds hardtop. Of course, he competed in the Sweepstakes races when possible.

More and more the Pettys were becoming a team act, as Lee ran 42 Grand National races and managed to add four convertible events to his busy schedule. Richard Petty finished fourth in the convertible season's points chase while he finished the season in 15th slot in the Grand National standings.

Lee Petty won the third and final NASCAR championship of his career in 1959 with 11 wins, 27 top fives, and 35 top tens. He also finished the 1959 season in 30th place in the convertible division with one win, one top five, and 2 top tens.

On the other hand, Richard finished fourth in the convertibles with one win plus six top five and seven top ten finishes. By contrast he managed a 15th place in the 1959 Grand National points total, recording no wins, six top fives, and nine top tens.

It looked as if the young second-generation driver finally had his first Grand National win June 14, at the old Lakewood Speedway in Atlanta. Richard had looked strong through-

1957 OLDSMOBILE SEDAN

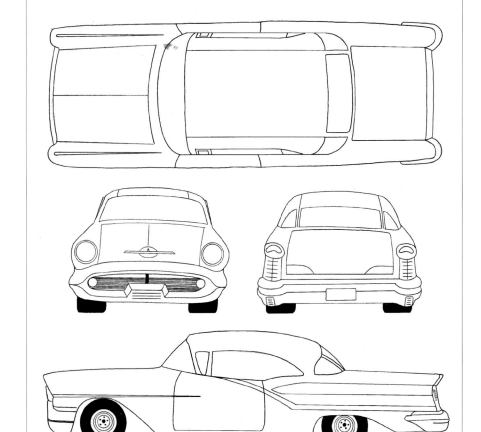

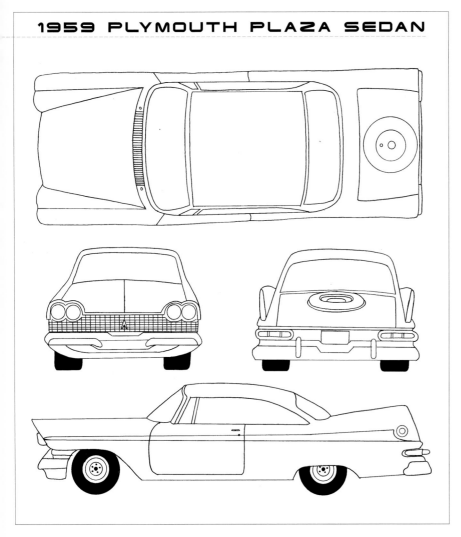

1959 PLYMOUTH PLAZA SEDAN

position near the midpoint of the 200-lapper on the old half-mile dirt track at Columbia, South Carolina. Jack Smith hounded Richard for the last half of the race, but young Petty prevailed for his first career win ever.

While making do with the three-year-old Oldsmobiles, the Petty organization was hard at work preparing two new '59 Plymouths. Lee Petty debuted in his new Plymouth hardtop in a 100-miler on the half-mile dirt track at Richmond, Virginia. Richard's '59 Plymouth was finished just in time for the Firecracker 250 at Daytona International Speedway on July 4. Richard was forced to drop out after just 78 laps with a faulty fuel pump. Lee finished only 77 laps in his Plymouth debut, retiring with engine failure.

Early in the season it was clear the future of the convertible division was in jeopardy. In late March NASCAR announced that 1959 would be the final season for the ragtops. The Darlington track continued to host a 300-mile spring convertible race through the 1962 season.

Richard Petty's impressive performance during the 1959 season garnered him the Rookie-of-the-Year title and a check for $250. Petty was told that the rookie title was second in prestige only to the national title his father had won. Young Petty was heard to remark that he wasn't sure about the prestige of the rookie title, but the payout was certainly a lot less than second place in the GN series!

As preparations were being made for the 1960 Grand National season, it was clear that Petty Engineering had two strong contenders wherever it competed. The association with the Plymouth division of Chrysler Corporation, reconsummated during the 1959 season, would prove to be long and celebrated.

out the 150-mile race on the one-mile dirt oval. Shortly after the checkered flag fell, the second-place finisher lodged a protest contesting the final race standings. NASCAR officials conducted a thorough recounting of the scorecards, and an hour later the official results were reversed — declaring the protesting Lee Petty the victor! Richard was relegated to second place.

Richard Petty had to wait until July to experience his first official trip to victory circle. In only his second race in a brand-new 1959 Plymouth convertible, Richard ran strong throughout the entire event. Starting from the seventh position, Petty moved quickly through the field, taking over the lead

The younger Petty begins his winning ways

Changing of the Guard

Lee's Plymouth sedan sits in front of Richard's convertible on pit lane. In the early years there were events in which both classes ran together in the same race.
The Richard Petty Private Collection

The Petty organization, flush with a lucrative factory deal with Plymouth, was fully focused on preparations for the 1960 NASCAR Grand National season. After racing part of a season successfully with dated Oldsmobile equipment and the remainder of the 1959 season with newly built Plymouths, the Level Cross operation now concentrated on putting together two very strong 1960 Plymouth Belvederes, one number 42 for Lee Petty and one number 43 for Richard Petty. No one from Petty Engineering was ever expected to campaign in hand-me-down race cars again or make do with anything but the best that he could build. For the first time the Pettys (father and son) would compete not so much as a team but as equals, with either Petty Plymouth capable of winning races week in and week out.

Plymouth advertising touted its brand-new cars as "The Solid Plymouth." Styling on the 1960 Plymouth might be best described as extravagant. The newly styled body shell had sprouted enormous mile-high vertical fins at the rear. The nose of the car featured wing-like brows that swept back over and around the leading edge of both fenders to hook around odd-shaped front wheel well openings.

The biggest change from 1959 to 1960 affecting race car construction was more structural than decorative.

With the introduction of the 1960 line of Chrysler Corporation cars, unibody construction was now applied to all the corporation's passenger cars. After preparing new race cars for the latter half of the 1959 season with body-over frame construction, the Pettys were now looking eyeball-to-eyeball at their first encounter with building Grand National stock cars minus frames!

Little could be transferred (except perhaps the drivetrain) from the new Plymouths constructed for the 1959 campaign. Stiffening up the more flexible unibody for competition undoubtedly presented a real challenge for the Petty race car builders. Soon it was found that the front subframe could be indirectly attached through the roll cage to the rear subframe, thereby tightening the entire substructure on the race car.

By 1960 the Pettys were already experimenting with larger displacement engines out of sheer defense against the overwhelming muscle of the competition. Pontiac had its 389,

Ford had a newly developed Police Interceptor 390, and Chevrolet was getting a lot of power from its "punched-out" 348 Chevy truck engine. The Pettys had already outfitted a Plymouth with the larger 413 V-8 from the Chrysler New Yorker. The Petty Plymouths didn't have an edge with more "cubes" under the hood, but they were definitely more competitive. It was still a fact that the blue Plymouths were no match for the Pontiacs, Fords, or Chevrolets at tracks such as Daytona and Darlington.

With the demise of NASCAR's convertible division, the lineup for the

Richard finds himself sandwiched between the #42 Plymouth of his father and the #4 Chevy of Rex White at Daytona. Note that Lee's Plymouth is painted differently than Richard's, Lee's having white paint around the headlights and grille. Both cars ran with silver wheels.
Richard Petty Private Collection

1960 PLYMOUTH FURY HARDTOP

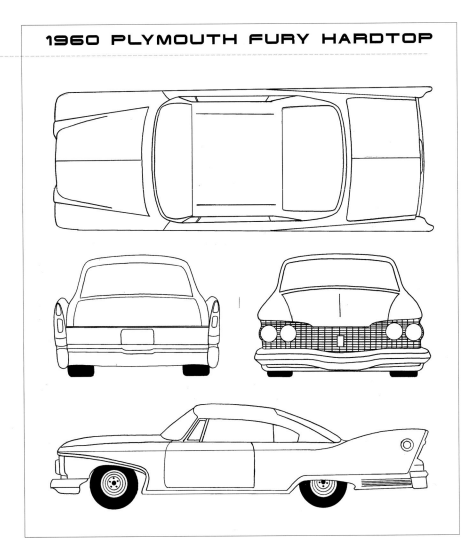

1960 Daytona 500 was exclusively hardtops. After pole qualifying and the two mandatory 100-mile qualifying races, the 40-car starting field was led by pole sitter Cotton Owens in a new Pontiac and by Jack Smith on the outside front row in what else — a new 1960 Pontiac!

The Pettys were relegated to starting much farther back from the leaders, with Lee in 14th and Richard in 19th. Though unable to mount serious or sustained challenges to the faster Pontiacs, Fords, and Chevrolets, the Pettys managed surprising third and fourth-place finishes as Junior Johnson marched to victory in a one-year-old Chevy. Johnson inherited the lead on lap 172 when a wind pocket sucked the rear window from race leader Bobby Johns' '59 Pontiac. The freak occurrence caused Johns to lose control momentarily in the second turn, but he was able to recover and finish ahead of Richard in third and Lee Petty in fourth.

The good finish for Richard Petty at Daytona undoubtedly propelled him to his first Grand National victory at the old half-mile dirt track in Charlotte, North Carolina, two weeks later. Richard Petty, not one to waste anything usable, drove his '59 Plymouth to the surprising victory over the Chevrolet of Rex White. Richard Petty took the lead from White with 18 laps remaining and held him off to the finish.

The 40-race Grand National schedule remained a season-long seesaw battle between Rex White and second-generation driver Richard Petty, who clearly came into his own during the 1960 season. White recorded the most wins for the season with six, as fifth-place Ned Jarrett and sixth-place finisher Lee Petty were next highest with five victories each.

White added to his six wins 25 top-five and 35 top-ten finishes in beating Richard Petty for the 1960 title. Richard Petty, by contrast, had only three victories for the season and 16 top-five and 30 top-ten finishes, placing second to White.

Richard runs on the high side of the banking at Daytona. His car is now painted the shade of blue he became famous for. **The Richard Petty Private Collection**

Until 1959 and 1960 NASCAR's Grand National series was primarily a dirt-and-pavement, short-track series. There were only three big tracks the series competed on, and by the late '50s two of them had gone out of business. Only Darlington's 1.375-mile paved oval had managed to survive NASCAR's formative years. Both the Raleigh Speedway (a one-mile paved banked oval and the 1.5-mile steeply banked dirt oval) and the Memphis-Arkansas Speedway were unable to make it during a time of sustained growth for NASCAR's premier series.

It was viewed as risky business when two brand-new paved race tracks opened for business during the 1960 racing season. Many hang-ups, from cash-flow problems to weather and construction delays, prevented either of the new facilities from hosting races until the very end of the NASCAR season.

The new Charlotte Motor Speedway was the first on board with a 400-mile event on October 16, the 42nd race of the 1960 Grand National season. Fortunately the championship was all but decided by the time this race took place. Because little of the landscaping had been completed by race time, strict rules were issued by NASCAR forbidding anyone from entering pit road through the unsodded infield running between the front straightaway and pit road. Richard Petty managed to finish second to Speedy Thompson's '60 Ford in the inaugural event. Lee dropped out early in the race with brake problems, placing 36th. All this was to no avail: both Pettys were disqualified by NASCAR after the race for spinning into the infield and making an "improper" entrance onto pit road.

Even more problems kept the new Atlanta International Raceway in Hampton, Georgia, from holding a major race until the end of October. The Atlanta 500 on the fast 1.5-mile facility was race number 44 and the final points-paying event of the season. Lee and Richard Petty finished nose-to-tail in sixth and

When the Pettys started running more than one car, they painted each one differently to easily spot them from a distance. Note that Richard's headlight pods are white and not painted blue like the rest of the car. The Richard Petty Private Collection

seventh places respectively. Rex White finished in fifth position in the final event and captured the 1960 driving title.

The new superspeedways did encounter their share of problems getting on board the demanding NASCAR Grand National series schedule. However, their mere existence added to the prestige and importance of facilities like Darlington, and the year-old Daytona International Speedway drew national attention to the series for the first time.

CBS television decided to include live coverage of the pole qualifying along with a pair of compact-sedan races from Daytona in late January 1960. Swarms of technical people descended on the Florida speedway to cover the festivities. A two-hour live telecast was hosted by announcer Bud Palmer, and the program was devoted entirely to the stock car racing at Daytona as part of the network's highly acclaimed "CBS Sports Spectacular." Surveys determined that more than 17 million viewers were glued in front of their TVs for the two-hour show. Big-time television had discovered big-time racing!

The new-found interest by the national news media in NASCAR Grand National stock car racing would be a key ingredient to increas-

SIGNIFICATA

- Chrysler switches to unit body construction on all its intermediates.
- Ford hires the Wood Brothers to conduct stock car tests, before returning to the circuit.
- Full-floating rear hubs become mandatory.
- Charlotte Motor Speedway and Atlanta International Raceway open and host their first Grand National races.
- Richard wins his first Grand National Race at the Charlotte Fairgrounds half-mile track in a 1959 Plymouth.
- Lee's final Grand National win comes at the same track where he won his first race — Heidelburg Speedway in Pittsburgh, PA. Richard comes in second in the same race.
- Driving a Chevrolet, Rex White wins the Grand National Championship over the course of 44 races. Richard Petty finishes second in his first full season and Lee Petty finishes sixth in points.

ing national exposure and interest in what had long been a regional phenomenon of the southeastern United States. This exposure would also play a major role in propelling young Richard Petty into the national spotlight.

A life-threatening accident leaves Richard holding the reigns at Petty Engineering

A Bleak Year at Best

The year 1961 was a bleak year for the auto industry. Car sales for the year were off significantly from the previous year, down to about the level of sales for 1959. It was much worse at Plymouth. After sustained growth and sales that maintained the division's third place behind Chevrolet and Ford, Plymouth lost nearly 37 percent in sales and slipped to seventh overall in sales.

Plymouth styling on its big cars — the ones that were being raced on the nation's race tracks — experienced one of the most drastic changes in the history of the division. Gone were the huge fins prevalent since 1956. In front was a completely new grille, bumper, and headlight treatment. Every type of design theme seemed wrapped up in one busy styling exercise. In the back, the huge fins of the year before were gone for good. The 1961 Plymouth Belvedere and Fury featured a flat rear deck and rear fender side panels with a heavy concave section that wrapped all the way around the rear of the body.

Whether the new styling for 1961 was pleasing or not is a matter of personal choice. Undoubtedly, the new body shape(s) threw a curve at the Pettys, who once again were working with a car body whose contours bore absolutely no resemblance to the race cars from the year before.

To say that 1961 was a disappointing year all around would be an understatement. The new 1961 Plymouth wasn't the most stable race car the Pettys had ever built, as shown in practice at Daytona International Speedway for the first big race of the season. However, Lee and Richard both felt the new race cars were stout and strong.

In the first of the 100-mile qualifying races used to determine starting positions for the Daytona 500, Richard Petty started from the 14th position in the first qualifier. When the green flag waved, Richard was able to maneuver his Plymouth into the sixth position. He quickly moved out to the high groove near the retaining wall, content to run his own race until the front runners either had mechanical problems or made mistakes. Young Petty was unable to keep the more powerful front runners in sight and gradually lost the all-important draft.

By the final circuit of the 40-lap event, Richard Petty, though two laps down to the leaders, had managed to stay in contention. As Fireball Roberts led second place Junior Johnson past Petty for the final time Richard tried once more to get hooked up in their draft. As the trio entered the first turn, Johnson's Pontiac swerved as the front tire was punctured by track debris. Petty tried frantically to avoid the spinning car by heading for the infield grass. Johnson's Pontiac struck the blue Plymouth in the right rear quarter panel, spinning it around, and sending it heading directly toward the outside guard rail.

The number 43 Plymouth mounted the guard rail and rode atop it for some distance before suddenly catapulting into mid-air and sailing skyward toward the parking lot below. The impact with the pavement totally demolished the car. Richard Petty scrambled to get out of the twisted hulk, stumbling and twisting his ankle. After being checked out by the track medical personnel, Richard hobbled back to the Petty pits.

The second qualifier was about to begin as Lee Petty offered Richard the chance to get back in a race car and run the second event. A still dazed Richard declined the offer, choosing to sit it out. It was a good choice, because suddenly his eyes began to hurt so badly he had trouble seeing. After another visit to the infield care center, doctors discovered hundreds of particles of broken glass fragments in both of young Petty's eyes.

After the glass fragments had been removed, Richard left the care center once more. As he stepped outside he heard the track announcer say there was one final lap left in the second 100-mile qualifying race. This announcement was followed by the sound of a deafening crash. Richard looked up to see his father Lee's number 42 Plymouth entangled with Johnny Beauchamp's Chevrolet as they disappeared from sight up the race track and over the guard rail.

Bad ankle or not, Richard Petty ran full speed to the crash site, which was not far from where his race car had landed a short time before. There was little of the number 42 left intact.

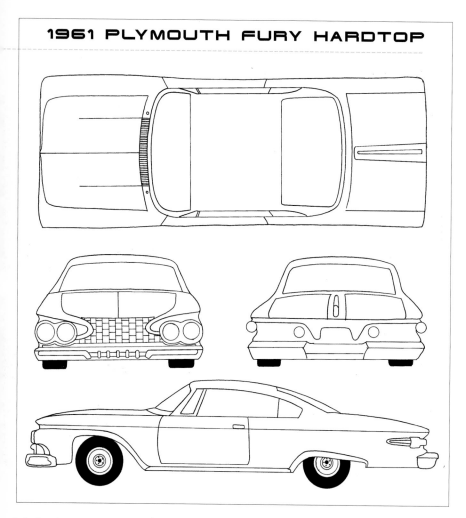

1961 PLYMOUTH FURY HARDTOP

Medical personnel were busily removing a gravely injured Lee Petty from the wreckage.

Richard Petty, confronted with the possible death of his father and mentor, quickly realized that he and brother Maurice had inherited the awesome task of literally picking up the pieces and pulling the Petty operation back together.

As Lee Petty lay near death in a local hospital, the Petty family rallied together and immediately began to deal with the situation at hand. Members of the family sat with the Petty patriarch around the clock. Lee, when coherent, continued to dictate the orders. He instructed Richard to take Maurice and get back to Level Cross and start getting a car ready for the next NASCAR event. Though many months of recovery lay ahead, the elder Petty was convinced he would be ready to race at the end of the next week.

Though there were no Petty Engineering race cars in the 1961 Daytona 500 that February, Bob Welborn did ask Richard Petty to drive relief for him during the race. Richard Petty got in the car for a few laps before returning home.

When the brothers returned home there was a new and different environment at Petty Engineering. As their father had instructed, Maurice and Richard learned by his example and began building race cars. Though it was a bleak year at best, Petty Engineering did compete in 41 of 47 scheduled events, with Richard Petty now assuming the primary role as manager and driver.

Richard Petty managed only an eighth-place finish in the final Grand National point standings. His 41 starts garnered just two wins, 18 top fives, and 23 top tens. His first win of the season didn't come until April 23, as he lapped the field in the 100-miler on the dirt at Richmond Fairgrounds' half mile. Victory number two came in a 100-mile qualifying event for the upcoming World 600 at the 1.5-mile Charlotte Motor Speedway on May 21. Petty outran Ralph Earnhardt, taking the lead on lap 44. The victory gave Petty the coveted pole position for the World 600.

Though Richard Petty experienced a lackluster year in 1961, it is to his credit that Petty Engineering survived and returned to competitive status in the tough Grand National series. With only one car competing and the eighth-place finish, the Petty operation didn't earn much money during the 1961 season. However, the abrupt change of circumstances gave Richard, Maurice, and their cousin Dale Inman the experience of building fast and durable race cars and competing consistently all season long without Lee Petty's leadership.

The year 1961 was truly a changing of the guard not only for Petty Engineering but for the entire Grand National series. Ned Jarrett won his first NASCAR title, defeating Rex White, who placed second. Other new names were also appearing in the winner's circle. Drivers like David Pearson, Jim Pardue, Fred Lorenzen, and Marvin Panch were poised to leave their individual marks on the sport as the 1962 season approached.

Richard gives 'em a run for their money

A Savoy Season

Petty on pit road in Charlotte. Note the two hood pins that now secure the hood in 1962. Much of the chrome trim has been removed or painted black. Bob Tronolone

There was a much different atmosphere at Petty Engineering preparing for the 1962 season. The fortunes of the Level Cross racing operations had fallen to the brothers Petty. But especially, the on-track success of the family business rested squarely on the shoulders of one Richard Petty.

Lee Petty's horrific qualifying accident prior to the 1961 Daytona 500 had all but ended the elder Petty's competitive career. Lee Petty did not return to the cockpit during the 1961 NASCAR Grand National season. Richard, and for a brief stint, Maurice, assumed responsibility for whatever success or failure Petty Engineering experienced on the nation's race tracks.

In 1962 Plymouth misread public tastes, anticipating a strong demand for more compact, full-size cars. A totally new design was introduced featuring a very pronounced long hood-short deck configuration, making the full-sized Plymouth line strongly resemble the compact Valiant series.

Plymouth engineers shrank the wheelbase some eight inches and trimmed nearly 600 pounds from the car's curb weight. The new 1962 Plymouths now rode on a diminutive 116-inch wheelbase. A buying public, still clamoring for large cars, turned to Chevrolet, Ford, and even Buick. Plymouth slipped to ninth in sales from eighth in 1961, even though the auto industry had rebounded from a

lackluster performance the year before.

Petty Engineering was again confronted with constructing brand-new cars for the new season. Virtually none of the chassis or sheet metal could be carried over to the new cars. The Pettys had chosen two-door hardtops for competition in '61, but a businessman's special (the lowly Savoy two-door post sedan) became the standard bearer for Richard Petty for the 1962 season.

Again, as had been standard practice in previous years, Richard Petty did not abandon his year-old race cars, getting yeoman duty from the seasoned mounts. Maurice and Richard competed in the first event of the 1962 season in November 1961 in a 100-miler at Concord, North Carolina. Later in November '61 Richard again drove the year-old Plymouth in a 100-

miler at Weaverville, North Carolina. On a handful of other occasions the 1961 Plymouth was entered in competition, but nearing mid-year the new 1962 Plymouth became the Petty's race car of choice — and for good reason.

Pontiac, Ford, and Chevrolet still had the edge on horsepower, especially on the high-speed tracks like Daytona International Speedway. What Richard Petty's blue Plymouths lacked under the hood, the team's considerable skills in setting up a race car and Richard's uncanny ability to quickly adapt to the draft allowed him to stay in the hunt.

When the series arrived at Daytona in preparation for the 500, it was evident the Petty race cars were still 40 to 50 horsepower short even with the reduced size of the 1962 Plymouth Savoy. Richard finished a respectable fourth in the second 100-mile qualify-

ing race. Starting from the tenth position in the big race, Petty, in the underpowered Plymouth, managed to lead three times for 27 laps. Though Glen "Fireball" Roberts was untouchable at Daytona, sweeping every competitive event he was entered in, Petty clung to Roberts' rear bumper to finish on the lead lap and take second place. Petty often has described the 1962 Daytona 500 as his favorite race.

Though the use of both the 1961 Belvedere and 1962 Savoy sedan was commonplace in the early part of the 1962 season, the little two-door became the race car of choice nearing mid-season. Also, by this time Petty Engineering was fielding a two-car team for virtually every event. The primary driver for team car number 42 (or sometimes 41) was veteran driver Jim Paschal, though a few times the name of Maurice Petty was listed as the driver of record. Lee Petty made one appearance in 1962, starting in fifth place for the 250-mile event at Martinsville, Virginia, in April, but he asked for relief from Jim Paschal shortly into the event.

The year 1962 proved to be an excellent one for Richard Petty and Petty Engineering. After the second-place finish at Daytona, Richard went on to finish second at Concord, North Carolina, to Joe Weatherly and second to Rex White's Chevy at Hillsboro, North Carolina. Finally, in mid-April, Petty relished his first victory of the season in the Gwyn Staley 400 at North Wilkesboro, North Carolina.

That first win and consistent string of seconds seemed to motivate Richard Petty as he finished second to Jack Smith's Pontiac at Myrtle Beach, South Carolina, in late April and then a day later won again at Martinsville, Virginia. He followed that with a string of top-five finishes, culminating with a fourth in the World 600 at Charlotte in late May. Petty continued scoring top fives through June.

July got off to a poor start. Petty went only six laps in the Firecracker 400 at Daytona before being involved in a crash that put him out of the event. After a DNF at Columbia, South Carolina, and a third at Asheville, North Carolina, Petty bounced back to

win the 200-lapper at Greenville, South Carolina, by three laps over the field. The Petty operation seemed to be on a roll as it fielded three cars for the Southeastern 500 at Bristol, Tennessee, in late July. Jim Paschal in car 42 beat Fred Lorenzen to the checkered flag, with Richard a close third, as Bunkie Blackburn brought home the 41 car in eighth place.

The Paschal and Petty combo rolled on to a one-two finish at Nashville, Tennessee, with Richard in a solo effort taking the 200-lapper at Huntsville, Alabama in early August. Jim Paschal returned to the seat of number 42 to win at Weaverville, North Carolina's Western North Carolina 500 with Richard in seventh. Petty bested the field at Roanoke, Virginia, in mid-August and followed that win with back-to-back victories at Winston-Salem's Bowman-Gray Stadium for a 200-lapper and a 100-mile half-mile dirt race at Spartanburg, South Carolina.

Petty seemed to be putting on a stretch drive for his first championship as he finished second to Ned

Richard passes Red Foote during the World 600 at Charlotte Motor Speedway. He eventually finished 4th. Bob Tronolone

1962 PLYMOUTH SAVOY SEDAN

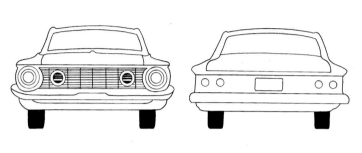

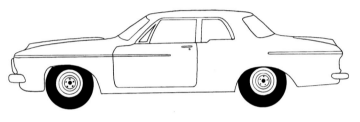

SIGNIFICATA

- Ford introduces the Starlift roof kit designed to improve racing aerodynamics. NASCAR bans the kit after just one race.

- Ford's big-block grows to 406 cubic inches and gets cross-bolt main caps.

- Ford officially announces it will no longer follow the AMA ban on racing.

- Chrysler follows suit with Ford, making a similar announcement. The factory-backed wars resume.

- Nashville is paved.

- Driving a Pontiac, Joe Weatherly wins the Grand National Championship over the course of 53 races. Richard Petty finishes second in points.

A good overhead shot of Richard's 1962 ride. Note how the hood markings indicate the horsepower rating. This would soon change to the size of the engine in cubic inches.
The Richard Petty Private Collection

Petty wrapped up another impressive year in NASCAR Grand National competition. He competed in all 52 scheduled races with eight victories, 31 top fives, and 38 top tens. But again his efforts fell short as Joe Weatherly scored his first championship title, winning nine times with 39 top fives and an amazing 45 top tens to beat young Petty out for the top prize.

As they say, "Close but no cigar!" For the second year, Richard Petty had put on a hard charge to win his first career Grand National title, but it was not to be. It was clear the young Tarheel driver had all the skills and talent to do the job. What was lacking was an engine that produced the kind of horsepower the competition had.

As the 1963 season approached, rumors spread that Chrysler was working secretly on the great equalizer for Richard Petty. Was it true? And would the much needed boost for Petty race cars arrive in time to turn around the results of the 1963 season? Or would things remain the same?

Jarrett at Valdosta, Georgia, in late August. It was a pair of second-place finishes again for Petty at Augusta, Georgia, and the second visit for the series in Martinsville. Petty cruised to victory next at North Wilkesboro in the Wilkes 320. Things slowed a bit as the team again fielded three cars with Jim Paschal taking sixth, Speedy Thompson in ninth, and Petty coming home in 16th at Charlotte for the National 400 in mid-October.

14 wins leave no doubt as to who will be a future champion

Poised on the Pinnacle

Richard poses by his 1963 Plymouth at Daytona prior to the 1963 Daytona 500. Although the doors were bolted or welded shut, they still carried the door handles and still had roll-up glass windows.
Richard Petty Private Collection

For Petty Engineering, the sheet metal change resulted in a slightly cleaner body shell and possibly a more aerodynamically competitive race car for 1963. Chrysler also attempted to help the Pettys get more competitive by tweaking its venerable 426 c.i.d. wedge engine in what was called the "Stage 3" version. The changes, which increased the horsepower substantially, promised to make the blue Plymouths a force to be reckoned with for the new season.

The NASCAR rule book for 1963 restricted engine displacement to 428 c.i.d. Electric fuel pumps remained on the not-permitted list, for fire was still every driver's nightmare. Concern that an electric fuel pump might continue to do its job after a crash dictated the ruling. Fuel cells were still something used only on Indy and F1 cars. Stock cars were still required to run production gas tanks. Dry-sump oiling systems were also not permitted. Interestingly, no special treadless tires were permitted; only "standard" treaded tires were allowed.

Once again the vehicle of choice for Petty Engineering was the base-line Savoy two-door sedan, not necessarily the Plymouth performance "image car." Plans for 1963 included putting three blue Plymouths into the field for many of the races where feasible.

The season opened in November 1962 at Birmingham, Alabama. The Petty organization made its presence known as Jim Paschal won by a lap over second-place Richard Petty. Maurice Petty, who started in eighth place, finished 14th after being taken out on lap 186 by a crash in the 100-mile event.

One week later Richard reversed the roles on Paschal by winning the 200-lapper at Tampa, Florida. Paschal and Petty finished on the same lap, with Joe Weatherly coming home third. Maurice Petty finished sixth, two laps off the pace.

After a near miss, falling short of 1962's top prize in NASCAR Grand National stock car racing, Richard Petty was without doubt poised near the pinnacle of success as the 1963 season approached. The young second-generation driver had challenged the ultimate titleholder Joe Weatherly until the very last race of the '62 season.

At Chrysler, Elwood Engle made the move from Ford to the v.p. of design position with the number-three auto maker, replacing Virgil Exner, who resigned at the end of 1962. Engle's arrival brought a major freshening of the entire product line, and especially lowly Plymouth. The stunning new Plymouth styling by the man responsible for the "Thunderbird look" at Ford resulted in Chrysler's bread-and-butter line increasing sales 50 percent over 1962 and moving from eighth to fifth in yearly sales.

During practice at Bristol, Richard and the crew prepare to adjust the front-end of his Plymouth. Richard is walking over to the tire on the left. That's Lee on the right. Richard Petty Private Collection

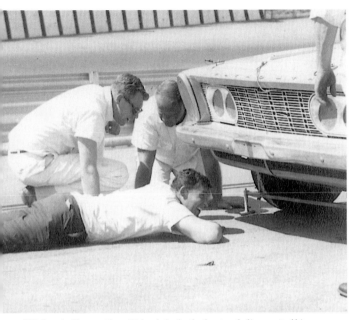

"High-tech alignment" — Richard checks the front-end alignment of his Plymouth. Note the white stripe on the center of the tire and the pointer on the bar. Note that the car still carries the PLYMOUTH letters on the edge of the hood. Richard Petty Private Collection

Jim Paschal came back on November 22 to score a two-lap victory in the Petty number 41 Plymouth at the Randleman, North Carolina, Tar Heel Speedway. Maurice brought the 42 car home in fifth; Richard Petty lasted only 188 laps, going out with transmission problems.

Then the 1963 series made its customary January appearance on the 2.7-mile paved Riverside International Raceway road course in California for the Riverside 500. Paul Goldsmith and A.J. Foyt started from the front row, but sports car and Indy specialist Dan Gurney won the first of his many stock car triumphs in the storied event. Richard Petty started the race in 15th spot but managed only a 41st-place finish as his transmission went sour on lap 27. Jim Paschal didn't fare much better, being involved in a crash on lap 81 and finishing 36th.

The Grand National series moved back to the Southeast for the annual Daytona 500. USAC driver Jim Hurtubise was recruited to pilot the 42 car. In the first 40 lap qualifying race, Richard Petty finished 12th, two laps off the pace. Hired gun Hurtubise managed only 17th place behind the "boss," also two laps down. Jim Paschal, driving the 41 car in the second qualifier, didn't fare much better than his teammates: he started 23rd and wound up 23rd, going out on lap 28 with engine failure.

For Petty Engineering, it was a ho-hum Daytona 500. Richard Petty finished a respectable sixth, two laps behind surprise winner DeWayne "Tiny" Lund, after starting 23rd. Hurtubise lasted only 113 circuits, going out with engine trouble and finishing 28th. Jim Paschal never really got warmed up as his blue Plymouth expired on lap 72 with ignition problems.

Ford had managed to sweep the first five finishing places with Fred Lorenzen, Ned Jarrett, Nelson Stacey, and Dan Gurney completing the top five. Lund, remarkably, was a replacement for Marvin Panch, the regular number 21 Ford driver who had been seriously injured in a fiery crash ten days earlier while testing a Maserati sports car. Lund, in fact, pulled Panch from the flaming race car. From a hospital bed, Panch

SIGNIFICATA

- Ford's big-block grows to 427 cubic inches.
- Ford's Galaxie gets a more aerodynamic "convertible" roofline at midyear.
- Chrysler introduces a 426 cubic inch version of its wedge engine.
- Chevy brings out a short-lived, race-only powerplant called "the Mystery Motor", the 427 Mk IV. GM gets nervous about its obvious violation of the AMA ban and completely withdraws from racing.
- Cars were required to weigh no less than the listed shipping weight from the factory.
- Hoods and trunk lids are required to have stock hinges and some form of positive locking device beyond the stock latches or locks.
- Numerals indicating the horsepower rating of the factory manufactured engine are to be painted on both sides of the hood in numerals at least eight inches high.
- Header dump pipes are 4 inches in diameter.
- Bucket seats are now compulsory, but must be factory made.
- Stock frames required, with no cutouts allowed.
- Single-bar bracing on either side of the roll cage is required.
- Driving a Pontiac, Joe Weatherly wins his second Grand National Championship over the course of 55 races. Richard Petty finishes second in points.

asked the Wood brothers to let Lund drive his car in the 500 mile race.

After the lackluster showing at Daytona, the Petty team got rolling. Richard Petty scored his first '63 calendar year win at Spartanburg, South Carolina, by one lap over Ned Jarrett's Ford. Jim Paschal came home in third place in the 42 car. The next day at Weaverville, North Carolina, Petty

Six days later Richard Petty returned to his winning ways in the Virginia 500, a 250-mile event at Martinsville. Jim Paschal managed only eighth place, surprisingly needing relief help. More surprising was the relief driver. . . Lee Petty!

Again Richard Petty was on a hot streak! After the Martinsville win, he won by a lap at North Wilkesboro in

As June came to a close at Atlanta International Raceway in Hampton, Georgia, for the Dixie 400, the two-car team of Petty and Paschal finished a disappointing 12th and 30th, respectively. Back at Daytona for the Independence Day Firecracker 400, the Ford teams feasted on the competition; David Pearson and Richard Petty were the only non-Ford products in the top ten. Petty struggled to eighth place, six laps off the pace of race winner Fireball Roberts. Petty never led a single lap in the 400-mile event.

As the series moved back to the short tracks, bad luck followed Richard Petty at the Myrtle Beach, South Carolina, half-mile dirt track. Petty crashed on lap 60. Ned Jarrett's Ford beat back the challenge of Buck Baker's '63 Pontiac. Petty continued to struggle in the 100-mile race at Savannah, finishing dead last after a crash on lap 38. Petty continued to struggle with mechanical problems and misfortune until late July at Bridgehampton Race Circuit in New York, as he scored a solid victory over Fred Lorenzen and Marvin Panch, both in Fords. The Bridgehampton race was notable for one other special reason. Lee Petty finished sixth in a Petty team car.

Richard races the Ford Galaxie of Fred Lorenzen. Richard Petty Private Collection

outran Buck Baker's '62 Chrysler to win the 200-lapper. One week later, Jim Paschal finished second to race winner Junior Johnson's '63 Chevy as Richard Petty hung on for third place at Hillsboro, North Carolina.

In mid-March the Petty team again fielded three blue Plymouths for the Atlanta 500 at Hampton. Richard started eighth and finished there. Jim Paschal started 11th and wound up 14th. Jim Hurtubise started in 10th and finished a disappointing 22nd.

A week later at Hickory, Richard Petty raced winner Junior Johnson to a second place. Jim Paschal took a fourth after starting from eighth place. Richard Petty scored a series of top fives through the next four events until he took the measure of the field at South Boston, Virginia, outdistancing runner-up Jim Paschal by two laps. It was Paschal's turn the next day at Winston-Salem, as he won the 200-lapper at Bowman-Gray Stadium. Richard Petty lasted only 185 laps, going out with fuel pump trouble.

the 400-lapper and followed that with a solid win at Columbia a few days later in a 200-lapper on the half-mile dirt.

Jim Paschal made it six straight victories for a Petty Engineering race car by cruising to a four-lap triumph at Randleman, North Carolina. Unfortunately, Richard Petty spent 30 laps in the pits only one lap after the green flag flew with serious fuel pump trouble. Richard finished 13th, 29 laps behind Paschal.

The Rebel 300 in early May at Darlington saw Richard Petty finish third to eventual winner Joe Weatherly as Jim Paschal brought the team car home in sixth. The next week Richard Petty was back on track with a win at Manassas, and followed that with a second at Richmond, but he managed only a 36th place at the World 600 at Charlotte in early June. Paschal recorded 3rd, 14th, and 42nd place finishes in the same events.

Petty came back to the front at Birmingham by winning the 200-lapper over Junior Johnson's '63 Chevy.

Next, Richard Petty took a second at Bristol, Tennessee, and returned to the winner's circle at Greenville, South Carolina, for his 11th win of the 1963 season. Jim Paschal returned to the Petty team car, finished right behind Petty at Bristol, and bested the "boss" at Nashville as Richard Petty followed Paschal, Billy Wade, and Joe Weatherly across the finish line to a fourth.

It was number twelve of the season for Richard Petty at Columbia in early August as he won the Sandlapper 200 over David Pearson and Bobby Isaac. Three days later at Weaverville in a 250 miler, Petty and Paschal were second and third to Fred Lorenzen's '63 Ford.

The remainder of August and all of September were slim pickins for Richard Petty and the Petty Engineering race team. Along the way Jim Paschal left the team to drive Cliff

1963 PLYMOUTH SAVOY SEDAN

Stewart's Pontiacs. Bob Welborn was hired to pilot the second Petty team car. Richard Petty didn't return to the winner's circle until early October with a win in a 200-lapper at Randleman, as Welborn came home in third.

Petty led a three-car team into the National 400 at Charlotte, North Carolina, in mid-October. Junior Johnson pushed his '63 Chevy to the victory of the Fords of Lorenzen, Panch, and Roberts. Richard Petty could manage only a sixth-place finish, ten laps off the pace. The other two team cars managed only 23rd and 26th places in the 52nd Grand National race of the 1963 season. But Petty returned to top form at South Boston, Virginia, beating David Pearson by three laps in the 150-mile event.

One week later the Petty cars finished second and sixth to Joe Weatherly at Hillsboro in what would prove to be Little Joe's final Grand National career victory. Bob Welborn was one lap behind Weatherly at the checkered flag; Richard Petty was 21 laps down at the finish.

The series then took a final Western swing, arriving at Riverside for the Golden State 400, the last race of the '63 season. Only Richard Petty made the trek for the team, and his efforts were short-lived. The number 43 Plymouth lasted only five laps, retiring with transmission trouble. A mix of Mercurys and Fords swept the field in the 148-lap event.

With 14 wins, 30 top fives, and 34 top tens for the 1963 NASCAR Grand National season, it seemed a sure bet Richard Petty would record his first championship title. Unbelievable as it may seem, Joe Weatherly beat out Petty for the title with only three wins, 20 top fives, and 35 top tens in the season's statistics. Remember, points were awarded under a completely different system than is used today.

What makes Joe Weatherly's '63 championship that much more amazing is the fact that Joe did not have a regular ride. Joe Weatherly won the 1963 Grand National championship driving for eight different teams! Ironically, many of the cars Weatherly coaxed to top finishes were backmarkers at best, often fielded by teams that were unheard of before.

The other major news from the 1963 season was the ascendance of Fred Lorenzen to the top of his game. The Chicago native, driving for Holman-Moody, became the first Grand National driver ever to top the $100,000 mark in winnings for a single season. This was considered quite a feat in the early '60s. Lorenzen ran only 29 races of the 55 scheduled, winning six times and recording 21 top five and 23 top ten finishes. He also finished third overall in the season's points chase.

At the conclusion of the 1963 season, surely the Petty Engineering team knew what it took to win a championship, even though this one got away. Richard Petty had proved he knew how to win, but he still didn't have the equipment to be competitive on the superspeedways. Longstanding rumors during late '62 and most of the '63 season would have made one believe that in the 1964 season, this final obstacle for Richard Petty might have a definite solution.

Petty wins his first Daytona 500 & Grand National Championship

It's My Turn Now

T he 1964 NASCAR Grand National season was truly one of triumph, technology, and tragedy. Richard Lee Petty's years of consistent hard work and "stick-to-it-tiveness" resulted in the first of many triumphs. Petty won his first major race, the 1964 Daytona 500, convincingly and recorded his first of seven Grand National (now Winston Cup) championships. Never again would Richard Petty be known just as Lee Petty's son!

Rumors had been rampant from late in the 1962 Grand National season about an impending change in Chrysler's racing program. Many of those rumors continued to fly back and forth throughout the 1963 season. Chrysler had never been as deeply involved in supporting its teams in major league stock car racing as had Pontiac, Ford, Mercury, and Chevrolet. Petty Enterprises, since devoting its full attention to Plymouths in mid-1959, had managed to get the utmost out of everything Chrysler had given them to work with. Richard Petty's early victories in Plymouths were the result of superior handling on the shorter tracks. A lack of pure horsepower kept him from being considered a serious contender on the superspeedways.

The season's point chase in those days started in the fall of the preceding year. Four events had already taken place before the "traveling circus" trekked out to Riverside for the

Richard at speed in his championship-winning 1964 Plymouth Belvedere. Compare this photo to the #41 car and note some subtle differences between the cars. This car has been carefully massaged, including the removal of the chrome side molding. Richard Petty Private Collection

Lee stands by an early 1964 Belvedere just prior to leaving for Daytona. Note Lee's fancy shoes. Richard Petty Private Collection

During the '64 season, the #41 Petty car was first driven by a number of drivers that included: Buck Baker, Jim Paschal, Maurice Petty, and Lee Petty. In the first half of the season, the younger Petty stuck to the short tracks, while Baker raced the bigger tracks and longer races. In the second half, Jim Paschal drove most of the races. Lee's last ride came in the #41 car at Watkins Glen, New York. Richard Petty Private Collection

This shot of Lee making adjustments under the hood of one of the '64s shows a few interesting details. The inside of the car is white, not blue, with the hinge assembly painted black. Also note the location of the battery in its stock tray. Bill Coulter

An interesting shot of a late '64 Plymouth due to the Champion Spark Plug decal. Not one you would likely find at your local parts store. Richard Petty Private Collection

Richard pits during the Southern 500 at Darlington on his way to a third place finish. Richard Petty Private Collection

Service taking place at the old Richmond Fairgrounds. Note that the roll cage is shorter from front to back than on current cars; also note the Firestone tires. Richard Petty Private Collection

The Petty Engineering cars had a reputation for being well prepared. Here is Richard in his '64 Belvedere at Daytona. Note how the numbers are painted over the chrome side molding. It's also one of the few cars to ever carry Richard's name. It's in small letters (Richard) under the vent window. Bill Coulter

When Lee retired from racing, he didn't just stand on the sidelines. Here he jacks the team's second car. Bill Coulter

first calendar event of 1964, the Motor Trend 500. For those first five races of the 1964 points chase Richard Petty soldiered on with the old 426 wedge engine that had taken him to numerous short and intermediate track victories the year before. But what Petty challengers found out at Daytona surprised none but devastated many.

On a secret five-mile-long test track in Texas, Chrysler Corporation had been testing a new version of its venerable hemispherical-head 426 V-8 engine. Word had leaked out that on the long straightaways the massive power plant was pushing the slippery Plymouths and Dodges at unheard-of speeds of over 185 mph, about 20 mph better than the competition was running at superspeedways like Daytona.

The Pettys installed the new engine in their 1964 Belvedere and promptly found after a few practice laps that the head gasket was leaking. The crew discovered the block wasn't quite big enough to cover the gasket on the cylinder head. They quickly set about heating brass and welding it to make the block fit up with the gasket and

cylinder head. The parts were reassembled, and Richard went on to win his first Daytona 500. And remember, that was the only hemi engine available, and it won the race.

Richard endured a grueling, season-long battle with Ford ace Ned Jarrett and Dodge driver David Pearson. Though Jarrett won 15 times to Petty's nine victories, Richard competed in all 61 events on the grinding schedule, while Jarrett appeared in only 59. Both drivers were unbelievably consistent: Petty had 37 top five finishes to Jarrett's 40, and 43 top ten finishes to Ned's 45. But it was those extra starts that clinched the first title for the young North Carolinian.

Richard Petty considers his 1964 Plymouth Belvedere two-door hardtop one of his favorite race cars. Petty feels styling changes in the intermediate body shell for 1964, such as the pointed nose and sloping rear window, made a major difference in aerodynamics. The Petty team in 1964 was concentrating on such things at a time

The engine that made it all come together for Plymouth was the Hemi. Its incredible power gave Plymouth the edge that was missing for a long time. Bill Coulter

when the competition struggled to improve engine performance.

The hemi engine was the last piece of the puzzle needed to make Richard Petty competitive. But the engine wasn't without problems. On the shorter race tracks, especially on dirt, Petty fell out of numerous events with rear-end trouble. It took time for the team to harness the mammoth engine's 500-plus horsepower. The wheels never quit spinning at full throttle as the huge engine delivered massive amounts of torque. Such awesome power produced similar problems even at Daytona, and the crew was forced to add 100 pounds of lead to the rear bumper of the

Petty's crew swings into action on a pit stop. Note the rear window bracing already present in 1964. The Richard Petty Private Collection

SIGNIFICATA

- Chrysler debuted their new 426 cubic inch Hemi engine even though no street-going hemis are produced.
- Ford introduces the 427 High Riser engine. Threatens to introduce a SOHC version of the 427.
- Cars with a 114 inch wheelbase limited to 396 cubic inch engines.
- Cars with a 116 inch wheelbase or larger use the 428 cubic inch engine.
- Plastic glass now allowed in the rear window.
- Three bars now required on the driver's side of the roll cage.
- Watkins Glen rejoins the schedule for a second time.
- Richard Petty wins his first Grand National Championship over the course of 62 events, the largest number ever run in the Grand National Division in a single year.

At Daytona, Buck Baker poses with the second Petty car which he drove in the race. Both cars ran on wheels that were painted silver. Bill Coulter

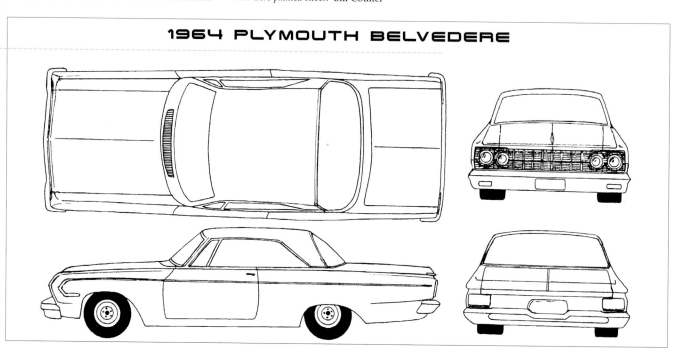

1964 PLYMOUTH BELVEDERE

Note the nearly complete lack of sponsor decals on the front fender of Petty Belvedere in this photo. *The Richard Petty Private Collection*

An unadorned Belvedere swings through the turns at Bridgehampton during practice for the road course race held there. The Richard Petty Private Collection

Richard shows his strength by stretching his lead going into a turn at Daytona. The Richard Petty Private Collection

Belvedere in an attempt to stabilize the problem.

Richard confirms that his 1964 Daytona 500 car was virtually stock in shape and configuration. But the team had massaged the car thoroughly upon returning to Daytona International Speedway for the Firecracker 400 in July. The blue Plymouth was now a "real" race car, lower with the body shifted on the chassis for even better aerodynamics.

Technologically, the race cars of 1964 were increasingly non-stock. The machine's aerodynamics and brute power exceeded the ability of Goodyear and Firestone to build tires that could hold up under high-speed competition. Remember again, with the introduction of the Chrysler 426 hemi, average lap speeds at Daytona increased 20 mph from the previous year.

In some part, this technology led to tragedy not seen again in NASCAR's premier league until the early 1990s. Gone in 1964 as the result of savage, sobering accidents were top drivers such as Joe Weatherly, the 1963 NASCAR Grand National champion

killed in the first calendar event of '64 at the Motor Trend 500 at Riverside, California. Billy Wade, the sensational 1963 rookie of the year, was killed driving a Bud Moore Mercury while testing tires at Daytona International Speedway, and Jimmy Pardue, who finished second to Richard Petty in the Daytona 500, lost his life while participating in tire testing at Charlotte. Glen "Fireball" Roberts died from severe burns nearly a month after being trapped in his flaming race car during the World 600. The 1964 season was a costly one. Something had to be done to make these race cars safer.

Blame for the catastrophes focused first on tires and the stock production fuel tank, which was so very vulnerable to fire. The cry continued for some method of slowing the race cars down. NASCAR thoroughly reviewed the rules late in the season and issued major revisions for the 1965 season. The proposed new rules appeared to eliminate the advantages enjoyed by the Chrysler race cars. The stage was now set for perhaps the most unusual and disruptive season in Richard Petty's career.

NUGGETS

Light on its feet...

As the winner of the Daytona 500 and with all the hoopla about the Hemi engine's raw power, it would be easy for younger readers to dismiss Richard's first championship as a result of the gobs of power coming from the Hemi with Richard and his Plymouth tearing up every major superspeedway in the country. Compared to the cars of today, the Belvedere was a big, heavy car with a huge engine. But when compared to the cars of that same time period, the Plymouth was actually a light-weight — and a good part of his success in 1964 came from the combination of a super strong powerplant in a sturdy, but lightweight car.

For that matter, consider that all of Richard's wins in 1964 other than the Daytona 500 came in races under 200 miles in length, and most of those were 100-milers. It's hard to think of the '64 Belvedere as a lightweight sprint car, but when compared to the Fords and Mercurys that won most of the long distance races in 1964, that's exactly what it was.

NASCAR outlaws the Hemi. Chrylser boycotts & goes drag racing

Outlawed!

Richard stands beside the first Barracuda drag car built at the Petty shops. The strange-looking scoops on the hood were air scoops that fed the normally aspired hemi-engine. Richard Petty Private Collection

Even before the last event of the '64 Grand National season, NASCAR president Bill France Sr. announced the newly revised 1965 rules for the stock-car sanctioning body. The new rules eliminated both Chrysler's hemi and all Ford hi-riser engines from further competition. Ford officials quickly applauded the decision, but just ten days later, Chrysler's racing boss, Ron Householder, issued a public statement blasting the 1965 rules. He made it abundantly clear that factory-sponsored Dodges and Plymouths would not take part in any future NASCAR events until the rules were adjusted. Clearly the lines were drawn for another major confrontation over who would govern the premier racing series, Detroit or Daytona Beach.

For Richard Petty the Chrysler decision was without debate — the Level Cross operation was on the corporation's payroll. Though Richard would have preferred to defend his newly acquired title, the decision was made in the late fall of '64 to go drag racing, something that would prove to be immensely popular with fans and drag strip promoters across the Southeast. Both the Pettys and Chrysler officials were willing to wait it out during the 1965 season, feeling NASCAR would eventually come around and see things their way.

In late 1964 Ford had declared it would not compete in Grand National racing in 1965 as long as the Dodges and Plymouths were allowed to use their Hemi engine. In turn Chrysler wasn't about to compete without the "great equalizer." Bill France Sr. was also banking on General Motors re-entering the arena because the rules appeared to favor that automaker specifically over Ford and Chrysler. It wasn't long before things began to take shape, and for NASCAR the pressure was quickly on to find a solution.

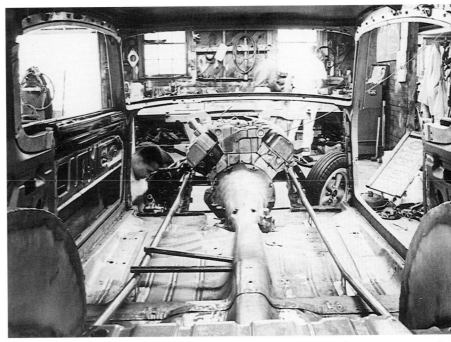

A rare photo of the first Barracuda being built in the Petty Shops in Level Cross. The stock 'Cuda was stripped and then modified along the lines of a stock car. Clearly evident are the inner support rails and the new rear wheel tubs. Richard Petty Private Collection

The 1965 season began at Riverside in mid-January for the annual Motor Trend 500. No factory-backed Mopars showed up. It was a Ford and Mercury romp! At Daytona in mid-February, again no factory-backed Mopars. And again it was a FoMoCo cakewalk as Fords and Mercurys took the first ten finishing positions.

As the new season unfolded and the series moved to the short and medium length tracks, it was quickly apparent the paying customers were not willing to spend their money to watch one Ford outrun another Ford. In addition there was a lack of harmony among factory drivers. Egos and tempers were on the ragged edge. It wasn't any fun just beating each other across the finish line — there needed to be a real adversary!

Promoters and race track officials were howling mad at NASCAR. As the attendance dropped, gate receipts and revenues were plummeting. Something had to be done and fast! It was the worst possible equation: unhappy racetrack owners plus

NUGGETS

Two life-saving changes that became part of NASCAR racing with the 1965 season were the racing tire inner liner developed by Goodyear and the bladder-style gas tank, commonly referred to as the "fuel cell." Both innovations went a long way to make this form of motorsports safer for everyone, especially the drivers.

unhappy drivers plus unhappy car companies plus unhappy fans! What was a poor sanctioning body to do?

At the same time, the Pettys were touring the Southeast with the sweetest little blue rocketship this side of the Mason-Dixon line. During the winter months, Petty Engineering had taken a production 1965 Plymouth Barracuda and turned it into a hemi-powered single-seat missile capable of

Maurice Petty makes an adjustment to the massive Hemi stuffed into the little Barracuda. Dale Inman looks on. Richard Petty Private Collection

like no other 1965 Barracuda because it was stripped of every ounce of unnecessary weight, reinforced with heavy-duty parts from the Petty's stock-car-building experience, and propelled by a monstrous 426 Hemi V-8 utilizing every trick that Maurice Petty's engine department knew. At first the car was equipped with with dual carbs and a Torqueflite automatic transmission. Ultimately the refined dragster was further lightened with a fiberglass front end, Hilburn fuel injection, and a Chrysler four-speed stick.

The first time out for "Outlawed" was at Piedmont Dragway in Greensboro, North Carolina. The best speed of the day was almost 140 mph. During that season the car continually drew standing-room only crowds all over the southeastern United States in exhibition runs, match races, and sanctioned events.

Richard Petty continued to compete in drag racing into late summer of the 1965 season, but only in a few special events. As a stock car driver though, Richard's desire was to get back to driving races that lasted a little longer than a few brief moments in time.

Back in Grand National competition, Bill France had tried everything he could think of to help promoters lure fans back to the grandstands. Nothing worked, not even reinstating Curtis Turner from a lifetime NASCAR banishment. Turner had been penalized for daring to organize a drivers' union. Upon his return to active competition, Turner said it was like getting out of prison.

Finally in late July, NASCAR rescinded its no-hemi mandate, allowing the Chrysler fleet of factory-backed race cars to compete again, but under some limitations. On Sunday, July 25, Richard Petty and the rest of the Chrysler crew returned from exile to race in the Volunteer 500 at Bristol, Tennessee.

For Petty it was an inauspicious debut. He lasted only 338 laps before retiring with differential failure. Richard Petty went on to compete in the last 14 races of the 1965 season,

running the quarter mile in the then-incredible time of 10 seconds at over 140 mph.

The Pettys built a real crowd pleaser that received tons of publicity and cut into Ford's territory in a different area. The little Plymouth was successful winning titles, trophies, and big

money events. Rumor has it that Richard was outrun only about a half-dozen times down the quarter mile.

They named the little blue Plymouth "Outlawed" and later "43/JR," this one looking very much like a shrunken version of Petty's Grand National Belvederes. It was

Waiting patiently to do a drag run in a beautifully appointed race car. It even had black carpeting. Richard Petty Private Collection

Early in its career, the 'Cuda already had bigger air scoops fitted and holes cut into the hood to keep the hood from lifting at speed. You can also see the simple roll bar through the windshield. Richard Petty Private Collection

winning four times, finishing ten times in the top five, 10 times in the top ten, and registering 38th place in the championship title chase.

The France announcement included the new rules for the 1966 season. Of course, these were the new and improved rules designed to keep everybody happy. Ford had already announced its intentions to introduce a new overhead cam 427 engine for competition, and it was rumored that Chrysler was ready with a double overhead cam hemi should the Ford behemoth be approved for competition.

And again the stage was set for another unsettling and highly unusual season for Richard Petty as the curtain rose on NASCAR Grand National competition for 1966.

1965 PLYMOUTH BARRACUDA

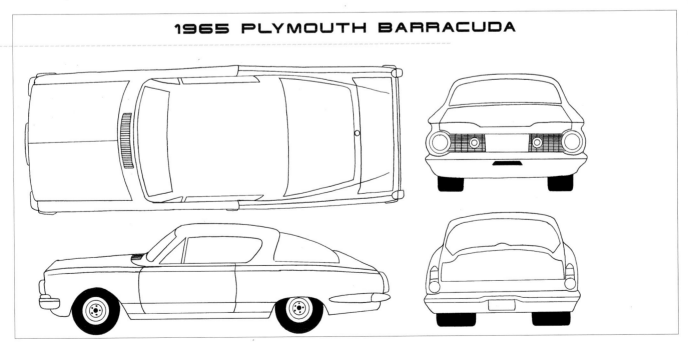

Bobby Isaac stays close to Richard as the Chrysler teams return to Grand National racing in the later half of the year.
Richard Petty Private Collection

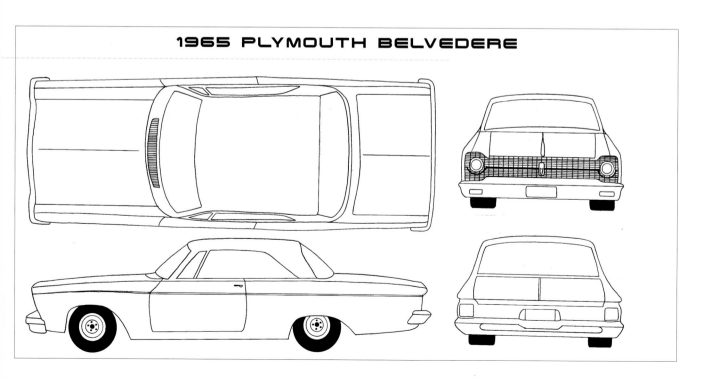

1965 PLYMOUTH BELVEDERE

Back end details on the Barracuda. Note the scoop on the left rear fender. Richard Petty Private Collection

SIGNIFICATA

- Engines now limited to a max of 427 cubic inches.
- Short track cars limited to 116 inch wheelbase, superspeedway cars to 119 inch wheelbase.
- Only engines of "production" design allowed. Hemi, SOHC, and Stagger Valve banned from competition.
- Chrysler boycotts first half of season.
- Ford runs the 427 "Wedge" engine.
- Minimum weight of 3900 pounds is established.
- Maximum rim width of 8.5 inches established.
- Holman and Moody perfect the "rear steer" suspension parts that become standard for the next decade and a half.
- North Carolina Motor Speedway at Rockingham opens and hosts its first Grand National event.
- Driving a Ford, Ned Jarrett wins his second Grand National Championship over the course of 55 races. Richard Petty finishes 38th in points, competing in only 14 events. He still managed four wins and ten top-tens.

*The second Barracuda, shown at the Pocono Drag Lodge, had a distinctly altered wheelbase than the first car and carried a fuel-injected version of the mighty hemi (the stacks covered by a cloth in this photo.) Compare the placement of the rear wheels in this photo to the photo taken in January of the "Outlawed" car. Though not immediately noticeable, the rear bumper chine is much longer in this picture.
Tommy Martin*

This side shot, taken in January 1965, shows just how far back Richard was sitting in the car. It now carries the "Outlawed" lettering as well, but this is still the first Barracuda. Richard Petty Private Collection

Stock cars went through some major changes in the mid '60s in an effort to make them safer and more durable, while still keeping the spirit of being "stock." A new cluster of instruments had replaced the stock items. Note, however, the key in the ignition.
Richard Petty Private Collection

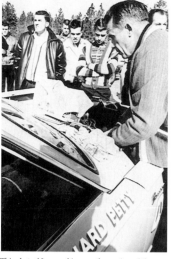

This is the car Richard drove when he was finally able to go stock car racing in 1965. The Richard Petty Private Collection

This shot of Lee working on the engine of the Barracuda also shows one of the rare times that Richard's name was painted on a car. The Richard Petty Private Collection

The battery in this era was supposed to be under the hood or in some location approved by the NASCAR inspectors. Some batteries were placed in the trunk on the driver's side to aid in weight distribution. The Richard Petty Private Collection

The single brake master cylinder was a small unit mounted on the firewall. Note the standard street hood hinges. The Richard Petty Private Collection

Cars rode on leaf springs in the rear during that time. This shot shows the spring shackle and the standard-type gas tank used at the time.
The Richard Petty Private Collection

Dale Inman adjusts the carbs on the Barracuda. Note the wingnuts that hold the intake scoops in place. The Richard Petty Private Collection

The gas cap on cars at that time were wired to the car so that they could be flipped on and off with a twist and not be lost in the process. The Richard Petty Private Collection

This shot was taken under the car from the rear looking towards the front. Header pipes exit either side of the car ahead of the rear wheels.
The Richard Petty Private Collection

Richard poses with his '65 Barracuda. The Richard Petty Private Collection

Lee Petty tinkers with the Hemi engine in the Barracuda. Note the plug boots in going through the valve covers.
The Richard Petty Private Collection

The upper portion of the roll cage behind the driver's seat shows the padding used even at this time. The Richard Petty Private Collection

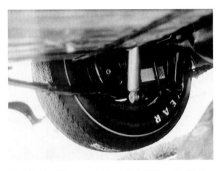

The left side of the rear axle shows that all the parts didn't always match. Note the color of the one shock compared to the other. The Richard Petty Private Collection

The front of this '65 Plymouth had a set of air scoops to cool the brakes located directly under the corners of the front bumper. The Richard Petty Private Collection

As each year passed, the number of bars included in a typical roll cage increased. This shows the arrangement of the bars behind the driver's seat.
The Richard Petty Private Collection

The brake-cooling ducts were a bit of genius. Aimed at the backing plates, the air was captured from the inside of the cockpit and driven down to the brakes by a drum fan.
The Richard Petty Private Collection

Another shot of the trunk shows the brake ducting and the production hinges required at the time on the trunk lid.
The Richard Petty Private Collection

A shot of the front upper A-arm assembly also shows how much of the inner wheel wells and sheet metal has been removed.
The Richard Petty Private Collection

By this time the cockpit was a strange mix of stock and racing components. The steering column, dash-board, door trim, and ignition switch are all stock while the rest is typical racing gear. The Richard Petty Private Collection

This photo shows how the seat was mounted and how the seat belts were attached to their hard points in the cockpit. The Richard Petty Private Collection

A truck bucket seat was reinforced and padded to help hold the driver in place. The Richard Petty Private Collection

The right side of the rear axle shows the twin shocks and the drilled backing plates on the drum brakes which were the standard at the time. The Richard Petty Private Collection

Petty and the Hemi return with a vengeance

Repeat Performance

To understand and interpret the NASCAR Grand National rulebook for 1966 required a lot more than a simple grasp of the language. What had started out as a "strictly stock" series in the late 1940s with a few easily understood rules had now become a linguistic maze.

The new rules announced in late 1965 allowed Chrysler to use its disputed hemi engine even on the superspeedways — but reduced to 405 cubic inches on tracks above one mile long. Ford could use its new OverHead Cam 427 engine in the big Galaxies but with a weight penalty pushing the heft over the two-ton level.

Bill France was emphatic that any special high-performance engines used in Grand National competition had to be production line items. To emphasize this point he made a trip to both Chrysler and Ford assembly plants. Chrysler had long been rumored to be offering the Hemi in mid-sized Plymouths and Dodges for 1966 as a production-line item, and France saw this firsthand during his trip to Chrysler. Ford on the other hand had never planned to actually install the OHC engine on the assembly line but rather offer approximately 1,000 units for sale to the public as a separate item.

Chrysler's boycott of the 1965 Grand National season had been a financial disaster and a situation NASCAR did not wish to repeat. With

this in mind as the 1966 season began, France held off making a repeat performance of the 1965 season. As an additional "carrot" the new rules would allow Ford to use two four-barrel carbs on its wedge-type 427 power plant. But Ford was adamant about the use of the OHC engine and continued to petition France as the 1966 season got under way.

Richard Petty won the season-opening event in Augusta, Georgia, in a year-old Plymouth. Dan Gurney kept the unbroken Ford string alive by winning the Motor Trend 500 at Riverside for the fourth straight year. But by the time everyone arrived in Daytona and had time to test and tune, it again became evident to Ford that its race cars were no match for the new lightning-fast Chrysler siblings on the superspeedways. Richard Petty

Richard plays leader of the pack to an assortment of makes, models, and years at Daytona. Chuck Torrence

The 1966 Plymouth sits on its trailer at Trenton Speedway in New Jersey. Richard Petty Private Collection

At the front of the pack - a position the Belvedere was in for most of the season. The Richard Petty Private Collection

While the '66 didn't look aerodynamic, it was smaller and didn't require as much effort to push it through the air. Note the gas cap and cable at the rear of the car. Chuck Torrence

continued right where he left off at the end of his first championship season by annihilating the competition and scoring his second Daytona 500 victory.

Ford did not take this situation lightly. The automaker immediately withdrew from a handful of short-track events just to show that it could be 1965 all over again. And when ACCUS (Automobile Competition Committee of the United States) recommended and NASCAR accepted a weight handicap on Fords if the OHC engine was used, Ford withdrew its factory-backed teams from further competition on April 15.

Though Ford said it could not compete under these rules, its decision to keep factory-supported race cars away didn't have the effect on attendance that the Chrysler boycott in 1965 did. A few big-name Ford drivers found other rides and with some measure of success. Curtis Turner went to work driving a Chevelle for Smokey Unick. Defending 1965 champ Ned Jarrett managed to work out deals with independents like Henley Gray to get back into action. Petty Enterprises fielded a second blue Plymouth for Marvin Panch, and he won the World 600. No doubt 1966

was a Dodge versus Plymouth battle, and this fact is reflected in the win column. Ford had only 12 wins, Mercury had 2 victories; Dodge had 18 and Plymouth won 16 races. The one exception was a handful of victories by a young modified ace named Bobby Allison driving a small block 1965 Chevy Chevelle.

The championship went to David Pearson, wheeling Cotton Owen's white number six Dodges. Media reports show a season-long battle between Pearson and Richard Petty. The final points total, though, doesn't necessarily reflect that fact. Rookie-

The nimble #43 Plymouth races against Fred Lorenzen in the #28 Holman-Moody Ford.
The Richard Petty Private Collection

Richard leads the field behind the pace car on the parade lap of the Daytona 500.
Richard won from the pole. The Richard Petty Private Collection

Sponsor decals were already starting to take over the front fender of the cars by the mid sixties. This photo shows who was helping Richard's efforts in 1966.
The Richard Petty Private Collection

SIGNIFICATA

- Firestone and Goodyear begin producing tires with inner liners.
- NASCAR makes inner-liners mandatory at superspeedways.
- Standard Class – 119 inch wheelbase, 430 cubic inches, 4000 pound minimum
- Intermediate Class – 115 inch wheelbase, 430 cubic inches, 4000 pounds or 405 cubic inches, 3500 pounds.
- Compact Class – 115 inch wheelbase, 335 cubic inches, 2500 pound minimum.
- Hemi allowed back in, however Chrysler had to use the Fury and Polara on the Superspeedways while smaller Chrysler cars had to use the 426 "Wedge".
- Chevy allowed to use the 427 "Stagger Valve" again.
- Ford allowed to use the SOHC 427 in Standard Class cars only. Cars run with a significant weight handicap.
- All manufacturers must produce 5,000 units to qualify.
- 426 Hemi and 427 SOHC use 1 carb., 427 Stagger Valve uses 2 carburetors.
- Fuel cells now mandatory.
- Four bars now required on the driver's side with one bar required on the passenger side.
- Dual master brake cylinders are now recommended.
- Reinforcing of the stock frame is now permitted.
- Seat belts, crash helmets, and shoulder harnesses are now mandatory.
- Top of hood must be at least 31 inches high from ground.
- Ford teams boycott over engine rules. It doesn't have the same effect as Chrysler's walkout.
- Bud Moore builds a Mercury Comet intermediate race car. When Ford teams end their walkout, they return with similar "half-chassis" intermediates fitted with 1965 Galaxie front frame clips.
- Deck lid spoilers allowed on Dodge Chargers.
- Driving a Dodge Charger, David Pearson wins his first Grand National Championship over the course of 49 races. Richard Petty finishes third in points.

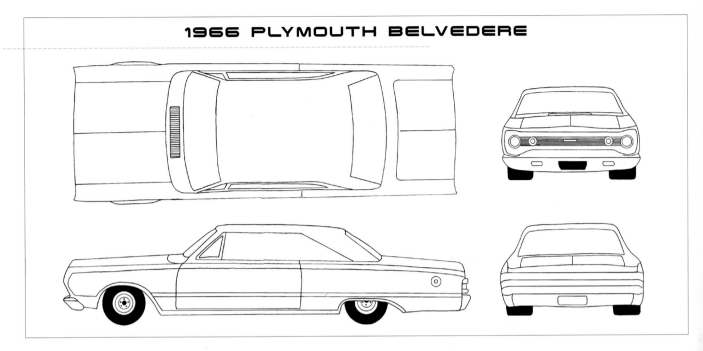

1966 PLYMOUTH BELVEDERE

sensation James Hylton in a year-old '65 Cotton Owens-built Dodge Coronet finished second to Pearson. Hylton didn't win a race all season long but his consistency had him around when it counted — at the finish.

Of course, the other major bright spot for Chrysler Corporation in 1966 was Richard Petty's second Daytona 500 victory in his Hemi-powered Belvedere. Richard won just eight races out of 39 starts in '66, but many were in high-profile events at Daytona, Darlington, and Atlanta. He also registered an incredible 19 poles and 15 outside pole starts as well as 20 top-five and 22 top-ten finishes.

To appreciate just how far NASCAR was willing to go for first-line Ford machinery, Junior Johnson showed up in August at Atlanta with a '66 Galaxie so radically modified that it soon became known as the "Yellow Banana." The top had been severely chopped and the nose of the car had a decided downward incline to it. The rear end of the car swept up into what must have been the world's largest spoiler on a stock-bodied race car! That the car sailed right through NASCAR inspection raised many eyebrows. But when Cotton Owens was asked by inspectors to raise the front ride height of Pearson's Dodge

Charger by a scant 1/4 inch, the incensed car owner promptly loaded up and headed for home.

Though the "Yellow Banana" had a short and uneventful life in racing, it did have a major impact on the NASCAR Grand National rulebook. Shortly thereafter, a new inspection procedure and lexicon were added to the NASCAR routine. Mandated body templates reportedly derived from the profile centerline of their production counterparts were used to authenticate the shape and contours of Grand National race car bodies. This procedure remains an integral part of the sports inspection procedures.

By September factory Fords began returning to the NASCAR fold. Initially, a few Fairlanes and Comets appeared, each with a hand-crafted chassis that again stretched the "strictly stock" interpretation of the rulebook. At first NASCAR refused to approve these race cars for competition. Eventually, though, the sanctioning body realized this new breed of "stock" car was the wave of the future, especially from the safety standpoint.

When the NASCAR rules for the 1967 season were in place, many of the references to "production-based" parts had vanished from the rule-

book. The new Ford chassis was in reality an adaptation of the highly successful unit used under the full-size 1965 and '66 Galaxies, much like the design that has carried the sport into the 1990s.

One other important innovation to come out of the 1966 NASCAR Grand National season was a small strip of sheet metal that in future years would become an integral part of all NASCAR race cars. The new Dodge Charger was without doubt the aerodynamic "bullet" in NASCAR Grand National racing for the 1966 season. The car's smooth nose and fastback profile seemed to make it the ideal choice for high-speed racing. Unfortunately, at those lofty speeds the new Charger was about as stable in the handling department as the proverbial "fat lady on skates." NASCAR officials learned that without some means of stabilizing the car at high speeds it was not only not very competitive — it was downright dangerous! The 1966 Dodge Charger soon sported the first approved "spoiler" on the trailing edge of the deck lid in NASCAR competition.

As everyone awaited the 1967 season no one, not even Richard Petty, could anticipate the adventure that lay ahead.

Richard
becomes "The King"

Richard poses beside the car that completely dominated the 1967 season. Note that the chrome trim has been replaced by a set of pin stripes. Richard Petty Private Collection

Petty's cars rarely ever had his name on them, but there were exceptions. Here he sits in his Plymouth at the NASCAR 500 in Riverside, California. Bob Tronolone

Richard Petty was ready to go racing, the team having built three new cars for the 1967 season. Though he had experienced his share of headaches during the previous year, the Petty team felt things were really beginning to come together during the last half of the '66 season. Richard had won 15 poles in 1966 and handful of races on the short tracks in July and August, even though mechanical problems sidelined him in 17 events. Furthermore, the rule squabbles that nearly destroyed the sport over the span of the previous two seasons seemed finally at an end.

There were some very grim faces at Chrysler, though, just two races into the new year. Indy 500 star Parnelli Jones outran everyone in the Motor Trend 500 at the Riverside race. Then in the second event of the season fellow USAC veteran Mario Andretti pushed his Holman-Moody Fairlane to victory in the Daytona 500.

After the lackluster start of the newly built '67 Plymouths, the Pettys decided to hang new sheet metal on the year-old car they'd had such good success with near the end of the previous season. The next race after Daytona was a 150-miler at Weaverville, North Carolina. Richard

and the " '66 with a facelift" were both revitalized, and together they won by two laps. Indeed there was something special about that ol' blue Plymouth. Anything and everything the Pettys did to this particular race car worked and only seemed to make it race better!

Even with this convincing win no one, not even Richard Petty, had the slightest idea of what was in store for the balance of the 1967 season. History was soon to be made and records were about to be set that would probably never be equaled or broken.

But the threat of a boycott nearly stopped the most impressive season

Final preparations for sending a race car to the track. Note the extended cab Dodge truck the team used as a hauler with a trailer towed behind it.
Richard Petty Private Collection

in the history of major-league stock-car racing by a Chrysler factory-backed race car. Obviously due in part to the early-season success of Ford race cars, Chrysler complained loudly that its rival's engines were illegal and that NASCAR inspectors weren't checking the Fairlanes and Comets closely enough with the newly mandated body templates. Chrysler kept up the rhetoric even though Plymouth and Dodge race cars managed to find their way to victory in six of the nine races after Daytona.

Chrysler declared that all factory-supported Dodge and Plymouth teams would boycott in the upcoming Atlanta 500 on April 2 unless NASCAR quickly addressed the complaints. All the Chrysler teams defied the parent company's declaration and raced at the Georgia 1.5 mile track. Many teams and drivers, after sitting out most of the 1965 season and dealing with the controversies of 1966, felt it was time to go racing and stop arguing.

Out of the 48 events held in the 1967 NASCAR season, Richard Petty won an unprecedented 27. This was at a time when NASCAR's premier series was still running on just about every type of racing surface there was: small paved bullrings; dusty, dirty, pot-hole infested dirt tracks; and superspeedways such as Daytona, Darlington, and Atlanta. Along with the 27 victories Petty posted in 1967, he finished in the top five 38 times and 40 times in the top ten. He completed 41 of the 48 races in 1967.

After the win on pavement at Weaverville, Petty had four victories in April at Columbia, South Carolina; Hickory, North Carolina; Martinsville; and Richmond, Virginia. In May Richard won for the first time in his career in the Rebel 400 at Darlington. It was also the first time any Petty had recorded a victory at Darlington, and the win broke another long-standing

Lee stands beside the newly completed '67. If you look into the cockpit you can see a tube-style headrest. Richard Petty Private Collection

Richard in turn six at Riverside for the NASCAR 500 in January 1967. The unusual numbers were an experiment that seemed like a good idea but were later dropped in favor of the tried and true style that remains the Petty trademark. Bob Tronolone

Maurice anchors the front end of the race car to the trailer with chains as the rest of the car gets covered with plastic. Richard Petty Private Collection

Richard blows by on the outside of Tiny Lund's Ford at the Trenton Speedway. Ray Masser

NUGGETS

A wolf in sheep's clothing

When we asked Richard and Dale what made the 1967 Plymouth so potent a race car, they both chuckled and looked at one another. Dale finally answered by saying, "The 1966". They went on to explain that the crew had built a couple of new race cars for the 1967 season. They were identical to the cars they built in '66 except for some new sheetmetal, but for some quirky reason the new cars were not as good as the older ones. They finally decided to reskin one of the older '66 cars with the new '67 bodywork — not that there was a lot of difference. But with that change, the "new" '67s suddenly ran a lot better — and started winning races.

History shows that the '67 Plymouth — specifically Richard's '67 Plymouth — dominated the sport that year. But the truth being told, the cars that won most of the races were really year old race cars . So, what was it that made them so good? All we got was a chuckle, a shrug, and a "Damned if we know." from one of NASCAR's best crew chiefs.

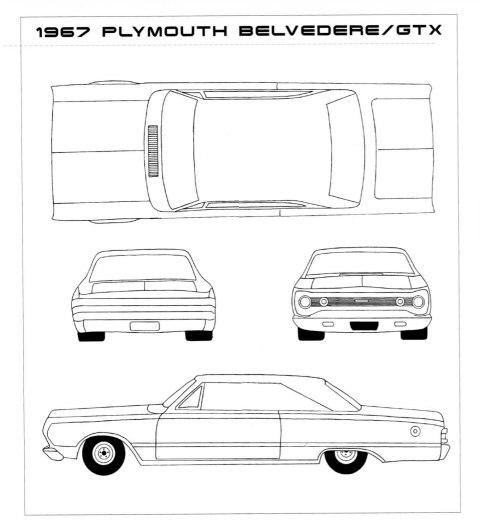

mark. This visit to victory lane at Darlington was Richard Petty's 55th career win, topping his father Lee's career record of 54.

The 250-mile race at Nashville lends more perspective on how intimidating the Petty juggernaut was becoming. Early in the race the blue Plymouth blew a tire and hit the wall, knocking the front end out of alignment and breaking a rear spring. The crew wanted to park the car but Richard said no. With a guess at realignment and some baling wire on the rear spring, Petty re-entered the race seven laps behind. Petty ran the field into the ground. One by one the front-runners had trouble and dropped out of sight. When it was all over Richard Petty had not only made up his seven laps and won the race, but he had won by five laps over the second-place finisher!

Winning 27 races in one season is an amazing accomplishment for any NASCAR driver, but Richard Petty

topped that by recording ten of those wins in a row. The string started with a victory at Winston-Salem on August 12. Then it was Columbia, South Carolina, and Savannah, Georgia, followed by the Darlington win. Next was Hickory, North Carolina; Richmond, Virginia; Beltsville, Maryland; and Hillsborough, North Carolina. The streak ran through number 10 at North Wilkesboro on October 1, 1967.

Though the Pettys and Chrysler officials were overjoyed at the success Richard was experiencing, Ford teams and FoMoCo factory-types were beside themselves. Richard Petty and his trusty car were beating the best drivers and equipment Ford could field. Everyone was beginning to wonder if anything could stop the blue tidal wave.

The final showdown came at Charlotte on October 15 for the running of the National 500. Ford had all the regulars in top form and had

The '67 in its final race in January 1968 at the NASCAR 500. Note the broad white stripe and the fuel fill on the right side of the car. Bob Tronolone

A good shot of the back of the car. Note that there are no numbers on the rear light panels as there are today.
The Richard Petty Private Collection

Richard poses with one of his most successful race cars. In two seasons with this body style, he won an amazing 35 races.
The Richard Petty Private Collection

Richard out in front of the field. Grille screens were typical at the time.
The Richard Petty Private Collection

At speed in 1967; Note the increased number of sponsor decals on the front fender.
The Richard Petty Private Collection

This was a very common scene in 1967 — Richard taking the checkered flag ahead of the rest of the field in a seemingly unbeatable car.
Richard Petty Private Collection

Another shot of the '67 Plymouth, at Trenton. Note the number of decals here compared to the photo above. Ray Masser

imported other well-known drivers like Jim Clark, Mario Andretti, and Jack Bowhser in an attempt to put an end to the Petty-Plymouth rout. None of them finished the race. Richard completed only 268 laps, leaving the race due to engine failure. Buddy Baker won the National 500 in a Dodge, chased closely by another Dodge driven by Bobby Isaac. Only two Fords finished in the top ten. The other eight positions were filled with Dodges and Plymouths.

Richard Petty did not win again as the 1967 season concluded. It was a moot issue at this point. His total dominance during most of the season had guaranteed his second championship title in four years.

The 1966-67 Plymouth that Richard Petty drove to at least 30 victories over two seasons is currently on permanent display in the Joe Weatherly Museum in Darlington, South Carolina.

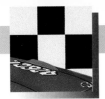
Some said the Pettys were two years ahead of everybody else. Plymouth's lax attitude blows the advantage for all.

And Plymouth Slept

T he late '60s were a time when muscle cars were all the rage on American streets from Boston to Los Angeles and back to Daytona. There was no doubt that racing was helping to shape the types of cars that were prowling the streets, but at the same time, street cars were definitely helping to shape what was showing up on the track. Just about every auto manufacturer was focused on making their particular fleet of cars the fastest around the block or the track. Body styles were changing in an effort to make the cars more competitive. With a season like the Pettys had in 1967, it appears that Plymouth may have been over confident about their approach to racing, at least where NASCAR's Grand National series was concerned.

The Plymouth GTX was greatly improved from the slab sided version of the year before. The body was significantly smoother and cleaner than the car that had just trounced the circuit with a 27 win season. With a cleaner front end and a sculpted rear window, the car appeared more graceful and sleek. Plymouth was confident in their equipment and in their #1 team that could milk the most out of their cars. After all, the Pettys were the best in finding slick, sly, and ingenious ways to make a car go fast and 1968 would be a season that would underscore just how good the Pettys were at their craft.

Looking a little war-torn, Richard and Lee Roy Yarbrough dive into a turn at Trenton Speedway. Note that the roof of the car has returned to the usual blue. Ray Masser

Dodge, the other Chrysler division, was pulling out all the stops to catch up with their Charger to produce a more aerodynamic body. The fastback Charger from 1966 and 1967 had terrible handling problems and Chrysler assigned its engineers to get the Dodge program into the winner's circle.

All the technical concentration on Dodge didn't escape the attention of the Petty team. It appeared to the Pettys that they were being left to fight Plymouth's battles alone while Dodge was getting all the help one could ever hope for. Since racing is all about getting the most advantage over your opponents, this situation didn't exactly lend itself to the Petty's getting their fair share of advantage.

Petty asked Chrysler factory officials to let him switch to a Dodge Charger for the 1968 season. They flatly rejected this idea, contending they already had all the Dodge teams lined up for 1968. Anyway, he was their number one "Plymouth guy." Hadn't

Richard Petty made a name for himself for years at the wheel of various Plymouth race cars? There was no Dodge in Petty's future, at least not for 1968.

Petty's request to switch did alert Chrysler enough to insure that any engineering bells and whistles that Dodge benefited from should be shared with the Plymouth camp as well. As a result, Chrysler assigned a select group of factory engineers to expend their considerable talents and imagination toward making the new Charger and GTX race cars as good as possible. Considerable effort was applied to better aerodynamics and improved handling. Every attempt was made to stay (barely) within the "intent" of the NASCAR rulebook. The body shells were lowered over the chassis pan. The body shells were repositioned on the wheelbase. And suspension and engine mounting points were skillfully repositioned. The results were impressive and

Richard's Road Runner at Daytona sported a black roof that looked like vinyl, but was actually a type of texture paint. The theory was that air would fill the textured surface and create a slicker surface over the top of the car. Richard Petty Private Collection

though the Plymouths benefited from the effort, the Dodge Chargers gained the most from these bits of engineering sleight-of-hand.

To its credit, Petty Enterprises further massaged the new intermediate body shell and ultimately outdistanced the other factory-backed Plymouths and many of the Chargers. Whatever the mandated templates didn't touch, body panels were sculpted. The undersides of the blue Plymouths were treated to some "smoothing" and an attempt at enclosing the rear of the chassis with a type of "belly pan" was employed. Richard and Dale Inman both admit that the 1968 Plymouth was the most "trick" car the team ever fielded. However, the competition wasn't about to take all of this lying down.

Ford Motor Company had not taken well to the licking experienced in 1967 solely at the hands of the now-acknowledged "King" of major league stock car racing and his seemingly unstoppable blue Plymouth. Ford and its Mercury division had been hard at work redesigning their respective intermediate hardtop coupes. If they couldn't gain an edge under the hood, a slippery fastback body shape similar to the sloped back on the popular 1967 Mustang might just make up for a lack of horses. The 1968 Ford Torino and Mercury Montego shared a new slick wind-cheating "fastback" silhouette that quickly reaffirmed the theory that it takes much less effort to propel a dart than a brick.

As everyone descended upon Daytona and the '68 season began, it

SIGNIFICATA

- Engines limited to 430 cubic inches.
- Ford's 427 SOHC engine virtually disappears. Engine is too expensive and not readily available to teams. All Ford teams use 427 Wedge instead.
- Ford debuts new Torino and Mercury Cyclone.
- Minimum weight now 3650 pounds.
- Car numbers of at least eighteen inches are still required on the trunk deck lid.
- No weight or displacement handicaps were placed on any car or engine.
- Midseason 426 Hemi and 427 Stagger Valve could use two 4 barrel carburetors.
- Late in the year, Dodge introduces the Charger 500 version of their car with cleaned up aerodynamics to run in 1969. Ford counters with the Talladega version of the Torino.
- Richard Petty asks Chrysler to allow him to switch from Plymouth to Dodge because of new Charger 500. Chrysler says no, so Petty switches to Ford for 1969.
- Driving a Ford, David Pearson wins his second Grand National Championship over the course of 49 races. Richard Petty finishes third in points.

Petty chases after Bobby Isaac in the #71 K&K Dodge. Note that the door handles have been removed and the areas blanked off. Chuck Torrence

The texture paint idea was repeated at the Firecracker 400 at Daytona in July, but with a different twist. This time the roof, hood, and tops of the rear fenders were all painted white. Here the crew services the car early in the race. NASCAR Archives

With a white top, the car was definitely cooler in the July heat, but the experiment ended early when Richard's engine failed, dropping him from the race. Note the off-centered number on the roof of the car. NASCAR Archives

The 1968 Road Runner was one of the most tricked out cars ever run by Petty Enterprises. Note the rake of the car and the Hemi markings on the hood. Bill Coulter

became clear that Ford had its act together. Practice speeds for both the Torinos and Montegos neared the 190 mph range. Cale Yarborough took the pole for the Daytona 500 with a speed just a tick over 189 miles per hour, nearly ten mph faster than the pole speed just one year before.

In the race itself, nothing was any match for the Fords and Mercurys. Cale Yarborough, LeeRoy Yarbrough, and Bobby Allison vied for the first three positions. USAC driver Al Unser in fourth was the only Mopar driver to finish on the lead lap, driving the #6 Cotton Owen's Charger. Richard Petty finished in eighth place, two laps down.

That's not to say that the Pettys were whipped on the speed of the Fords alone. The team arrived at the Florida tri-oval with their first two-toned race car in nearly twenty years. With black vinyl tops being a popular option on the street, speed engineers pointed out that there may be a way to make the car more slippery. Aerodynamicists will tell you that air slips over air better than it does anything else. If the surface is like a golf-ball, air will fill the various pockets and cause the airflow to slip over the surface much more efficiently. To take advantage of this principle, Inman had the roof of the car painted with a black texture paint that closely replicated the vinyl roofs of the nation's street cars. In fact, it looked so much

like the real thing that many believed that it actually was a real vinyl roof used to hide an unusually thin metal roof.

According to Dale Inman, a weld had been missed on the front edge of the roof because of the way the front bar on the roll cage had been installed. From the moment the car made its first runs at the track, it had a distinct whistle. Like air getting caught on something, it was loud enough that Richard could hear it while driving. As the car sped by, the crew in the pits heard it also. With the weld missing, the roof — which was the standard thickness of sheet metal used at the time — would pucker and gap slightly as the car slipped through the air at nearly 190 mph. The entire team tried to find the source of the problem, but to no avail. Early in the race the paint-

ed roof panel began to separate and peel back like a tin can. Inman was shocked on one pit stop when, while changing the right side front tire, he looked up to discover Richard standing on the hood of the car stomping on the front edge of the roof with his boot! Many pit stops were necessary to duct tape the leading edge of the roof back into place so that Petty could continue the race at competitive speeds. The stops did the team in for the day.

Later in the year, the team tried the principle again. At the Firecracker 400 they used white texture paint on all the upper surfaces except the trunk lid. It was, without a doubt, one of the most unusual-looking Petty cars ever raced and the white paint did help cool the interior of the car.

The Road Runner sends off a shower of sparks as Richard hits the retaining wall at Daytona. The roof had already been taped with duct tape to try and keep the sheet metal from peeling back when the car was at speed.
Bill Coulter

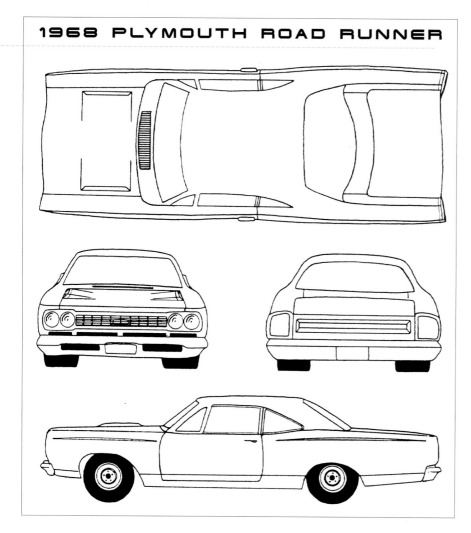

1968 PLYMOUTH ROAD RUNNER

Unfortunately, a blown motor put an end to that race earlier than expected.

With Ford's dominance of the Daytona 500, the tone was set for the balance of the 1968 season. Fords and Mercurys ruled the longer tracks, where sheer speeds were the determining factor. Chrysler cars won only three times on the superspeedways. Cale Yarborough drove his Mercury to four such victories. LeeRoy Yarbrough, David Pearson, and Donnie Allison won one race each.

By season's end, Pearson and Petty had each won 16 events while Bobby Isaac, driver of the K&K Insurance Dodge who finished second in the points race, won only three races. Pearson and his Holman-Moody Ford were in 47 races of the 49 scheduled, but he had more top five and top ten finishes than either Isaac or Petty, thereby winning the 1968 Grand National championship. Most of Petty's 16 victories came on the short-paved or dirt bull rings, where aerodynamics played less of a role in overall performance.

As the season began to draw to a close, the development of the cars and what the auto makers were going to unleash on both the tracks and the streets continued in high gear. The problem was that Plymouth didn't have much to offer in the way of improvements. Dodge had developed an even slicker version of their Charger. The 1968 version of their car was famous for the sails on either side of the rear window. While it looked distinctive, the turbulence generated by this arrangement played havoc with balance of the car. By moving the backlight so it formed a smooth, flush rear window and by moving the front grille so it too was flush with the front end of the car, Dodge created the 1969 Charger 500. These simple changes proved effective enough to add five miles per hour to the top speed of the car at Chrysler's test b ick. Chrysler

was so confident of the new Charger and what it would do that it took the unusual step of unveiling the car in October. Plymouth, on the other hand, had nothing to show and it was equally apparent that Petty would not get a chance to run one of the new Chargers either.

Richard Petty continued to feel frustrated especially since he was being denied the assistance he felt he needed and also was not being allowed by Chrysler officials to switch to Dodge. Ford, seeing an opportunity, spoke to Petty about running a Ford and revealed that more work was being done to further improve the Torinos with a long nosed version that would be named the Talladega.

On Monday, November 25, 1968, Richard Petty made an announcement that he felt was the only option he had left. After ten years with Plymouth, the Pettys would be fielding Ford Torinos for the 1969 season. Petty's announcement about the switch from Plymouth to Ford sent a shock wave through the sport and the new season was awaited with great anticipation.

During a routine pit stop in the Firecracker 400, Richard's crew services his white-topped Road Runner. Bryant McMurray

Note that the number is biased to the driver's side of the roof. This is the only time that Richard's car appeared in this paint scheme. Bryant McMurray

If it weren't for the unbelievable 1967 season, the 1968 Road Runner would probably be remembered as being one of the most refined race cars of its time. The Richard Petty Private Collection

Chrysler's decision not to give the Pettys the fast car they wanted prompts them to move to Ford

The Year of the Torino

The King cuts a corner close as he rounds turn #8 at Riverside, California driving a short-nosed Torino. Bob Tronolone

Richard sits behind the wheel of his 1969 Ford Torino. Note how the door handle and keyway have been blanked off and the addition of the switches on the dash panel, much the same as they are today. Richard Petty Private Collection

No two Torinos were ever marked alike. In fact, the markings changed constantly. Here Richard runs a Torino at Trenton, New Jersey. Ray Masser

Richard leads Lee Roy Yarbrough through Riverside's turn #8 using a different line. This was his first outing in the car. He eventually won the race. Bob Tronolone

At the beginning of the 1969 season the sport of auto racing was still a buzz concerning the stunning announcement made by Richard Petty in late 1968. Unbelievable! Richard Petty leaving his trusty Plymouths behind? Richard Petty in a . . . FORD?

As was the usual practice at the time, NASCAR'S premiere division began in the fall of the previous year and since Petty Enterprises didn't have its new Torinos ready to race, Richard won the first points race of the season at Macon, Georgia, in his tricked-up 1968 Plymouth. He followed that win with a second-place finish at Montgomery, Alabama, in early December.

Between that first week in December and early February, Petty Enterprises was a virtual beehive of activity with all the changes that were taking place. The Pettys were gearing up for the 1969 season in a completely new way. Instead of building their new race cars from the ground up as they always had since Lee Petty began racing, they took delivery of a couple of bare-bones Holman-Moody chassis. From that point on they custom-built their own version of a 1969 Torino NASCAR Grand National race car — hanging the sheet metal, installing the drive train, and adding all the suspension pieces, wiring, plumbing, etc.

The frequent arrival of Ford delivery vans from Charlotte bound for Level Cross were an unusual sight. They were dropping off engines, sheet metal, and chassis parts and anything else that was needed to build the new make of race cars. The casual observer must have wondered if he was in the right place. Level Cross wasn't exactly known as Ford country.

Upon arrival at Riverside, California, for the '69 Motor Trend 500, Richard did seem to have a few things to learn about his new mount. During practice around the legendary nine-turn road course in preparation

1969 FORD TORINO

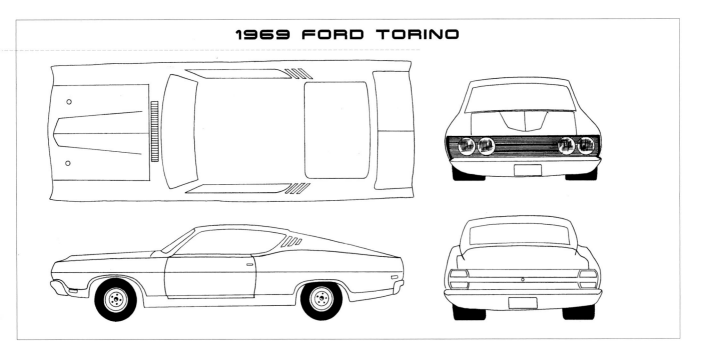

The long-nosed version of the Torino was called the Talladega. Although they were usually marked as such, occasionally they weren't. Chuck Torrence

for qualifying, Petty found himself engaged in what is commonly called "agricultural racing." He sorted out the new Torino and found that its driving and handling characteristics were very different from what he was used to in the family Plymouths.

But Richard Petty always was a "quick study." After starting from the fourth position he moved quickly to take command of the race. Though he

did experience a couple of close calls, including spinning off course twice, he recovered both times to maintain the top spot. Leading 103 of the 186 laps, Petty won his first Grand National race for his new car maker. His only serious threat came from four-time Indy winner A.J. Foyt in a Jack Bowsher-built Torino. Though Foyt continually overrode his brakes attempting to catch leader Petty, he

managed to keep the # 43 Ford in sight and finished on the same lap with the victor.

Both Ford and Dodge introduced new variations of their chosen race cars for use on the superspeedways for the 1969 season. Dodge had already unveiled its Charger 500 in October of the previous year hoping that the slicker Dodge would catch the fast Fords. But Ford had a new weapon too. As Dodge was unveiling the Charger 500, Holman-Moody had been busy tinkering with the Torino. By utilizing the longer front fenders of the Mercury Montego and fitting the front grille flush as on the Charger 500, Holman created what would become known as the Torino Talladega. In addition to the nose job, Holman re-rolled the rocker panels (the area under the doors) so that the clearance was raised one inch. With this change incorporated into the production cars, racers would be allowed to drop the front end of the car even further and thereby add to the wind-cheating rake of the car.

Petty seemed to be off to a flying start, but Daytona would be a much different story. From the time they arrived Richard and the Petty team

The Petty Enterprises crew services Richard's Talladega during a pit stop. The slope of the front valance panel is very apparent here. Bryant McMurray

Oops! Richard's slick Talladega after a close encounter of the concrete kind at Rockingham after blowing a right front tire. It finished his day. Chuck Torrence

had power problems with the Holman-Moody engines they were being provided. It seemed that the powerplants weren't as stout as some of the other Fords on the track, perhaps a reaction to Petty blowing the Ford regulars into the weeds at Riverside. Qualifying twelfth, Richard managed to bring the new car home in eighth place, four laps down to LeeRoy Yarbrough who won the race in Junior Johnson's '69 Ford Talladega.

The folks at Dodge were aghast. Thinking they had the winning combination with the Charger 500, they were disappointed again when the Fords were so dominant. Chrysler's racing executive Robert M. Rodger sent his staff back to the drawing board to create whatever it would take to thwart the Fords. By April, Bobby Isaac had tested a new version of the Charger that included a pointed fiberglass nosecone and a high-mounted rear spoiler. Called the Daytona, Dodge scrambled to get the car into production in time to do battle with the Fords before they walked away with another championship. But it would be September before the car would make its racing debut at Bill France's new superspeedway in Talladega.

The powerplant problem experienced at Daytona was eventually solved when Maurice got a handle on how to get some serious power out of the Ford engines and the team didn't have to rely on engines supplied by Holman-Moody. By then it was the end of April in the Virginia 500 at Martinsville when Richard finally visited victory lane again. During the drought, Petty took a back seat to the ensuing battle among the Dodges of Bobby Allison and Bobby Isaac, the Torino of David Pearson, and the Mercury of Cale Yarborough. However, Petty was always near the front and did manage to hold onto the series points lead.

By the time the series returned to the tri-oval at Daytona for the Firecracker 400 in July, Richard Petty was still clinging to a slim lead in points by consistent finishes and with three wins. But again it was evident the team was having problems getting the new car to behave at high speeds. Petty finished a disappointing fourth, four laps off the pace. LeeRoy Yarbrough backed up his impressive Daytona 500 victory by covering the field and winning the Firecracker 400 over Buddy Baker at the wheel of the Cotton Owens' Dodge Charger.

Richard's fifth win of the season finally came in late July at the inaugural Mason-Dixon 300 at Dover Downs Raceway in Delaware. The blue Torino finished a full six laps

SIGNIFICATA

- Minimum weight is set at 3900 pounds and maximum engine size of 430 cubic inches.
- Dry-sumps now allowed. This also allowed engines to be mounted lower.
- All engines must use one 4 barrel carburetor.
- Drivers must start race on the tires that they qualified on.
- Three specialty cars debut: Ford Talladega, Mercury Cyclone Spoiler II, & Dodge Charger 500.
- Dodge debuted a new car at Talladega race: the Dodge Daytona.
- In-car radio systems are experimented with at Talladega.
- Racing slicks are tried for the first time at Talladega.
- Ford introduces the Boss 429 Hemi and first uses it in the Mercury Spoiler II.
- Rim width is expanded to 9 inches.
- Car numbers of at least eighteen inches are still required on the trunk deck lid.
- Four bars now required on passenger side of roll cage.
- Michigan International Speedway in Brooklyn, Michigan, Dover Downs International Speedway in Delaware, and the Alabama International Motor Speedway in Talladega all open and host their first Grand National events. Drivers claim Talladega is too rough to race on and the tire companies scramble to make a tire that will hold up under race conditions. All major drivers boycotted first race. The surface is later fixed.
- Driving a Ford, David Pearson wins his third Grand National Championship over the course of 54 races. Richard Petty finishes second in points.

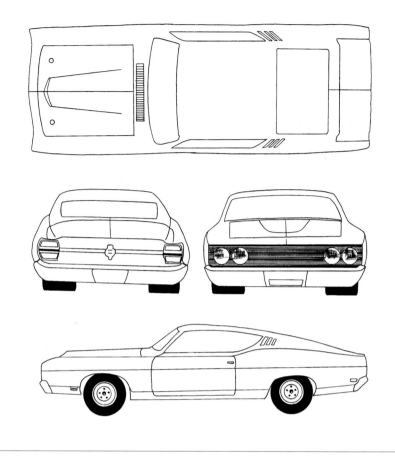

over the field. Again though, the Petty Torino experienced tire blistering problems. Three times Petty had to duck into the pits because of excessive tire wear. The victory was his 94th career win.

As the '69 season headed into the month of August Richard Petty had pushed his Ford to three more wins and a series of third-place finishes looking at the back bumpers of the Yarbrough and Pearson Fords or the Isaac Dodge. Finally on August 22 at Winston-Salem, North Carolina, Richard Petty hit a career milestone no one had ever come close to before. In the "Myers Brothers Stock Car Spectacle" Petty battled all race long with rivals Pearson and Isaac. Bobby Isaac had pushed his red Dodge to a two-lap lead at mid-race over Pearson and Petty. While gambling on fuel mileage, Isaac ran it too close. Forced to pit, Isaac was unable to regain his advantage. Petty outran Pearson to the checkered flag. For Richard Lee Petty it was career victory number 100.

As September approached, Bill France Sr. was putting the finishing touches on what many considered the finest closed-course race track on the map near Talladega, Alabama. The 2.66-mile high-banked tri-oval was billed as the ultimate experience for high-speed stock car racing. France had invested millions and the track was scheduled to open for business in mid-September to host the first-ever Talladega 500.

Some weeks earlier in a motel room in Michigan, in preparation for the first event at the brand-new two-mile track, Richard Petty and many other principal NASCAR Grand National drivers formed the Professional Drivers Association (PDA). It wasn't so much a labor union for the premier series drivers as it was an organization devoted to improving the sports image and conditions inside the series.

The PDA garnered little attention until practice began for the Talladega 500. Many of the drivers were vocal about speeds approaching the 200 mph mark and a track surface they deemed too coarse and bumpy. Numerous tire problems repeatedly caused alarm for drivers, teams, and the Goodyear and Firestone tire companies.

As president of the PDA Richard Petty asked that something be done about the drivers' concerns. Bill France made it clear that he had little tolerance for someone telling him how to run his business, especially his new showplace. When the drivers felt that little was being done about the problems, Petty suggested that PDA members might forego participation in the inaugural event.

The events that followed saw Richard Petty eyeball-to-eyeball with Bill France Sr. Both Goodyear and Firestone were scrambling to find tire compounds that could withstand the grueling pace of sustained laps of nearly 200 mph. Everyone wondered if there would be a race. Would the drivers and teams boycott, or would the tire companies refuse to provide racing tires?

Dwarfed by all this hyperbole was Dodge's long-awaited introduction to racing of its new Charger Daytona, originally offered for sale to the public in April. NASCAR rules mandated a waiting period, forcing Dodge to delay racing the new car until September. The high-tailed, shark-nosed missile was scheduled for debut at Talladega to garner the maximum effect and as a jab at Ford, which had named its main-line race car after the new facility.

The race proceeded on schedule, albeit without most of the name drivers and only one tire company. Just before the race France gave the drivers and crews an ultimatum: either race or leave. Led by the Petty transporter, nearly all the major competitors headed for home.

Richard Brickhouse, driving the Ray Nickels Dodge Daytona vacated by Charlie Glotzbach, won the first Talladega 500 over a field of only 13

Welcome - sort of...

It shocked most of the racing community when Petty Enterprises became a Ford team for 1969. It left a lot of fans stunned by the idea that Richard would be driving a Ford. But that was nothing compared to what the other Ford drivers thought. For the rest of the Ford crews, having the Pettys join their party diluted what they felt they could get from the great blue father in Dearborn. There was also a very real fear that the Pettys would find a way to improve on Ford's "Better Idea" and not bother to let everyone in on it.

When Richard trounced his competition at Riverside the first time out, the rest of the Ford clan howled in protest. So when Richard got his engine from Holman-Moody for Daytona, it seemed to be down on power compared to some of his fellow Ford drivers. Thinking something was up, the team "barrowed" an engine marked for someone else — and promptly gained a few MPH on the track. Once Maurice mastered building a Ford engine the supply/power handicap went away and Richard started winning again.

Fords ran three different engines in 1969. Here a Talladega is equipped with a Boss 429, Ford's version of the Hemi. Bryant McMurray

The tail ends of the Talladega and the Torino were the same. Note the fuel overflow pipe on the museum car exiting where the tail light should be and the extra sheet metal that blends the bumper edges into the body to reduce drag. Tim Bongard

The nose of the Talladega was extended and the vertical cross-section reduced, making the car cut more cleanly through the air. This is the car on display at the Petty Museum. Tim Bongard

At Talladega, Richard is interviewed by Ken Squier about the conditions at the track.
The Richard Petty Private Collection

Grand National cars and 23 NASCAR GT series pony cars. The debut of the new race track and Dodge's new weapon was tarnished but not permanently damaged.

For the balance of the season Richard Petty was able to stay within striking distance of Isaac and Pearson with many top finishes and five more trips to victory lane. Ultimately, in the final stretch of the season, Petty outdistanced Isaac but finished second to Pearson in the season's points chase. David Pearson recorded his third and final NASCAR Grand National title, again driving Holman-Moody Fords.

The season's final stats showed Pearson competing in 51 of 52 events. He had 11 victories with 42 top-five and 44 top-ten finishes. By contrast, Richard Petty had competed in only 50 of the scheduled races. He recorded 10 victories with 31 top-five and 38 top-ten finishes.

None of Richard Petty's 10 wins came on the superspeedways in spite of the team's switch to Ford race cars. And whatever happened to Plymouth? Without Richard Petty winning races for them, Plymouth had nothing the PR folks could write about, a fact made even clearer with a drop in new car sales. Seeing the need to regain what had been lost, Plymouth began making overtures to Petty even before the end of the 1969 season. Chrysler officials now came around with "their hat in their hands." They asked what it would take to get Petty back in a Plymouth? Petty, knowing he could have whatever he wanted, shrewdly made two requests: he wanted Plymouth to build him a "Daytona" to go racing in 1970 and for Petty Enterprises to become the parts distributor for all of Mopar's racing parts. Plymouth couldn't afford to say no.

Richard runs the Plymouth Road Runner and the Superbird

A Tale of Two Birds

In the late sixties and early seventies this was the classic scene — Richard in his Petty Enterprises Mopar doing battle with David Pearson in his Wood Brothers Mercury.
Bryant McMurray

The most memorable cars of the "aero wars" were Chrysler's Plymouth Superbird (Petty's #43) and the Dodge Charger Daytona (Fred Lorenzen's #3, Buddy Baker's #6, and Charlie Glotzbach's #99.) With their pointy noses and huge wings, they were a sight to behold. Richard Petty Private Collection

The Plymouth division of Chrysler Corporation kept its promise to Richard Petty. During the off-season before the 1970 Grand National series, Plymouth and Petty Enterprises collaborated to build one of the most recognizable race cars in the history of motorsports.

Strikingly similar to the 1969 Dodge Charger Daytona, Plymouth's Road Runner Superbird took all the lessons learned by its sister division the previous year and applied them to the Plymouth "B body" in grand fashion. The new "winged warrior," with its distinctive long pointed nose and mile-high rear-wing spoiler, looked to be just what was needed to get the Petty operation back in high gear — especially on the superspeedways, where it had lagged the previous two seasons.

But even with the new race car, the 1970 Grand National season was not going to be a runaway for Richard Petty. Ford had discovered early on that their newly restyled Torino Cobra was no match aerodynamically for the older but "cleaner" Talladega. Ford found using year-old technology was no handicap. In addition, late in the 1969 season NASCAR had approved Ford's use of the new Boss 429 Hemi engine in both the Talladega and Mercury Cyclones. Ford was ready with the right mix of weapons to do battle with both Dodge and Plymouth.

Richard Petty acknowledged that the '69 Ford with such an engine would be formidable competition. But he was thoroughly convinced that the new Superbird was more than a match for the FoMoCo siblings. Besides, Richard believed the 'Bird had a stability and handling edge over the Fords and Mercurys.

Chrysler, in an attempt to cover all bases, hired master road racer Dan Gurney to drive the number 42 Petty Superbird in the 1970 season inaugural event — the Motor Trend 500. This was also in part due to Gurney's new Trans-Am Barracuda deal to run the 1970 SCCA pro-series.

In spite of the new race cars and Gurney's seeming ownership of victory lane at the California road course, A.J. Foyt took Jack Bowsher's 1970 Torino to victory for the Ford camp. Richard Petty, who started sixth, ran near the front most of the event — only to blow an engine with just seven laps remaining. Even with the DNF, Petty placed fifth in the final standings. The hapless Gurney ran into mechanical problems all day, never leading a single lap in spite of his pole start, and he wound up behind Petty in sixth place.

The next race, the Daytona 500, was a tossup during practice, qualifying, and the two 125-mile qualifying races. Would Mercury, Ford, or Dodge have the edge? The new Superbird, though consistently smooth and fast, had shown no flashes of brilliance at the hands of either Richard Petty or brand-new contract driver Pete Hamilton in the Petty team car number 40.

Cale Yarborough's commanding win in the first qualifier at the wheel of the Wood Brothers' '69 Mercury Cyclone must have given a shot of adrenaline to the Mercury contingent, especially after he had also grabbed the pole position over the competition.

The second qualifier, when sorted out, looked like a reunion of year-old race cars: a quartet of 1969 Dodge Daytonas swept the first four positions. In neither of the two shakedown races did the new Superbird appear to have anything to show the other competitors.

Sunday's 500-mile race was another story altogether. Richard Petty lasted only seven laps when his engine died, relegating him to 39th place. While many expected Petty to call his new teammate in and take over that ride as relief driver, Richard simply let Hamilton do what he was hired to do and race. Petty's confidence was rewarded handsomely. The young Massachusetts native outran David Pearson's Talladega to score a decisive victory for the new Plymouth Superbird race car.

SIGNIFICATA

- NASCAR uneasy about all of the factory specialty cars. Requires 1,000 examples or 1/2 the number of dealerships, whichever is greater, to qualify.
- Plymouth hires Petty back and debuts new Plymouth Superbird.
- Ford has 3 racing engines; 427, 428, & 429. Talladega & Spoiler must use 428 and Torino & Cyclone can use 429. Ford races 1969 cars because they are faster and more aerodynamic than 1970 versions.
- Exhaust pipes must now exit in front of rear tires.
- Windshield safety clips for the front windshield are now required. Three on top and two on the bottom.
- Door handles must now be removed and the holes covered over with a piece of aluminum.
- Headlight openings may be used to pick-up air for brake cooling.
- Padded headrest now mandatory.
- Trunk lid number still required. Tail and headlight cover numbers also required.
- Exhaust and fuel filler on left side of car for superspeedways and on the right side for road courses.
- Restrictor plates are now mandatory for superspeedway races.
- Ford withdraws by cutting back racing budget 75%. Chrysler cuts back to backing Petty Enterprises only.
- 12.1 inch tire sidewall established as standard.
- Wheel size expanded to 9.5 inches.
- Firestone withdraws from NASCAR racing completely.
- First race held at the Richmond Fairgrounds Raceway in Virginia this year.
- Driving a Dodge Charger, Bobby Isaac wins the Grand National Championship over the course of 48 races. Richard Petty finishes fourth in points.

At Riverside in June, Richard in a Superbird and Don Tarr in a Dodge Charger race side by side; notice how the modified nose section added to the overall length of the car. Note Richard's window net.
Bob Tronolone

Richard slides through a turn on the dirt at Columbia, South Carolina in his Road Runner. This was one of the last races run on dirt for the Grand National Division.
Richard Petty Private Collection

After knocking out a chunk of the pit wall his Road Runner tumbled with such force that he was nearly thrown from the car.
Richard Petty Private Collection

Hamilton went on in 1970 to record two more victories for the Petty team in just 16 starts. All three of his wins were high-profile events, the kind that made dream headlines for the Plymouth advertising gurus. After his impressive Daytona 500 victory, Pete drove his Petty Superbird to victory in both races held at Alabama International Motor Speedway, the Alabama 500 and the Talladega 500.

Petty took to the new Superbird himself like the proverbial duck to water, scoring 18 wins in forty starts of the 47-race schedule, while recording 27 top-five and 31 top-ten finishes. Petty's many victories came on varied track types in places such as the mile at Rockingham; the half-mile paved surface at Macon; Martinsville's nearly flat paved half-mile; Dover Downs' monster mile; the tight little quarter-mile paved track at Bowman-Gray

Stadium in Winston-Salem; the Falstaff 400 at the Riverside road course; and the final Grand National dirt track event ever in NASCAR Grand National competition.

Richard shared his thoughts on the significance of this final dirt track race run in the Grand National Division at the State Fairgrounds Speedway in Raleigh — a type of racing surface that not many years before was the backbone of the sport. Petty said at the time that this victory was as significant to him as his first Daytona 500 win in 1964.

Petty competed in only 40 of 47 races in 1970, for good reason: he experienced the most memorable and devastating crash of his 33-year career. As the series moved into Darlington for the Rebel 400, Petty had recorded back-to-back wins in the previous two races. During a routine

1970 PLYMOUTH ROAD RUNNER

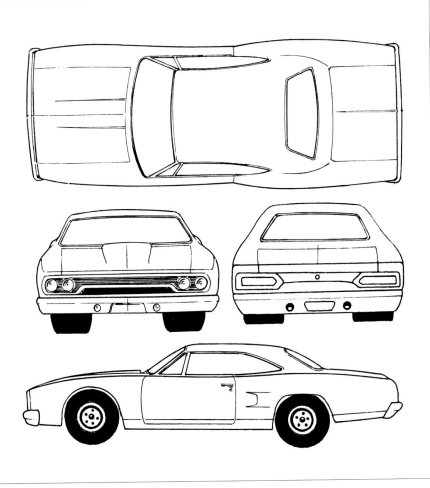

When the tour returned to Riverside in January 1971, Richard brought the Road Runner. Bob Tronolone

As time passed, there were a few obvious differences in the Superbirds of Hamilton and Petty. Hamilton's car sported a red nose panel and a unique spoiler/splitter to help direct air flow on the nose.
Richard Petty Private Collection

practice session around the legendary track often referred to as the "lady in black," Petty lost control and ruined his primary car, one of just two Superbirds the team had available for competition. The team hurried home, returning for the final practice laps with Richard's trusty and usually reliable '70 Road Runner coupe. The Pettys continued to struggle to adjust to the substitute race car and fine-tune the handling.

In nearly the same track location as his earlier accident, Petty hit the outside wall entering the fourth turn very hard and came off the concrete at an angle. His race car careened almost head-on into the concrete barrier in front of pit road. The resounding impact took out a sizable chunk of the wall and sent the driver and race car out of control into a series of barrel rolls. A shower of auto body and chassis parts flew in all directions. Onlookers could see the unconscious Petty through the car's side windows as he was tossed around like a rag doll. When the car finally came to rest on its top, Richard was still held in by his seat belt and wearing his helmet, but he was hanging nearly a third of the way outside the left side of the car. Until this incident window nets had been only a suggestion. They now became a mandatory part of the NASCAR rule book.

Richard poses beside his Road Runner. Note the three bar headrest.
Richard Petty Private Collection

Petty returned to Plymouth when they were able to give him a machine that could race with the Ford Talladegas and the Dodge Daytonas.
Richard Petty Private Collection

The two Superbirds in the Petty stables were driven by Richard in #43 and Pete Hamilton in #40. Richard Petty Private Collection

Miraculously, Petty survived the horrifying crash. The resulting injuries, however, forced him to miss six crucial races, which without doubt cost him any hope of winning the 1970 championship. His fourth-place finish in the season's point chase had to be viewed as a disappointment by both Richard and the entire Petty team.

Bobby Isaac recorded his only NASCAR Grand National champi-onship in 1970 over Bobby Allison in second, James Hilton in third, and Petty in fourth place. For winning the championship, Isaac received a check for $40,000 from Falstaff Brewing in a special ceremony in California at the conclusion of the season. He and the K and K Insurance team also received another surprise from Dodge for their efforts. They were informed they would no longer receive factory backing for the 1971 season.

The 1970 season also marked the first time a major commercial television network made a serious commitment to NASCAR's premier series. At the beginning of the season, ABC network officials met with NASCAR's top brass and signed a contract to televise 10 events. Most were part tape-delay and part live broadcast.

The season also marked the first appearance of treadless race tires for NASCAR stockers and the much-maligned restrictor plates.

Again the culprit appeared to be the 2.66-mile track at Talladega. First, Goodyear, attempting to create a larger "contact patch" on its race tires, concluded that there was only so much adhesion possible with a treaded tire. The introduction of the "slick" stock car tire came about as the direct result of the physical forces peculiar to racing at the Alabama track at 200 mph.

Even with better traction afforded by the new slick tires, the speeds increased again, only exacerbating the original problem. Many observers thought the only real way to allow drivers and race cars to compete with any degree of comfort was to slow them down — which meant reducing horsepower. Reducing the engine's ability to take in fuel and air reduces its ability to produce horsepower. The restrictor plate — with four holes considerably smaller in diameter than those in the four-barrel carb — met with broad approval by drivers, crews, and the sanctioning body alike.

The news received by the K and K team had more than a passing effect on Richard Petty and the Petty Enterprises team. With Chrysler's decision to reduce participation in NASCAR Grand National racing, the Pettys were in for a whole new set of conditions and circumstances as the 1971 season loomed on the horizon.

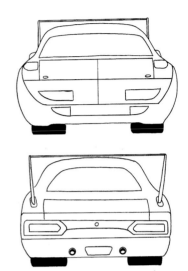

1970 PLYMOUTH SUPERBIRD

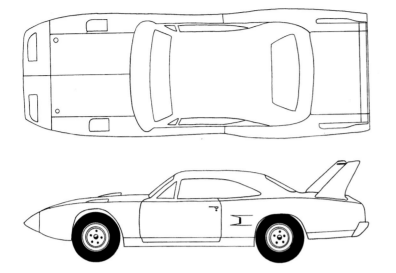

Superbirds are rare by any standards nowadays, so the best place to see one is at the Petty Museum where this one is kept and maintained. Richard Petty Museum

Richard helps push his Superbird out onto the pit lane at Darlington. Again, note how the chin spoiler on his car differs from Hamilton's on page 71. Bryant McMurray

NUGGETS

Big Bird

There is no doubt about it. Walk into the Petty Museum and you will be immediately struck by the shear size of the Plymouth Superbird. With the nose extension and huge wing on the trunk, the car looks like it's a block long. It felt that way driving it on the smaller tracks too — something Richard avoided whenever possible.

It's easy to fall into the trap of thinking that Richard was driving the Superbird in any of the races he won that year. But that isn't so. The plain old Road Runner, the beakless, tailless, version of the car won more than its share of races that year on tracks where trying to squeeze a Superbird through traffic would be like threading a needle with a rope.

Sometimes neither car worked well. At Darlington, Richard first wrecked his Superbird in practice. He then wrecked in the race in almost the same spot, this time in the Road Runner.

A fast bird without wings

The Hemi Road Runner

For 1971, Richard Petty found himself facing a fourth straight NASCAR Grand National season with a different race car, a new two-car team operation, a new teammate, more new rules, and a new NASCAR Grand National series sponsor.

The cutback of Chrysler's racing budget had widespread effects not only on 1970 champ Bobby Isaac and the K and K Insurance operation but also on the driver and team capturing the number two spot in the series points chase, who found themselves out in the cold as well. Bobby Allison had found a definite home with the Mario Rossi Dodge team, whose

1971 was one of the most interesting years to watch stock car racing because of the number of makes and models that could be found in any race. Here, Richard leads Fred Lorenzen in the STP-sponsored Nichels-Goldsmith 1971 Plymouth Road Runner followed by Bobby Isaac in the K&K Insurance 1971 Dodge Charger. Bobby Allison follows him in his 1970 Dodge Charger while his brother Donnie brings up the rear in Banjo Matthews' 1969 Mercury Cyclone. Bill Coulter

strong performance during the 1970 season marked it as a serious contender for the '71 title chase. With the Chrysler cutback, that too was not to be. Chrysler was willing to fund only one Plymouth and one Dodge race team, and they mandated that the entire operation would be operated from the Petty Enterprises compound at Level Cross.

The new 1971 Plymouth Road Runner represented the continuing challenge confronting the Pettys, who were struggling to stabilize their race car development efforts. In 1968, the restyled Plymouth intermediate had thrown a wrench into that equation. Again in 1969 the Pettys were sorting out a different race car with a Ford while still trying to remain competitive. Bingo! The 1970 season had brought them back to the Plymouth fold and the security of the legendary Superbird. All these situations lasted but a season before being disrupted. Would 1971 bring any relief for the Petty race car builders? Fortunately, the 1971 Plymouth Road Runner coupe powered by the

venerable Chrysler 426 cid hemi proved to be a match for all comers virtually "right out of the box." Though Richard had engine problems in the Riverside season opener in a year-old Plymouth, he arrived in Daytona a month later with the new car and a full head of steam.

Petty's victory in the 1971 Daytona 500, accompanied by teammate Buddy Baker in a Dodge for second place, marked Richard's third such accomplishment there as well as his 120th career triumph. The win marked the beginning of a truly dominant season, one the sport had not seen since Petty's legendary 1967 sweep of the series.

The 500-miler at Ontario followed on the heels of the Daytona event. A.J. Foyt, in the Wood Brothers' '69 Mercury, outdistanced both the Petty team cars to claim the victory. When the series returned to the East Coast in March for 500 laps at Richmond, Petty ruled the field, taking the victory over Bobby Isaac's Dodge by two laps.

From this point Petty ripped off two more impressive wins at Rockingham and later at Hickory. In all, Richard Petty scored 21 victories in 1971 in 47 scheduled races. Petty recorded wins at virtually every type of race facility on the series schedule. Petty's dominance is even more noticeable in the season statistics. He went on to record 38 top-five and 41 top-ten finishes.

At speed at Daytona, the '71 Road Runner was a natural race car.
Richard Petty Private Collection

The Road Runner of this era was the only car to appear in the traditional solid Petty Blue paint scheme seen here and the two tone red & blue schemes of the STP era a year later.
Richard Petty Private Collection

Who was Richard's first big corporate sponsor? If you said STP, you're not exactly right. A glance at the rear quarter panel a year before the STP deal will tell you it was Pepsi — at least for a few races anyway.
Richard Petty Private Collection

In the Dixie 500 at Atlanta on August 1, 1971, Richard Petty became the first NASCAR driver ever to win more than a million dollars in his career. He won the race that day as well. The victory was Petty's 551st start. His second million dollars in career winnings would come more quickly, actually after only 121 more races.

The only real obstacle in the path of Petty's stretch drive for the NASCAR Grand National title was Bobby Allison. The Alabama driver had campaigned in his own Coca-Cola-sponsored 1971 Dodge Charger before moving his sponsor and number 12 to the Holman-Moody Mercurys and Fords vacated by David Pearson. Allison climbed aboard the red-and-

gold race cars and immediately became the primary challenger to "The King." Allison responded to Petty's 21 victories with 11 of his own.

The other surprise of the 1971 season came from the Junior Johnson race car shops. Ford had announced its pullout from NASCAR Grand National racing prior to Chrysler's announced cutback. This move by Dearborn left many Ford and Mercury teams, unable to secure outside sponsorship, looking for a new direction. For Johnson it was a Chevrolet. Though this GM division had said publicly it wasn't taking an active part in the sport, the sudden appearance of a very competitive 1971 Monte Carlo seemed to indicate otherwise.

Indiana's Charlie Glotzbach was recruited to drive the new car.

Though the Chevy program never threatened the ultimate outcome of the championship, the added nameplate helped to increase attendance, and it also went a long way toward luring General Motors back onto the playing field. The new team entered 13 races in the second half of the season with one victory (at Bristol, Tennessee) plus seven top-five and ten top-ten finishes for 1971.

After the government banned much advertising of tobacco products, companies like R.J. Reynolds began looking for new ways to advertise their "forbidden" products. Shortly after Ford's announced pullout,

In September, Richard was among a group of famous racing drivers to be invited to the White House by President Nixon. On Nixon's right, admiring the famous #43, is Mario Andretti.
Richard Petty Private Collection

Berkline refinished Richard's seat in order to promote their line of durable fabrics. Also note the peace sign headrest, the window net hardware, and the decal on the fire bottle.
Richard Petty Private Collection

NASCAR and RJR joined forces to form what may well be the most important alliance in modern motorsports. Involvement with major-league stock car racing quickly proved to be RJR's ticket to reaching its customer base.

RJR, through its Winston brand of cigarettes, brought public attention to NASCAR like nothing before. The Winston Cup Series also revamped the structure of nearly everything in the sport. Winston was willing to establish a lucrative $100,000 driver points fund, limited to contested events of 250 miles and longer. The company wanted to showcase its products before the larger crowds. Instantly the death knell was sounded for events at many smaller tracks as well as the dirt tracks. The year 1971 was the last the series featured more than one event per week — and some weeks the teams even had a weekend off.

Richard continued to run in virtually every scheduled event in 1971. He admitted that the prospect of increasing his income and at the same time reducing his time spent at the race track was appealing. Petty had taken home nearly $130,000 for winning 27 races in his watershed season of 1967. By 1971, with the new system instituted by Winston, Petty pocketed $309,000 for just 21 victories. Richard never smoked cigarettes but he often said if he did, it would have been Winstons starting in 1971.

The sanctioning body continued trying to regulate race car technology in 1971. The restrictor plates were beginning to spark a lack of harmony. The various types of engines — especially those from Ford and Chrysler — all had varying sizes of openings in their respective restrictor plates as NASCAR tried to maintain a level playing field. The ultimate objective was to encourage the manufacturers to move away from the specialty powerplants like the Boss 429 and the Chrysler hemi.

The Fords and Mercurys were the first to move to less-restricted engines, namely the venerable 427 high-rise side oiler. The Chrysler teams were first to complain the loudest about their underpowered race cars. Eventually the Dodge and Plymouth teams saw the light, equipping their cars with the trusty 426 wedge engine from the Chrysler storehouse, which could run with many fewer restrictions. Quickly the likes of Petty, Isaac, Buddy Baker, and Pete Hamilton were blowing off the competition with regularity. Of course, then it was Ford's turn to howl.

Interest in the NASCAR Grand National series had now reached the highest places and most hallowed halls of America. President Richard Nixon, in an unprecedented move, extended a special invitation to the who's who of racing to visit the White House. Of course, as a major representative of NASCAR's premier series, Richard Petty was on hand to meet the President and show him around his trusty blue Plymouth.

Despite all the smoke you see, Richard and his blue Road Runner are on the way to a first-place finish in Trenton, New Jersey. Note the dark center panel on the hood. It was painted black on this particular car. Ray Masser

Part of what made the Road Runner so potent was its 426 cubic-inch Hemi engine. This one is on display at the Petty Museum. Tim Bongard

1971 PLYMOUTH ROAD RUNNER

As NASCAR mandated smaller engines, these massive powerplants were forced to run with diminutive carburetors. This eventually forced a switch to the 340 cubic-inch wedge engine. Tim Bongard

Richard Petty had the world by the tail in 1971, and prospects for the 1972 season seemed bright. There was, however, one missing piece from the puzzle — a major sponsor for the Petty racing team. The solution to that weighty problem would forever change the image of Richard Petty and the identity of his racing machines.

Petty on the high banks of Dover's Monster Mile in June. He finished 3rd in the race. Ray Masser

STP and Petty team up

The Racer's Edge

The very first Winston Cup championship belonged to Richard Petty after his convincing rout of the 1971 NASCAR Grand National field. The realization that he had won his third championship — Petty Enterprises's sixth title overall (counting the three won by Lee Petty) — and Richard's unprecedented three Daytona 500 victories created a confident atmosphere in the Level Cross race car shop as the '71 season came to a close. But the knowledge that 1971 was the last year Chrysler would financially support the Petty racing effort gave pause to everyone, especially Richard Petty.

These were uncharted waters the Petty operation was embarking upon. Remaining competitive without the wherewithal to continue technology development was the key. Would Petty Enterprises be able to field a competitive team properly, or might it have to trim the schedule? Would Richard Petty be relegated to the middle of the pack?

Running at Texas World Speedway for the final event of the 1971 season, Petty already had the NASCAR Grand National title wrapped up convincingly. The steady blue Plymouth number 43 had put 20 checkered flags under its belt at that point.

As the Petty team put the final touches on the car Richard would handle in the season finale, a surprise visitor appeared in the crowded garage area on the pretense of offering congratulations and encouragement. STP Corporation president and motorsports magnate Andy Granatelli made his appearance brief, not wishing to interrupt the beehive of activity surrounding the team's meticulous preparations.

Surely Mr. Granatelli was doing more than just scouting the stock car scene. STP sponsorship was no new thing to NASCAR Grand National racing. Fred Lorenzen had launched his comeback bid in Ray Nichel's number 99 STP Plymouth in 1971. Could it be "Mr. 500" wanted a larger involvement in the stock car game?

At Riverside in January, Richard's first outing with STP as his sponsor. There wasn't time to repaint the car, so it appeared in solid Petty Blue with STP decals on it. He also won the race. Bob Tronolone

The last Plymouth driven competitively by Petty was the 1972 Plymouth Road Runner. A great race car right out of the box, it still wasn't as sleek as the Dodge Charger. Petty would run both cars during the season and switch to Chargers full-time in 1973. Richard Petty Private Collection

All those questions would have to wait for another day. There was a race to run, and Richard Petty and his blue Plymouth were up to the task. Petty closed out his third championship season with a convincing victory on the two-mile oval at College Station. Richard Petty recorded 21 victories for the 1971 season.

It wasn't until a few weeks later, during the so-called off-season, that Richard Petty received a phone call in his Level Cross office from Andy Granatelli. Andy, never one to beat around the bush, wanted to know if Richard Petty would come to Chicago to talk turkey about STP sponsorship for his Grand National Plymouths. Richard Petty, mustering his coolest

demeanor, suggested he could work it into his schedule on the way to Riverside for the opening race of the 1972 season.

A couple of days before practice began for the Riverside opener, Richard Petty, Maurice Petty, and Dale Inman flew to Chicago to meet with Granatelli. It was clear from the outset that Granatelli wanted his company's name on Richard Petty's race car. It was equally clear that if Richard were going to remain in the top echelon of stock car racing, he needed exactly the kind of financial backing Granatelli had to offer.

The negotiations moved quickly, with general agreement on virtually every point except one. Andy

Granatelli wasn't about to put his company's name on any race car that was not fluorescent (STP) red. And Richard Petty wasn't about to drive any race car that wasn't Petty blue. This sticking point caused the otherwise congenial negotiations to run so deep into the night hours that Maurice and Dale had to leave and catch a plane to California.

Andy Granatelli, corporate mogul, and Richard Petty, businessman, continued the friendly tug of war until it came time for Petty, the race car driver, to head for the West Coast. At the last moment, Granatelli offered a compromise that would create one of Richard Petty's career trademarks. Granatelli suggested the race car be painted Petty blue and STP red! Just that quickly was born one of the most recognizable color schemes in the world of motorsports. Simultaneously, STP vice president Ralph Salvino was poised at the Riverside race course to plaster the blue Plymouth with decals declaring the new sponsorship. The two-tone paint treatment would have to wait.

Petty made the most of his debut for new sponsor STP. Much like his first win for Ford at Riverside in 1969, he won right out of the box for Granatelli and company. Though the race was shortened by persistent fog, Petty took control of the race after Bobby Allison's Chevy developed engine problems. It was his 141st career victory.

The 1972 season differed from past seasons in a multitude of ways. The most significant was undoubtedly the new Grand National points system. In the past, points were awarded not on a team's participation but by the size of the race track and length of race. Naturally the longer races were held on bigger tracks and shorter events were predominantly contested on shorter tracks. Any race 400 miles or longer gave the winner 150 points. A 250-mile race victory carried only 100 points, while a 100 mile event rewarded the victor only 50 points for the win.

SIGNIFICATA

- Bill France, Sr. steps down as NASCAR president. The job is handed off to his son, Bill Jr.
- The schedule is shortened to 31 events and the entire schedule is then sponsored by R.J. Reynolds. This means all drivers will be competing for the Winston Cup, but it also means that the 100 and 125-mile Grand National events are gone.
- Trunk deck lid numbers still required.
- Ford intermediates revert back to full frames with rear coil springs.
- Bud Moore builds a Torino powered by a 351 Cleveland small-block.
- Minimum weight is lowered to 3800 pounds.
- Restrictor plates return. Sleeves abandoned.
- Chrysler officially withdraws from factory-backed racing.
- Standard Class and Intermediate Class rules still in effect.
- Holman and Moody split up.
- Driving Plymouth Road Runners and Dodge Chargers, Richard Petty wins his fourth Grand National Championship over the course of 31 races.

The STP stock car and Indy car pose together at the Pocono garage area. Note the design on the blackout panel on Richard's hood. STP via the Richard Petty Private Collection

The new system for 1972 was considerably more complex. All events were worth the same 100 points to the winner, but there was more. A complicated system of lap points was also devised. This additional system had six categories in which points were awarded for participation by lap, ranging from 0.25 points for short tracks to 1.25 points for tracks like Daytona and Talladega. To say that the season was confusing was complimentary. Shortly into the new season James Hylton led in the standings over Petty, without winning a single event. But Hylton had finished every lap of every race to that point. By contrast, Richard Petty had four wins in the first ten races and had finished ahead of Hylton in nine of the ten events.

Also during the off-season, R.J. Reynolds, in league with NASCAR president Bill France Sr., had completed revamping the series by eliminating many paved short tracks and all dirt facilities. The newly reborn Grand National series had only 31 races on the schedule.

After Riverside, the Daytona 500 was next on the 1972 schedule. The Petty team cars—Richard in the

Plymouth Road Runner and Buddy Baker in a Dodge Charger—hadn't practiced or qualified well. Both drivers started the race near the back of the pack in 31st and 32nd positions, since neither one had finished his qualifying heats. In the 500, Baker went out early due to a crash on lap 18. However, Petty made a spirited charge to the front, as A.J. Foyt's Mercury was clearly the car to beat early on.

Foyt cruised to his first Daytona 500 win after Petty went to the garage with a blown engine. The mighty hemi gave up the ghost just as Petty was about to close in on the talented Texan. The romp from the rear had overtaxed Petty's engine and he was through for the day.

Just as cream eventually rises to the top, the following week at Richmond was a Richard Petty show. He finished four laps ahead of second-place Bobby Isaac.

As the series moved through the spring and into June, it was clear that though Pearson (now piloting the number 21 Mercury) and Isaac in the bright red-orange Dodge would take their share of the wins, only two dri-

At Dover, Dale Inman times Richard's laps as Maurice looks on. Ray Masser

1972 PLYMOUTH ROAD RUNNER

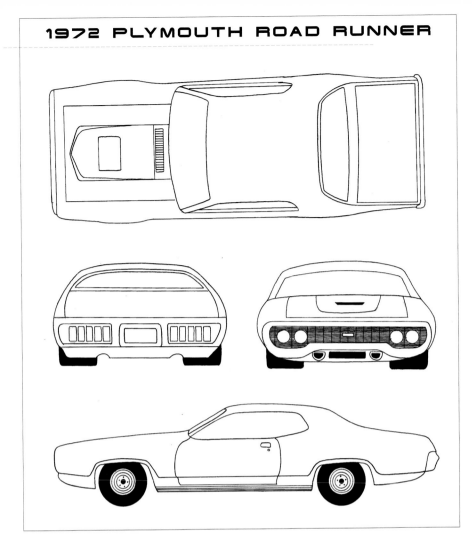

This collision looked like it would end Richard's day at the Richmond Fairgrounds. Actually, the team made repairs and Richard not only rejoined the race, but he won it! Harry Miller via the Richard Petty Private Collection

vers had their eyes fixed on the big prize. Week in and week out, Richard Petty and Bobby Allison traded the points lead back and forth. Allison won at Dover Downs, a full lap ahead of Petty. Pearson took the 400-miler at Michigan, with Allison in second and Petty a close third. By the end of June Petty beat Allison in the 250-miler at Texas World Speedway and on July 4 Petty took second to Pearson in the Firecracker 400 at Daytona. Allison finished third.

In the midst of this melee, Richard Petty changed horses in mid-stream. He debuted his new Dodge Charger for the Winston 500 at Talladega on May 7. Petty finished fifth in the new mount, two laps behind teammate Buddy Baker, who finished third on the same lap with the leader. The reason for abandoning Plymouth in which Richard Petty had campaigned for 14 seasons, wasn't completely clear. Petty did say he felt the Charger body was a bit cleaner aerodynamically than the Plymouth.

Through July Bobby Allison hit a real hot streak winning, at Bristol, Trenton, and next at Atlanta. Richard Petty was close each time but had to settle for second. Allison came back in late August to beat Petty at Nashville, and then he won the Southern 500 by holding off David Pearson for the win. Richard Petty finished third, seven laps off the pace.

By September the battle between the gold-and-red Chevy and the fluorescent-red-and-blue Petty cars as perceived by the media was at fever pitch. Most season highlights focus on the "blood sport" battle waged between the Allison Chevy and Petty Plymouth/Dodges during the stretch drive for the title. The word most often used in the media at the time was "feud." Both drivers denied that it was the case, though the determination of both drivers on the track seemed to undercut their claims.

At Martinsville, Allison started from the pole and led much of the race. Richard Petty was a full lap behind—he had to stop earlier with a

Another difference in the '72 Charger is the grille configuration. The center sections bulge more on the later cars. Ray Masser

Richard gets an assist out of the pits by Jimmy Martin, now Richard's public relations manager. Note the number on the trunk lid. Ray Masser

The Dodge Charger had sleeker lines than the Plymouth Road Runner. Note the hooded fuel overflow outlet. The taillight panel on this car was blue. Ray Masser

You can tell the '72 Charger apart from later versions of the car because it carries the engine size on the hood and it has a canted roof number. The wheels on this car were blue. Ray Masser

The Dodge Chargers were originally painted to look just like the Plymouth Road Runners. The paint scheme would be refined in the next season and essentially remain the same for a number of years. Bill Coulter

One of the first runs in his new Charger. Note that the grille trim is painted, not chromed. Ray Masser

One of his last runs in a Plymouth, Richard is shown racing at Dover in September. The team alternated between the Dodge Charger and the Plymouth Road Runner throughout the entire season. Ray Masser

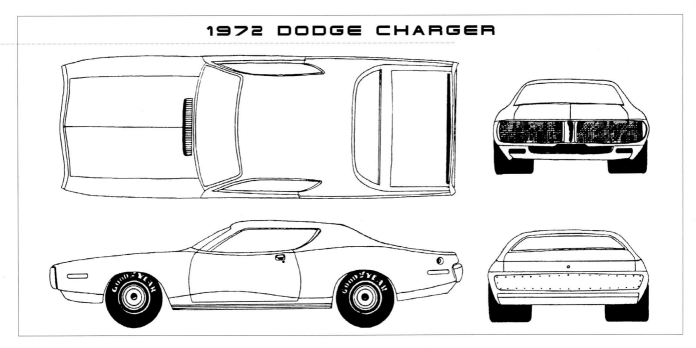

Richard on the high side of the K&K Insurance Dodge illustrates the similarities and differences in the two Mopar body styles. Bryant McMurray

cut tire. Allison was closing in to put a second lap on number 43. Petty, stubbornly refusing to let Allison get by, was able to make up his lost lap on the next caution. When the green came out again, the two drivers had the record crowd on its feet as they slugged it out for nearly 50 laps to the checkered flag. Petty went on to beat Allison by six seconds.

The "battles" ended at Riverside when Richard promised to slug the next person — regardless of what team he was on, his own or Allison's — if any of the "feuding" persisted. Everyone took him seriously and that ended that. Petty went on to record his fourth Grand National title and second consecutive Winston Cup championship with eight wins, 25 top fives, and 28 top tens.

Richard and Maurice pose in front of the STP Charger with Dale Inman and the crew behind the car. Note the blue gas cap, duct tape on the wheel weights, and the painted metalwork on the nose of the car. Richard Petty Private Collection

Allison had to settle for second in the title chase for '72 with 10 wins, 25 top-five finishes, and 27 top-ten finishes. However, Allison set a NASCAR record by leading at least one lap in the first 30 races of the 1972 season. When added to the nine races in a row he led at the end of the 1971 season, Allison led 39 consecutive races, which still stands as an all-time record.

For Richard Petty and Petty Enterprises it was another satisfying year. Winning the first race of 1972 for new sponsor STP and the national series title went a long way toward cementing the relationship between race driver and sponsor.

Winning with the big block Charger

Not Always Easy

The 1973 NASCAR Grand National season saw many new opportunities open up for Richard Petty as both driver and businessman. The Petty team, with Richard Petty driving, had really jelled. They were the people to beat, week in and week out. The financial backing was there to build competitive race cars, to expand engine programs, and to hire plenty of the right people in all areas of the operation. Richard Petty was truly at the top of his game as a race car driver. It appeared there were no weak spots in the Petty operation.

The competition was not resting, though; in fact, it was very hard at work. David Pearson had joined the Wood Brothers after A.J. Foyt exited the red and white Mercurys for the USAC Indy Car schedule early in 1972, and he was doing quite well, thank you! The team had entered only 17 races of the 31 scheduled in 1972, but Pearson had managed to be victorious in six while recording 12 top-five and 13 top-ten finishes. This team looked to be a formidable competitor for 1973.

Cale Yarborough, who two years earlier had left stock cars behind for the fast-lane world of Indianapolis cars, returned in late 1972 to compete in a few races whenever and wherever he could find an open driver's seat. When Bobby Allison left Junior Johnson's team to form his own, Cale quickly joined up with the Howard/Johnson team and appeared to be a solid threat for 1973.

As the new season opened in customary fashion at Riverside in late January, a new player joined the fray in the form of a Roger Penske-owned AMC Matador driven by the legendary Indy champ and road racer Mark Donohue. Fresh from great success with similar equipment in SCCA Trans-Am, Donohue took command of the 191-lap Motor Trend 500 early on. At the checkered flag, Donohue had shown his road-racing mastery by beating second-place Bobby Allison by a full lap. Richard Petty, who had started fifth, lasted only 95 laps and retired with engine trouble.

As the series made the trip back to Florida for the 1973 Daytona 500, many familiar names and faces appeared on the entry list. But since the '72 season many had played racing's version of musical chairs. Allison was in his own race car. Bobby Isaac had left the K and K team when it withdrew in mid-'72 after the team owner objected to NASCAR's rules interpretations. Buddy Baker, having lost his ride of two years with the Pettys, hooked up with a revitalized K and K team for 1973. Bobby Isaac was now at the wheel of Bud Moore's Ford Torino. Moore returned to NASCAR for selected races in 1972 after a few years fielding a car in the SCCA Trans-Am series.

When everything had been sorted out in the 1973 Daytona 500, the race was really contested among just four cars, Petty's Dodge, Isaac's Ford, Baker's Dodge, and Pearson's Mercury. By race's end, Petty easily won his fourth Daytona 500 when the engine blew in Baker's Dodge with just ten laps remaining.

The following week at Richmond was one of Petty's amazing comebacks. He made up two laps lost to an earlier crash to beat Buddy Baker to the checkered flag again.

When the series moved to Rockingham for the Carolina 500, Pearson and Yarborough began to show their collective muscle, finishing one-two with Baker in third and Bobby Allison in fourth. Petty fell prey to engine problems again, retiring from the 492-lap event on circuit 386 and finishing 23rd.

By late March, Richard finished second to Yarborough at Bristol but dropped out early with mechanical trouble at Atlanta on April 1, finishing a disappointing 34th. David Pearson won by two laps over second-place Bobby Isaac. By the next race at North Wilkesboro, Petty was back in form,

The early seventies saw Richard sporting a rather stylish Fu Man Chu mustache along with his trademark shades. Bryant McMurray

Richard circulates the Riverside road course in his '73 Charger. The bulges in the grille are very evident in this photo. Also note the natural metal door handle covers. Later cars had their patches blended and painted the same as the surrounding area. Bob Tronolone

taking the 250-mile event over Benny Parsons by four full laps.

In the Rebel 500 at Darlington, a slugfest, a late race crash took out many front-runners—including Petty. David Pearson won going away by 13 laps over Benny Parsons and 18 laps over third-place Bobby Allison. Petty still managed a seventh place, though he was 27 laps down at the end.

Pearson and Yarborough battled it out again for the win at Martinsville as Pearson's Mercury outdistanced Cale's Chevy to the finish line. The two competitors were five laps ahead of third-place Bobby Isaac. Richard Petty again experienced engine trouble, dropping out late in the race and finishing 21st.

A big part of what was quickly becoming a chronic engine problem for the Petty team may well have been the revised rules for the 1973 season. The new rules mandated a minuscule

Riverside in June. Another way to determine if the Charger you are looking at is a '73 is to look at the fuel filler. It's a '73 or earlier if you see a gas cap and cable. Quick-break fueling connections weren't regularly used until 1974. Bob Tronolone

SIGNIFICATA

- Mark Donohue wins the Western 500 in an AMC Matador equipped with four-wheel disc brakes. Other teams soon follow the example.

- Sealed ram air systems are outlawed.

- 430 cubic inch engines limited to smaller size carburetor bore. This is the "nails in the coffin" of the large engines. They are gone for good now.

- Engine displacement numbers on the hood become optional markings.

- Gas crisis forces manufacturers to produce smaller cars and engines.

- Trunk numbers are dropped as a required marking.

- Driving a Chevrolet, Benny Parsons wins the Grand National Championship over the course of 31 races. Richard Petty finishes fifth in points.

390 cfm carburetor for the big-bore wedge engines. These behemoths were on their way out. The sanctioning body was making every attempt to persuade competitors to use smaller displacement engines, preferably 366 cid or six liters.

The series next rolled into Alabama International Speedway for the Winston 500. Buddy Baker put the K and K car on the pole as David Pearson qualified for the other front-row spot. Richard Petty and Cale Yarborough started from the second row.

On lap nine of the 188-lap event, a chain-reaction accident, originally involving 21 cars, ultimately retired 19. Many of the front-runners were caught up in the melee as the faster cars overtook those at the rear of the 60-car starting field.

David Pearson miraculously maneuvered his Mercury through the debris. Hardly challenged — most of his primary competition was gone — Pearson went on to win by a lap over second-place Donnie Allison. Richard Petty was not as lucky as Pearson: the car ran over something on the track that punctured his dry sump oil system. After frequent stops for repairs the mighty Dodge finally went to the garage for good on lap 51.

Another driver, almost unnoticed, was quietly moving up through the weekly standings. Benny Parsons had teamed with L.G. DeWitt for the '73 season. They had no major sponsors, which spelled a lack of financing or equipment to match the top teams. Parsons was skilled at conserving his efforts while getting the most out of his equipment.

As the series continued, Cale Yarborough won at Nashville. Buddy Baker outran Pearson for the victory in the World 600 at Charlotte at the end of May. Pearson was in the money again when the series hit Dover Downs for the Mason-Dixon 500. Petty won by two laps at College Station in the Alamo 500 in mid-June. One week later it looked as if the "King" had the Tuborg 400 at Riverside in the bag until lap 81, when he hit the turn-nine wall and fell two laps off the pace as he pitted for repairs. However, Petty, charging back, made up the deficit and finished second to race winner Bobby Allison. Benny Parsons finished in third place, two laps down, but post-race stats showed that Parsons had quietly pulled out to a 200-plus point lead in the Winston Cup title chase standings.

From Riverside it was on to Michigan in mid-June, and David Pearson was again untouchable. The Mercury driver made it back-to-back wins by outrunning Richard Petty to the flag in the Firecracker 400 at Daytona. Though NASCAR had recently granted the Chevrolets an engine rules change, both Bobby Allison and Cale Yarborough, who started 1-2, were early casualties.

Benny Parsons' single victory of the 1973 season came at Bristol in the July 8 Volunteer 500. Richard Petty retired on lap 334 with chronic ignition problems. Both Allison and Yarborough went out after an accident on lap 343. Pearson and Baker were absent from the proceedings, but for different reasons. The Wood Brothers were competing only in the big-ticket events. The K and K team kept its race cars at home and its driver Buddy Baker out of competition in a disagreement over the engine rules changes NASCAR had made a few races earlier, which many felt favored the Chevrolets.

David Pearson continued his dominance of the superspeedways, taking the measure of the field by a lap in the Dixie 500 at Hampton, outside of Atlanta. Richard Petty was again plagued by engine failure, exiting on lap 72. Benny Parsons recorded one of his few DNFs of the season, retiring with oil pump failure on lap 248 of the 328-lap event. Dick Brooks pulled a surprise upset in a borrowed race car, inching past Buddy Baker and David Pearson through the tri-oval to record his first career Grand National win. Richard Petty was a disappointing 14th as points leader Benny Parsons recorded his second straight DNF, winding up 38th in the 50-car field.

David Pearson continued his mastery on the high banks by nearly beating Cale Yarborough at Darlington in the Southern 500 and following that up with another victory at Dover Downs in the Delaware 500. During this stretch, Richard Petty took a second at Nashville as Benny Parsons again "DNFed" with a terminal engine in that race. Petty finished fourth at Darlington, one lap ahead of Parsons in fifth. Richard came back to win at Richmond. Parsons was eight laps off the pace in fourth. Petty came home seventh at Dover, and Parsons was fourth. Petty lost out at the finish line to Bobby Allison at North Wilkesboro; Parsons finished a strong fifth.

Richard Petty appeared to be on a roll, taking the Old Dominion 500 at Martinsville by a lap ahead of Cale Yarborough in late September. The results were just the reverse for the two drivers at Charlotte in the National 500 one week later. Steady Benny Parsons again finished in the top ten with a sixth at Martinsville and a fourth at

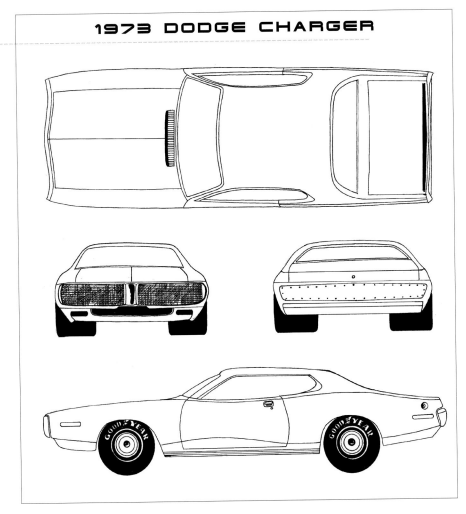

1973 DODGE CHARGER

resulted in Richard Petty's slide to fifth in the points with six wins in 28 starts, 15 top fives, and 17 top tens.

Though the '73 racing results were a disappointment for the Pettys, there were some other bright spots in 1973.

Richard Petty was one of the twelve drivers invited to participate in the inaugural running of the International Race of Champions (IROC). That first series was contested on the Riverside road course in 12 equally prepared Porsche Carrera RSRs. Mark Donohue emerged as the first IROC champ.

The movie, 43, the Petty Story hit theaters in fall 1973. This "low-budget thriller" didn't win any academy nominations, but it did feature a sterling cast of characters. Darin McGavin was recruited to play Lee Petty in the biographical film, and in true typecasting the part of Richard Petty was played by the "King" himself.

With the help of Richard Petty and the crew at Petty Enterprises, Chrysler Corporation appeared to make a serious attempt to break into the Chevrolet-dominated short-track racing business in 1973. The Chrysler "Kit Car" concept was officially announced in late 1973. Conceived by corporate engineering whiz Larry Rathgeb and developed by the Pettys, the program provided for ordering a competitive race car through a local Chrysler dealer.

The cars, whose construction relied heavily on the factory "parts bin," could be purchased either in kit form like a plastic scale-model kit or "turn key" ready-to-race from Petty Enterprises.

On an off-weekend from the regular Grand National schedule, Petty entered a stock car event at Pocono Raceway. The event was sanctioned by USAC's stock car division. It's a race the Pocono management will never forget. It's also a race USAC will never forget. Actually, it's a race Richard Petty won't forget either — he handily won the 500-miler over the best USAC had to offer.

Charlotte. All this action set the stage for a bizarre ending to the season, ultimately determining who would be the '73 series champion.

Only 195 points separated Benny Parsons and Richard Petty entering the last race of 1973 at Rockingham. Richard Petty put his two-tone Dodge on the pole, and David Pearson's Mercury was right alongside on the front row. The Allison brothers started side-by-side in row two.

Benny Parsons started in fifth place, but on lap 33 his Chevy tangled with the Mercury of Johnny Barnes. The result was not a pretty picture. Parsons' car was a shambles. The entire right side sheet metal was gone. There were parts of the car strewn everywhere. What wasn't broken was bent clear out of shape. The car was history — and Benny Parsons as '73

Grand National champ should have been too.

Parsons dragged his wounded mount back to the garage area. His team, along with a multitude of other crew members, pitched in to rebuild enough of the savaged race car to get Parsons back onto the track. After 136 laps in the garage for repairs, Benny Parsons rolled back out on the race track and completed 308 laps, finishing 28th — enough to capture the title!

While Parsons' car was being rebuilt, Richard Petty had retired on lap 133 with engine failure, thus destroying any chance he had at the title. Benny won the 1973 Grand National championship over Cale Yarborough by a scant 67 points. David Pearson bested Buddy Baker for the victory, his eleventh win in only 18 starts for 1973. The DNF

Small blocks and big power

Back On Track

By the early 1970s racing had become accustomed to many acronyms: STP, RPM, MPH, DIS, and RLP. You could add the stock car sanctioning body NASCAR to that list. Unfortunately, another acronym overshadowed all others in motorsports in the fall of 1973. OPEC (Organization of Petroleum Exporting Countries) announced a major reduction of oil exportation to Europe, the Far East, and most damaging, the United States. Many Middle Eastern oil-producing countries had decided they weren't getting paid sufficiently for their "natural resources." In other words, they were raising the price of doing business immediately, and if you didn't like it you could start walking to work.

American major-league racing quickly got its wagons in a circle to protect the future of the sport. Race historians recalled that due to the energy crisis in this country during World War II the only major sport to be padlocked was racing. Sanctioning bodies such as NASCAR, USAC, NHRA, IMSA, and SCCA moved quickly and decisively to present statistics ranking racing as number seven on a list of the energy usage of major sports. In late November 1973 President Nixon decreed that all gas stations would be closed between 9:00 p.m. on Saturdays until Sundays at midnight. This was definitely not a good situation for American motor-

Between 1974 and 1977 the cars remained basically the same with only minor differences. This is the car Richard drove in 1974 at Michigan's fall race. Bill Coulter

sports, and especially NASCAR Grand National, which ran most races on Sundays.

This timely move in presenting racing's case to the government and tempering public opinion also showed the sport was vitally interested in dealing with this national and global crisis. This unified and factual response ensured that motorsports would receive a fair shake. The numbers clearly proved that though racing's use of fuel was highly visible compared to other professional sports, the 40 race cars in events like the Daytona 500 actually consumed much less fuel than a sports team's one-way plane

flight from New York to California for a single game.

Without question the energy crisis had a profound impact on NASCAR Grand National racing. The first casualty was the financially plagued Texas World Speedway. The track's president announced the facility would close immediately and not reopen until the energy crisis ended.

The federal government had asked that all "leisure time activities" be reduced to conserve energy by 25 percent. NASCAR responded by announcing a modification to all scheduled Grand National events. All race tracks hosting Grand National

*The shapely Charger featured a slender nose that
helped slice through the air like the Torinos a few
years before.* Bryant McMurray

*A classic battle between Richard and David Pearson
in the #21 Wood Brothers' Mercury at Michigan.*
Bill Coulter

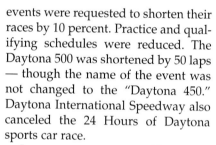

Pocono in August. Note the absence of the door handle patch, the quick-break fuel fill, and the flat header pipes. Ray Masser

You can spot early Chargers by the small size of the STP logo on the front hood as seen clearly in this photo. Bryant McMurray

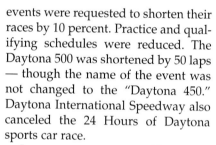

events were requested to shorten their races by 10 percent. Practice and qualifying schedules were reduced. The Daytona 500 was shortened by 50 laps — though the name of the event was not changed to the "Daytona 450." Daytona International Speedway also canceled the 24 Hours of Daytona sports car race.

In some ways more troublesome to Richard Petty and the other NASCAR Grand National competitors than the energy crisis was the sanctioning bodies' enactment of an entirely new points system for the 1974 season. This new way of awarding points was based on money won from track purses multiplied by the number of races a driver started; that final number was then divided by 1,000 to get the exact number of points earned per race. It wasn't too far into the new season that all concerned, even NASCAR, knew they had a dead skunk on their hands with the new points system. It wasn't that the system didn't reward the winners of the races, it was that the computations were complicated and so difficult to understand, that even the competitors had a hard time understanding it. If the competitors had a hard time, you can bet the average race fan was hopelessly lost. In the

end, the results turned out as they should have but the system would need to be changed yet again. But this was one of the few things NASCAR waited until 1975 to change.

Before the season had really begun to roll, there were no fewer than five major rules changes by NASCAR. The first change came in time for the Atlanta 500 in late March. The carburetor restrictor plates used since 1973 were removed. A new carb was developed for the big-block engines. On April 22, the second rules change allowed for more air for the big-blocks. By this time many teams had moved to small-block engines and even with the rules changes the small-engine cars ran away from those with big-displacement engines. At the conclusion of the Winston 500 the nearest big-block race car was 14 laps behind the small-block race cars.

NASCAR conducted tests after Talladega and decided to allow two new carburetors for big-block-engined race cars depending on the track size. And in late June, NASCAR also decided to reduce the maximum displacement for all small-block racing engines from 366 to 358 cid. Then in July the sanctioning body announced that no engine larger than

SIGNIFICATA

- All engines must use a standard size round air cleaner. No ducting of air allowed for engines.
- Suspension can be leaf springs, coil springs, or torsion bars.
- Specific carburetors are the only units allowed by NASCAR for competition.
- Electronic (transistorized) ignitions allowed only if used on the street version of the make or model.
- Maximum of 2 degrees of body rake is allowed.
- Openings left between the body and the bumpers is required to be covered over with sheet metal.
- Dry-break fuel fillers now allowed.
- Daytona 500 was limited to 450 miles because of fuel crisis.
- First NASCAR race at Pocono International Raceway in Long Pond, PA is held.
- Driving a Dodge Charger, Richard Petty wins his fifth Grand National Championship over the course of 30 races.

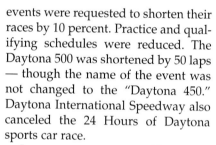

358 cid would be permitted to compete in the series in 1975.

For Richard Petty, the 1974 season got off to an acceptable start with a second-place finish to Cale Yarborough in the rain-delayed Winston Western 500. When the series returned to Florida for the annual Daytona 500, Richard responded by dominating the shortened affair. Petty's familiar STP Dodge Charger was almost a full lap ahead of the three-car battle for second among Cale Yarborough, Ramo Stott, and Coo Coo Marlin. The victory was Petty's 155th career win.

Petty was still using the familiar wedge-design big-block V-8 engine to power his trusty Dodge. The rules for '74 had dictated that engines over 366 cid were limited to one small four-barrel carburetor with a rating of 340 cfm. Petty had one of the few Mopars still competitive with a big-block engine.

Bobby Allison bounced back from a dismal showing at Daytona by taking the measure of Petty and Yarborough at Richmond Fairgrounds Raceway. Even though Allison won the race with the new points system, he actually lost ground: Petty earned more points for second place.

Richard Petty made it two-for-three, lapping the field at Rockingham in the Carolina 500. Again the Chevrolets of Yarborough and Allison were around at the end and came home second and third. With the new points system, Richard Petty's points lead had mushroomed to three times the total of second-in-points Bobby Allison.

Cale Yarborough led a ten-car Chevrolet sweep at Bristol in the Southeastern 500. The highest ranking non-Chevy was Ed Negre's year-old Dodge in 11th place. Richard Petty was sidelined before the one-quarter mark of the 500-lap event after getting involved in a multi-car accident. Though Petty finished 23rd, race winner Yarborough gained only ten points on him in the title chase.

The Atlanta 500 in late March saw Cale's Carling Black Label Chevrolet

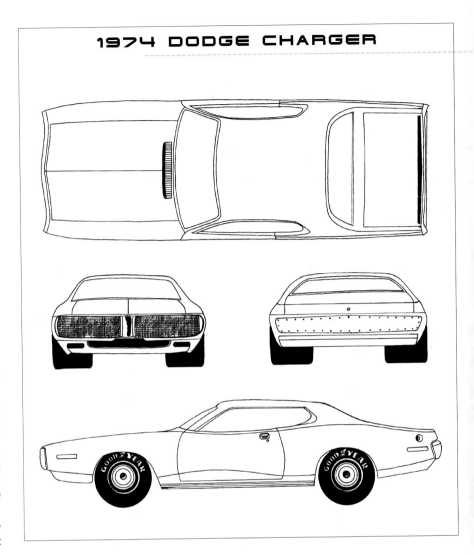

1974 DODGE CHARGER

in victory circle again. Second-place David Pearson in the familiar number 21 Mercury was the only driver on the same lap at the finish. Yarborough did gain considerable ground on points leader Petty who finished sixth three laps off the pace. Notable in this sixth race of 1974 was the use of a small-displacement engine in Pearson's Mercury. The new powerplant enabled the veteran Pearson to sit on the pole.

Pearson followed his good showing with the smaller 351 cid engine by beating back the challenge of Bobby Allison and Buddy Baker to win the "Rebel 450," the shortened version of the Rebel 500 at Darlington, South Carolina. Again Richard Petty's luck ran thin. He retired early with engine failure and finished 20th.

The message from NASCAR was finally delivered at Petty Enterprises. The sanctioning body did not want the non-production big-block V-8 used in competition. Chronic engine problems for Richard's Dodge had forced Maurice Petty to develop a 340 cid small-block engine in the race car. Richard Petty responded by winning at North Wilkesboro, taking a second at Martinsville, and capturing a third on the superspeedway in Talladega for the Winston 500 in early May.

The new small-displacement Mopar engine appeared to agree with Petty. He continued to run up front with a win at Nashville for the Music City 420, a third behind Yarborough and Pearson in the Mason-Dixon 500 at Dover Downs in Delaware, and a

Two of the key markings on the 1974 version of the Charger's paint scheme are the two small STP logos on the tops of the fenders over the wheel wells and the STP oval that stays within the striping on the nose. The Richard Petty Private Collection

The rear taillight panel was painted blue for most of the 1974 season, although the color of the panel was often dictated by the color of the decals that needed to go on this portion of the car. Note the STP logo and the size of the spoiler on the trunk lid. Ray Masser

second to Pearson in the World 600 in Charlotte. The streak ended with a DNF due to engine failure in the Tuborg 400 at Riverside, where Petty exited after only 49 laps. The poor finish on the California road course cost Petty the points lead. Yarborough moved into first with a 102-point lead over Petty. Petty didn't let all this turmoil get him down. He moved on to Michigan International Speedway to score a decisive win over Canadian rookie contender Earl Ross.

When the series paid its second visit to Daytona for the annual Firecracker 400, Petty and David Pearson waged a seesaw battle to the finish line, with Pearson taking his third straight 400. Petty had to settle

At Riverside in January 1975 Richard didn't fare too well. Here the battered STP Charger screams through one of the turns despite the damage. Bob Tronolone

for runner-up, his fourth in as many years in the July classic. In spite of Cale Yarborough's photo finish with Buddy Baker for third place, Petty took away the points lead from the Chevy driver.

At Bristol in mid-July Petty was third behind race winner Yarborough in the Volunteer 500. Cale made it two in a row, backing up his Bristol victory with a contested win over Bobby Allison at Nashville. Petty was involved in a multi-car crash on the state fairgrounds half-mile late in the race and had to settle for 13th place.

He bounced back just eight days later by outgunning rival David Pearson to win the Dixie 500 at Atlanta. Cale Yarborough experienced valve trouble with the new small-block Chevy engine and finished 14th. By virtue of the victory Petty was able to regain the points lead and extend the differential over Cale to 120 points.

Maurice Petty seemed to have the small displacement Dodge engine figured out, and combined with Richard's newfound momentum, the team went on a tear. Richard took

three decisive victories in a row. He not only won at Atlanta, but followed that with a win over Buddy Baker's Ford at Pocono in the Purolator 500 the next week. It was Petty and Pearson neck-and-neck in the Talladega 500 seven days later. Petty increased his points lead over Cale Yarborough to nearly 500 points.

The race was marred by the sport's largest incident of sabotage. The only cars affected were all those that might be considered front-runners, some 20 cars in all. The Roger Penske crew first discovered "foreign matter" in the fuel line of Bobby Allison's AMC Matador. It wasn't long before numerous teams discovered cut tires, cut oil lines, or foreign matter in many race cars' gas tanks. It was discovered that someone had "adjusted" the alignment on the Petty Dodge.

In late August David Pearson enjoyed some revenge by out-dueling Petty in the closing laps of the Yankee 400 at Michigan International Speedway. It was Pearson's 82nd career Grand National victory. Cale Yarborough managed third place,

finishing on the same lap with the two leaders.

Yarborough started fourth in the Southern 500 on Labor Day, going on to a one-lap advantage over second-place Darrell Waltrip, driving his own race car. The points system came under considerable attack once more at Darlington. Richard Petty finished 35th, sidelined after being hit by Richard Childress. Petty gained more points than Waltrip under the point system.

Richard Petty took off on another tear, winning again at Richmond in the Capital City 500 and once again at Dover Downs in the Delaware 500, then finishing a close second to Yarborough in the Wilkes 400 at North Wilkesboro, North Carolina.

Petty appeared to be continuing the streak after qualifying at Martinsville where he put his Charger on the pole for the event. However, his engine gave out after only 22 laps and would have given Yarborough a chance to make up some points if he too hadn't lost his engine with 80 laps to go. Petty then went on to place second in the National 500 at Charlotte and grab a third-place finish at the American 500 at Rockingham. He ended the year by starting the Los Angeles Times 500 at Ontario Motor Speedway from the pole and swapped the lead with A.J. Foyt, Cale Yarborough, and Bobby Allison throughout most of the race. With 12 laps to go, Petty's engine let go, which placed him 15th in the final finishing order of the race. It didn't matter though. In spite of all the rule changes and having to work with a new powerplant, Richard won his fifth championship.

The Charger and Petty become a fixture in victory lane

Hard Charger

I f 1974 appeared to be a great season for Richard Petty, 1975 was in a class by itself. The red-and-blue Dodge Charger with Richard Petty at the controls rolled over the competition like a tidal wave. Petty won early and often, wrapping up his sixth NASCAR Grand National championship when he won the National 500 at Charlotte Motor Speedway with four races still remaining in the season.

The year marked the first time Petty Enterprises fielded race cars with year-old sheet metal. The introduction of the new Chrysler Cordoba had forced cash-starved Chrysler Corporation to streamline its product line. Gone was the distinctive coke-bottle appearance of the Dodge Charger. In its place was a clone of the new Cordoba personal luxury car. Though both the 1975 Cordoba and Charger featured handsome body work, they were about as aerodynamic as a boxcar.

Fortunately, NASCAR Grand National rules permitted the use of a given year's body style for three years. This was good news for Petty Enterprises, especially since the outfit had developed such a winning combination with its version of the wind-cheating 1972-1974 Dodge coupe.

The Petty/STP relationship was now stronger than ever. Many other front-running teams were changing drivers or sponsors, desperately seeking either, or both. The main competi-

In 1975 the rear taillight panel was red most of the time as seen here in this pit stop at Dover in the spring.
Ray Masser

tion for winning races appeared to be Dave Marcis in a rejuvenated K and K Insurance Dodge; David Pearson again in the Purolator Mercury; and Cale Yarborough in the Holly Farms Chevy Laguna. Competition for the 1975 championship title would also come from men with names like Benny Parsons, Dave Marcis, Buddy Baker, Lee Roy Yarbrough, and a new one, Darrell Waltrip.

The much-maligned points system from the previous year was modified again, the fifth change in nine years. Gone were the complicated mathematical equations, and for the first time all 30 races on the schedule paid the same number of points for a win, whether Talladega or Martinsville.

This new points system, designed by veteran NASCAR statistician Bob Latsford, was designed to encourage competition for the Winston Cup instead of the big-purse races alone. Additional bonus points were paid for leading a lap and for leading the most laps during a race. The system proved itself and remains in use today.

The new season didn't start looking like anything special for the Petty team. During the running of the season-opening Winston Western 500 at Riverside, Richard lost 19 laps in the pits when he hit the wall. He wound up in seventh place behind race winner Bobby Allison.

In the next event, the Daytona 500, Petty proved to be the catalyst that determined its outcome. In the late stages of the race, second-place Benny Parsons appeared to have the only car capable of beating David Pearson's Mercury, but he would need some help. Petty's Dodge was obviously the fastest thing on the track. But he had a cracked cylinder head leaking coolant that required occasional pit stops for more liquids.

Petty blew past Parsons, who was nearly a quarter of a lap behind the leader, signaling him to hook up in a two-car draft. This mini-freight train quickly closed in on first-place Pearson, who then collided with Cale Yarborough on the back straightaway and spun into the grass. Benny Parsons then drove around Richard Petty and on to his only victory in the February classic. Petty managed to salvage seventh place in spite of mechanical problems.

Petty was back on target the following week. He won the Richmond 500, at the Virginia state fairgrounds track, by six laps over second-place Lennie Pond. A week later at Rockingham, Richard had to settle for third place; Cale Yarborough won a seesaw battle with David Pearson. Both drivers finished on the same lap, with Petty falling off the pace due to overheating.

Moving to Bristol in March, Petty got back in the groove, winning the Southeastern 500 by six laps over Benny Parsons. Next Petty rolled over the competition in the Atlanta 500 in Hampton, holding off Buddy Baker's Ford on a last-lap dash to the checkered flag. Petty's third win of the year, it increased his lead in the championship chase to nearly 200 points.

Richard Petty wasn't done on this stretch: he beat Cale Yarborough by three laps to win the Gwyn Staley Memorial 250 at North Wilkesboro. Petty led 310 of the 400 laps, and according to second-place Yarborough, he was untouchable. It was victory number four of the season and further increased his championship points lead.

Bobby Allison in the Penske Matador took a rare victory: the Rebel

The folks at Petty Enterprises pose with the Charger and transporter at Level Cross. Richard is in the front row on the left. The Charger in 1975 and 1976 carried a decal for the Muscular Dystrophy Association on or near the rear pillar. The Richard Petty Private Collection

500 at Darlington. But Petty crashed about one-third of the way into the event and suffered a DNF. The 26th-place finish for Petty and the sixth-place finish by Benny Parsons reduced Petty's lead in the title chase to 195 points.

Richard bounced back at Martinsville, to win the Virginia 500 in late April. A rising young driver from Franklin, Tennessee — Darrell Waltrip — again rose to the occasion by challenging Petty throughout the entire race and finishing a close second on the same lap.

In the 420-lap race in Nashville for the Music City 420, Richard's Dodge was plagued by chronic carburetor problems, and he finished seventh, 16 laps off the pace. Budding driver Darrell Waltrip took over the lead late in the race when the engine in Cale Yarborough's Chevy expired. It was Waltrip's first trip to the winner's circle in Grand National competition.

Petty won again in late May in the World 600 at Charlotte. It was the first time Richard had won there.

According to Petty, "We had been coming to Charlotte for over 15 years. It really felt good to finally win there." Petty finished a full lap ahead of Cale Yarborough in second. It was Petty's 170th career victory and again increased his points lead. The race was broadcast tape-delayed by CBS Sports television. Former Grand National star Fred Lorenzen provided the post-race interview with Petty from the winner's circle.

Petty followed up his Charlotte win with a rousing victory in the Tuborg 400 at Riverside on June 8, dueling with rival Bobby Allison's Matador throughout the entire event. Petty finally prevailed, leading the last 18 circuits around the 2.62-mile road course.

Next came a second to David Pearson in the Motor State 400 at Michigan International Speedway on June 15. The margin at the flag was only two car lengths. Petty returned to action two weeks later for the Firecracker 400 at Daytona Beach. Richard, who started the race from

There are always exceptions to the rules. At the August Pocono race, Richard's car ran without the MDA decal and with black Goodyear decals on the front fender — a rarity for the Charger. Ray Masser

Nashville 1975. A good color shot of the Mopar small block V-8 run by Petty Enterprises. Bill Coulter

13th position, managed to work his way to the front. He led for the first time on lap 85. Though Buddy Baker led 119 laps of the 160-lap event, Petty took over the front position on lap 148 and led the final 12 laps for his eighth victory of the season. The win moved Petty to a commanding 456-point lead over Dave Marcis, who was now in second in points.

Richard Petty continued his competitive streak at the end of July with a series of second-place finishes in the next three races. In the Nashville 420 Petty never led a single lap but did manage to finish second to Cale Yarborough, one lap in arrears. Richard followed that up with a second to David Pearson in the Purolator 500 at Pocono International Raceway in early August. On lap 191 of the 200-lap affair, with Pearson's Mercury in front, the red-and-white Petty car began trailing a telltale cloud of smoke. The NASCAR officials displayed the black flag with just two laps remaining. Since NASCAR gives a black-flagged race car four laps to observe the infraction, the timing of the black flag set off a controversy. In spite of the brouhaha, Petty's points lead continued to grow.

In mid-August, Petty recorded a third second-place finish by battling eventual winner Buddy Baker to the finish at Talladega. The rain-delayed event was a tragic one: veteran driver DeWayne "Tiny" Lund was killed after his Dodge spun down the backstretch and into the grass. As the car came to a rest, rookie Terry Link was caught up in the melee and slammed into the driver's door of Lund's stationary race car. Lund was pronounced dead at the track hospital of massive chest injuries.

When the series returned for its second visit to Michigan, Petty extracted a bit of revenge by getting past David Pearson on the last lap of the 200-lap event to win the Champion Spark Plug 400. Only half a car length separated the two cars at the line.

Petty started off September with a second-place finish in the Southern

500 at Darlington. Bobby Allison in the AMC Matador took the third victory of the season for the Penske-owned team. Richard Petty's 174th career win came next at Dover Downs in the Delaware 500. Petty was able to make up an unbelievable six laps during the later stages of the race. Earlier Petty had lapped the field by more than two laps when he ran over debris from Elmo Langley's blown engine, breaking a suspension part and sending Petty to the pits for repairs for six laps.

In the Wilkesboro 400, Petty started from the pole position. He led on occasion, battling with Cale Yarborough frequently. A miscue on a routine pit stop by the Junior Johnson crew allowed Petty to take the lead from Yarborough and Petty led 82 of the last 87 laps for the victory.

At Riverside International Raceway, Richard cuts one of the corners tight in the Tuborg 400 in June. The emblem above the STP sticker on the nose is a small Petty Enterprises decal. Bob Tronolone

Richard goes around James Hylton on the high side at Dover Downs in the spring race. Ray Masser

1974 DODGE CHARGER

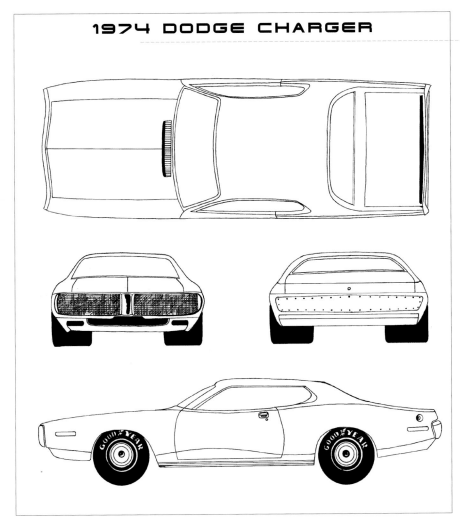

Grand National driver in history to win more than $2 million. At the close of the '75 season, Richard Petty had a sport- and career-high 177 victories.

Petty was again invited to compete in the IROC series in light of his fifth championship the previous season. The series opened with a 50-lapper at MIS in mid-September. David Pearson won the race over Bobby Allison, with Richard finishing seventh.

Round two began on Saturday afternoon in late October, this time on the road course at Riverside. Bobby Unser led the entire 30 laps to take the victory. This IROC race will be best remembered for attrition: all but five of the 12 race cars suffered damage during the event. At the conclusion of round two Richard Petty stood sixth in the point standings, which were led by Bobby Unser.

Round three took place the following day, again on the Riverside road course. Bobby Allison worked his way to the front and the victory. Richard Petty hit the turn-nine wall on lap 24 and had to settle for 11th finishing position. Petty, Jody Scheckter, and James Hunt did not make the final cut to nine finalists for round four the following February at Daytona.

Richard leads David Pearson's Mercury through the turns on Riverside roadcourse.
Bob Tronalone

Petty made it number 12 of the season by winning the National 500 at Charlotte in early October. The victory was a record for wins by a driver since the series had been reorganized and the number of events reduced to 30 each season. Petty led the final 111 laps and beat runner-up David Pearson by just three seconds at the checkered flag.

Petty dropped out of the next event on the schedule, the Old Dominion 500 at Martinsville in late September, with differential failure. Dave Marcis took the win for K and K Insurance, with Benny Parsons the only other car on the lead lap. Petty, who had started sixth on the grid, was not competitive all day, leading only once for one lap.

Darrell Waltrip made his second trip to victory lane in 1975 by winning the Capital City 500 at Richmond in mid-October. For the only time all season, Petty finished dead last by going out on lap 34, his Dodge suffering a

rare case of engine failure. Petty wasn't too upset about the poor showing: the 28th-place finish wrapped up his sixth championship with four races remaining on the 1975 schedule.

Richard Petty, never one to rest on his accomplishments, proved it by winning once more before the celebrated 1975 season concluded in Bristol, Tennessee. Petty came back in classic fashion after cutting a tire down early in the 500-lap event. Returning to the track, Petty caught Lennie Pond and took the lead position on lap 436, leading the remaining laps for his record 13th season victory.

Petty's sixth championship season marked the first time a driver had won nearly half the scheduled races: he took 13 checkered flags from the 30 events in 1975. Petty set a record of 11 straight first or second-place finishes. He wound up the season with 21 top-five and 24 top-ten finishes. In August 1975 Richard Petty became the first

The famous Pearson and Petty battles

The One That Got Away

For the 1976 season, Petty Enterprises and Richard Petty prepared for battle in the new season much as they had in recent years. Consistency had always been a hallmark of the Petty operation from the beginning. That consistency brought this premier racing operation the Grand National crown in 1971-72 and again in 1974-75. On paper there was no reason to think that 1976 would be different. The 1974 Dodge Chargers being built by Petty Engineering were identical to those used for the past couple of years by the team, but the venerable 1974 Charger was in its last year of eligibility according to NASCAR rules.

Unfortunately, other forces would further complicate the task ahead for the mighty men from Level Cross. Increasingly, Chrysler Corporation was swimming in red ink. The Arab oil embargo of 1973 had triggered a severe recession in America. Inflation had shot up, demand for goods and services was way down, and the auto industry was staring at sales figures similar to those of 1970. Instead of the United States auto industry sharing in the sales of 11 million vehicles, demand had dropped back to 6 million vehicles. Sales figures for 1975 and early 1976 were down sharply at both Ford and GM, and Chrysler's numbers were off 34 percent.

Surprisingly, the new Dodge Charger, the "Cordoba clone," sold fairly well, but not like the newly

What a selection of race cars! The parade lap at Riverside included Mercurys, AMC Matadors, Chevy Monte Carlos and Lagunas, Ford Torinos and, of course, a good number of Dodge Chargers led by Richard's in the second row. Lou Hart via the Richard Petty Private Collection

introduced small Chrysler. The boxy and formal Charger looked completely different from its namesake of just a few years earlier. For this reason, the Dodge Charger no longer appealed to the youth or performance market. Unleaded gasoline and the national 55 mph speed limit discouraged any-

thing that bespoke muscle or speed. And just as in 1975, the aerodynamics of the '76 Dodge Charger offered the racing community no more promise.

Chrysler's sales dilemma and a diminishing lack of factory support in drive-train research and development for the racing community put addi-

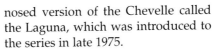

tional burdens on engine wizard Maurice Petty and company to coax increased performance from the Mopar small-block V-8. The smallest of our major auto manufacturers, with sales down by one-third, had to work around the clock to increase fuel mileage substantially in addition to complying with even stiffer federal environmental standards. More racing horsepower, even for the likes of Richard Petty, was the last thing on Chrysler's agenda.

With this backdrop to help usher in the new season, Petty's Dodge faced

the challenge of Pearson's Mercury, Yarborough's Chevy, and Baker's Ford. Early on it was evident that Petty's major challenge for the 1976 Grand National title would come from someone driving one of these three makes of race car. The odds swung decidedly in the favor of the Chevrolet teams for 1976 as they worked all the bugs out of a slope-

nosed version of the Chevelle called the Laguna, which was introduced to the series in late 1975.

In the Winston Western 500 at Riverside, Richard qualified in 27th place, retiring on lap 83 with a spent engine. He finished in 25th place. David Pearson dominated the show in his Wood Brothers' Mercury, beating Cale Yarborough to the finish line by 36 seconds.

The battle resumed in mid-February at the Daytona International Speedway's annual Daytona 500. Pearson and Petty swapped the lead many times during the course of the afternoon. In the closing laps it came down to a two-horse race between two of the sport's best pilots. Richard Petty took the lead with 13 laps left and appeared headed for another victory in the Super Bowl of stock car racing.

Pearson was content to "draft" Petty until the final lap around the 2.5-mile oval, obviously waiting for the traditional last lap to slingshot into the lead. As the two cars entered turn three, Pearson swung out and took the lead from Petty but drifted high. Petty countered by dropping low and moving alongside Pearson's Mercury. As the two cars came off turn four neck and neck, Petty's Dodge wriggled, then Pearson's Mercury bobbled. They touched, hit the wall, and began spinning wildly.

Both cars slid into the front-stretch grass, with Petty coming to rest some

distance ahead of Pearson, less than 100 yards short of the finish line. Petty was unable to re-start the wounded race car's engine. Pearson had managed to keep the engine running in his mangled Mercury, and he crept across the finish line for his first Daytona 500 victory. Many consider the 1976 Daytona 500 the most exciting on record.

Petty came back with a vengeance the following week at Rockingham. He won the Carolina 500 by two laps over second-place Darrell Waltrip. Bobby Allison, debuting the new Penske/Cam 2 Mercury, touched fenders with Cale Yarborough on the backstretch late in the race and slammed the outside wall. Allison spent three days in the hospital but was released no worse for the wear. The victory was Richard Petty's 178th of his career.

It was a long dry spell before Richard Petty would get win number two of the season or visit victory lane again. What followed the win at Rockingham for Petty was a prolonged string of top-five finishes and too many DNFs. Petty was second to Marcis at Richmond, but he crashed early at Bristol, finishing 27th and losing the points lead to Yarborough.

On March 21, Richard's engine let go in the Atlanta 500 halfway through the race and he wound up in 28th spot. Petty then bounced back to finish second to Yarborough at North Wilkesboro, one lap off the pace. Richard was still third in points as Parsons held a slim 36 point-lead over Yarborough.

The Rebel 500 at Darlington in mid-April wasn't kind to Petty. The engine expired again in his Dodge at the midpoint of the event. And who, you may ask, was taking home all the gold and virtually dominating the series? David Pearson had won four of the first eight races of 1976, and he hadn't even competed in three of the short track races. Actually, Pearson and the Wood Brothers' Mercury were four-for-five at this point.

At Martinsville on April 25, Richard Petty finished fourth behind

The '76 version of the Charger could be identified by the MDA decal on the rear window pillar and the white taillight cover panel. Here Petty goes through turn #8 at Riverside. Bob Tronolone

Dover in September. The spot in the middle of the roof numbers is a small antenna, one of the first times a radio was used by the team. Ray Masser

SIGNIFICATA

- Driving a Chevrolet, Cale Yarborough wins the Grand National Championship over the course of 30 races. Richard Petty finishes second in points.

Waltrip, Yarborough, and Pearson. Petty was again in fourth place as the series moved to Talladega for the Winston 500. Buddy Baker won in a Ford with Yarborough's Chevy and Allison's Mercury right behind.

Cale Yarborough retook the points lead over Parsons and Petty by winning the Music City 420 at Nashville in early May. Richard managed to keep Yarborough in sight all evening, but Yarborough prevailed, leading all but 22 laps. It was Yarborough's third win of the 1976 season.

Richard Petty could manage only a sixth-place finish in the Mason-Dixon 500 at Dover a week later. Benny Parsons beat David Pearson for the victory, and the win pushed him back into the points lead over Yarborough and Petty. The lead was a slim one, though, at just 24 points.

By Memorial Day, David Pearson was on a hot streak once more. He beat Petty in a seesaw battle in the World 600 at Charlotte. It was a battle of Mercurys at Riverside in mid-June as Pearson prevailed in his Mercury over

Bobby Allison's Cam 2 Mercury. Both Petty and Dave Marcis, the major contingent for Dodge, suffered mechanical problems that kept them off the pace. Petty, still running at the finish, was nine laps down in ninth place.

David Pearson took the lead from Cale Yarborough with 18 laps left in the Cam 2 Motor Oil 400 at Michigan one week later and went on to victory number seven in 11 starts. Petty briefly led twice in the late stages of the race but finished fourth. Yarborough's second-place finish gave him a 51-point lead over Parsons and Petty in the chase for the title.

Independence Day at Daytona, Cale Yarborough made it win number four in the Firecracker 400. Yarborough beat back challenges from both Mercurys of Allison and Pearson for the win. Unfortunately it was another DNF for Richard Petty. The engine died on lap 126, relegating him to 22nd place. Yarborough extended his lead in points over Benny Parsons to 90.

Benny Parsons led the final 100 laps to win the Nashville 420 two weeks later. Richard Petty was runner-up, 15 seconds behind at the finish. Richard did lead more than 70 laps in the early going but never seriously challenged for the victory after that. With Parsons' victory and Cale Yarborough's fifth place, Benny closed to within 70 points of leader Yarborough.

On August 1 in Pocono, the 18th race on the schedule, Richard Petty finally recorded win number two of the season. Petty battled with Pearson, Baker, and Parsons all afternoon before taking the checkered flag. In spite of the victory Petty remained third in points behind Parsons and Yarborough. The win was number 178 in Petty's career. Parsons' third-place finish combined with Yarborough's

The STP pit crew in action servicing Richard's Charger. Ray Masser

Another unique marking in '76 was the "Dodge by Petty" logo on the white taillight cover. It had been a while since the " ... by Petty" modex had been used. Bob Tronolone

25th place boosted Parsons into the championship points lead by just seven.

Misfortune struck Petty once again during the Talladega 500 in early August. Starting from 14th position, Petty was a factor in the race until a sour engine sidelined him with just 20 laps remaining. Parsons, Yarborough, and Pearson didn't fare much better. Only Yarborough was still running at the finish. Cale, who soldiered on most of the day with a sour engine, finished 26th.

David Pearson made it look easy, coming from nearly a lap down to win the Champion Spark Plug 400 at Michigan in late August. It was victory number eight for the season and career win number 95 for Pearson. Yarborough was second, Petty third, and Bobby Allison fourth. Again Petty remained third in the championship title chase: Yarborough regained the points lead once more as Benny Parsons finished ninth.

On the high banks of Bristol International Speedway, Cale

Richard and his Dodge Charger on the high side of Richard Childress in a Chevy Monte Carlo at Dover Downs. Richard Petty Private Collection

Yarborough's Chevrolet had no real competition in the Volunteer 400 one week later. Yarborough led from lap 28 until the end and cruised to a two-lap victory over second-place Richard Petty. The win, combined with Benny Parsons' fourth-place finish, increased Yarborough's lead in the points chase.

By winning his first Southern 500 at Darlington, David Pearson scored a "Triple Crown," having earlier won the Daytona 500 and World 600.

Richard Petty led early in the race for 21 laps, and for most of the afternoon he was able to keep the other leaders in sight. With 45 laps remaining Pearson took the lead from Waltrip and held onto it the rest of the way. Petty got around Waltrip on the last lap of the race to finish second. Due to a pit-lane accident, Cale Yarborough lost 60 laps for repairs, finishing 23rd. Petty's second moved him ahead of Benny Parsons in the title chase, but with all of Yarborough's misfortune

he managed to hold a slim 29-point lead over Richard.

If Richard had hoped to rally and recapture the lead in the points race, he would need Yarborough to have a run of bad luck. Unfortunately, just the opposite happened. Cale went on a tear that put the championship out of Petty's reach by winning the next four races in a row. He captured the trophies at The Capital City 400 at Richmond, the Delaware 500 at Dover, the Old Dominion 500 at Martinsville,

Dale Inman (center top), Maurice Petty (on left with hat), and the rest of the Petty crew take a break between pit stops. Note how the tools and equipment in the pits have evolved when compared to what crews use today. Richard Petty Private Collection

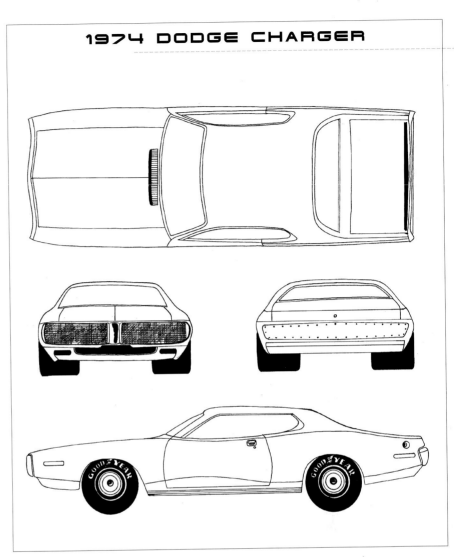

1974 DODGE CHARGER

and the Wilkes 400 at North Wilkesboro, while Richard claimed a third, second, fourth, and third, respectively, at those same races.

When the tour returned to Charlotte for the National 500, Cale finished second to Donnie Allison, while Richard finished eighth, six laps down.

Petty finally made up some ground at the American 500 at Rockingham by lapping the entire field on his way to a dominating victory while Cale finished fifth. But it was too little, too late. When Richard's engine let go on lap 157 of the Dixie 500 at the Atlanta International Speedway on November 7th, Cale only had to start the final race at Ontario Motor Speedway to claim the championship. In hindsight, the wreck at Daytona foretold the luck of the season and a championship that would just slip away.

A good high angle shot of the Charger at Dover in September. Note how large the STP oval on the hood has become. This was the size used in the '76 and '77 seasons. Ray Masser

The aging Charger gets another life

Running On Borrowed Time

NASCAR, in a desperate attempt to keep the front-running Mopar teams in competition, revised its eligibility rules from three years to four and also extended the racing life of cars like the 1974 Dodge Charger for one more year on the Grand National circuit. This move was appreciated by the Pettys, but other issues concerned them more in preparation for the 1977 season.

In 1977, cash-strapped Chrysler Corporation was busy shuffling nameplates, revising model lineups, and struggling to regain lost ground in the marketplace. The formal body styles introduced in 1975 for Chrysler, Dodge, and Plymouth intermediate two-door coupes continued on largely unaltered in the new model year save for cosmetic changes. There seemed little hope that Chrysler could produce a new car with the aerodynamics suitable for high-speed racing.

To compound things, as fewer teams raced Mopars, the cost of tooling or making racing parts for Chryslers began to escalate to a point that racing a Chrysler wasn't worth the investment from either a racer's or a manufacturer's standpoint. Some reports had the Mopar teams resorting more and more to reconditioning used parts as new items became scarce.

When the new Dodge Diplomat and Chrysler LeBaron were announced by Chrysler in the fall of

'76, faint hope was held out that the sanctioning body might approve this more shapely body shell for competition. But though the Diplomat/LeBaron rode on the same 112-inch size wheel base as the Chevy's Laguna, NASCAR considered the car's cross-section and silhouette too small for fair competition. Numerous reports claimed that Chrysler was working on a more race-worthy model to be introduced by mid-1977. If true, this was encouraging news but of little comfort as the new season got under way.

The trusty two-tone 1974 Dodge Chargers, with corporate backing from STP, were once again pressed into service to run head-to-head with

Richard leads Dick Brooks at Michigan. Note how dark Richard's windshield is compared to that of Brooks' car. This was one of the rare times the Charger appeared with the grille trim blacked out. Elmer Kappell

The Charger rounds a corner at Nashville in July of 1977. By now the car sports Goodyear decals over the front wheel wells and blue wheels that made occasional appearances. Elmer Kappell

Richard takes a drink as the crew services the STP Charger at Bristol. That's Bobby Allison's AMC Matador on the track beyond Petty's roofline. Bill Coulter

competitors who seemed to be constantly growing stronger. Reports circulated that the Pettys had fully evaluated Chevrolet and Ford racing equipment in the off-season. Their decision was to stay put, deciding to take their chances with proven (though somewhat dated) equipment. This move was seen primarily as a wake-up call to Chrysler from the Pettys.

At the season opener at Riverside for the Winston Western 500, David Pearson shot past a spinning Cale Yarborough 16 laps from the finish to record his first win of the new season. Yarborough recovered to finish second and Richard Petty took third, down a lap at the finish.

Petty's day ended too soon in the Daytona 500, the second event on the 1977 schedule. The ghosts of engine failure from the previous season continued to haunt the Level Cross race team. Petty finished 26th, lasting only 111 laps. On the short track at Richmond one week later, Yarborough led on four occasions during the rain-shortened event, but most importantly, he was leading when the red flag came out. Richard, on the other hand, came in sixth, two laps down at the flag.

In mid-March, Petty returned to championship form by winning a wreck-marred Carolina 500 at Rockingham, North Carolina. Richard led the final 58 laps as well as 281 of

the 492 laps to beat Darrell Waltrip by eight seconds at the checkered flag.

Petty then developed a mini-streak, taking the Atlanta 500 a week later by 12 seconds over archrival David Pearson. Richard started from the pole and led five different times for 112 laps to take the win. Richard then finished second at North Wilkesboro and repeated the 2nd place finish at the Rebel 500 at Darlington in early April.

While Yarborough dominated the Southeastern 500 leading all but five laps of the 500-lap event after starting from the pole position, Richard Petty finished third, nine laps in arrears at the finish. When the series moved to Martinsville, Petty again finished third.

A very competitive Richard Petty

Running On Borrowed Time

A familiar winning smile in the Winner's Circle.
Bryant McMurray

had to settle for 20th place when the engine in his Dodge expired with just 35 laps to go in the Winston 500 at Talladega on the first day of May. Things improved slightly at the Music City USA 420 at Nashville in mid-May. Richard finished in the fifth spot, four laps down at the flag.

Cale Yarborough fought a day full of adversity to win his sixth race of the season in the Mason-Dixon 500 at Dover in mid-May. Petty's third-place finish combined with Yarborough's win allowed the Chevy driver to increase his points lead to 202 for the Winston Cup.

If it looked as if the old Chargers of Petty Enterprises just didn't have anything for Junior Johnson's Chevys, guess again. Richard was not about to let Yarborough make a romp of the championship. At the World 600 at Charlotte on Memorial Day, it was a Pearson-versus-Petty show for most of the afternoon. Pearson had started from the pole, but it was soon apparent that Richard had the equipment to mount a serious challenge for the win. Petty took the lead from Pearson and led the last 130 laps of the race uncontested. Cale Yarborough was plagued by mechanical ills throughout the race. He was 50 laps down at the finish, and his lead in the championship battle was reduced to 108 points.

Petty backed up the Charlotte win with another convincing victory in the NAPA 400 at Riverside two weeks later. Petty took the lead position for good from Cale Yarborough on lap 33 and led the rest of the way for the win. The victory enabled Petty to cut Yarborough's points lead for the title to just 93.

Fortunes changed momentarily the following week at Michigan International Speedway in mid-June. Petty was unable to catch Yarborough in the closing stages of the Cam 2 Motor Oil 400 as Cale led the final 64 laps. It was Yarborough's 47th career Grand National victory and the win allowed him to increase his points lead to 103 over Petty.

Petty struck back by leading the final 19 laps of the Firecracker 400 at Daytona on July 4 to take the win. Petty led a finishing parade of seven cars that were all on the lead lap. Cale Yarborough was plagued with transmission problems that cost him dearly, dropping him 14 laps behind at the finish. Petty's victory and Yarborough's 23rd-place finish dropped his points lead to just 17 for the Winston Cup Grand National title.

The next week at Nashville, Darrell Waltrip won the Nashville 420 by one lap over Bobby Allison. Richard Petty placed third, two laps down. Cale

The parade lap at Ontario Motor Speedway in November 1977. That's Neil Bonnett beside Petty and A.J. Foyt on the inside of the second row with Pearson on the outside. Bob Tronolone

1974 DODGE CHARGER

The Charger's last ride. Dressed in full 1977 trim, Richard raced the Charger for the last time at Riverside in the NASCAR 500 in January of '78. Bob Tronolone

Yarborough recorded a fourth, three laps behind Waltrip at the finish. Yarborough's points lead over Petty was reduced to only 12.

In late July the series moved to Pocono for the Coca-Cola 500. It was Benny Parsons' turn to shine. Benny battled with Petty, Waltrip, and Bobby Allison over the last half of the event to record his seventh career victory. Cale Yarborough was sixth, two laps behind Parsons. The finishing order allowed Petty to take the title-points lead away from Yarborough for the first time during the season.

The heat of the points race was exceeded only by the summer heat in Alabama. In early August, Darrell Waltrip, driving in relief for an exhausted Donnie Allison, won the Talladega 500 at Talladega. Cale Yarborough managed a second-place finish, good enough to regain the points lead from Petty, who finished 11th, eight laps down at the flag.

The Champion Spark Plug 400 followed two weeks later. Darrell Waltrip outran pole sitter David Pearson to win. Yarborough was fifth, finishing on the same lap with the winner. Richard Petty settled for an eighth-place finish, two laps off the pace.

The following week Cale Yarborough bounced back to record win number eight of the season by taking the checkered flag in the Volunteer 400 at Bristol. Yarborough sharply increased his points lead over Petty; the Dodge driver exited early due to a crash on lap 118 of the 400-lap race. Petty was awarded 22nd place.

It was David Pearson in front at the checkered flag for the Southern 500 at Darlington on Labor Day. Richard Petty, with relief from Dave Marcis, finished fourth, two laps off the pace, and Cale Yarborough was right behind in fifth, five laps down. Then, on the second Sunday of September, young Bobby Allison protégé Neil Bonnett drove the Jim Stacy Dodge to a narrow victory over Petty in the Capital City 400 at Richmond. It was Bonnett's first Grand National career victory.

Richard leads the 1977 IROC race at Michigan.
Bill Coulter

Engine woes sidelined Richard early in the Delaware 500 at Dover in mid-September. The Dodge pilot recorded a 23rd-place finish, completing only 301 laps of the 500 circuits scheduled.

Heat exhaustion took its toll the next week at Martinsville as Bobby Allison had to relieve Petty. Cale Yarborough on the other hand, came back to win the Old Dominion 500 over Benny Parsons and David Pearson. With the victory Cale added 25 more points to his Winston Cup Grand National title lead, which was now up to 219 over second-place Richard Petty.

Petty started from the pole at the Wilkes 400 at North Wilkesboro in early October. He led for the first 76 circuits around the flat .625-mile state fairgrounds race track but was side-swiped by Bobby Allison on the 93rd lap. Petty lost control of his Charger and hit the front stretch pit wall. The impact caused the car to ricochet onto the track, where it was struck by Benny Parsons' Chevy. Petty was finally retired on lap 341 from the damage sustained.

Richard sits behind the wheel of an IROC Camaro in 1977. Never really comfortable in someone else's car, Richard eventually decided to pass on the IROC after a wreck and injury later in the '77 series. Bill Coulter

On the first Sunday of October the series returned to Charlotte for the NAPA National 500. Petty had opened up a substantial lead in the first 100 miles, only to fall victim to a broken shock mount. He ultimately was forced to retire on lap 107 of the 334-lap event, recording a 32nd-place finish. Cale Yarborough's second-place finish and Petty's continuing misfortunes further tightened the Chevy driver's grip on the championship points lead. Yarborough then iced the cake by finishing fourth in the American 500 at Rockingham. He had won his second straight Winston Cup Grand National championship. Petty ran a close second to winner

Richard smiles in victory lane at Riverside. It would be one of the last victories in the reliable old Dodge Charger. Bob Tronolone

Donnie Allison, but it was too little, too late, to challenge Yarborough for the title.

By late October there were just two events left on the schedule, and the title was no longer in question. In Atlanta, Cale Yarborough came in fifth with Richard Petty in sixth, both on the lead lap when the race was shortened to 268 laps by threatening weather and impending darkness.

The final event of the season was the Los Angeles Times 500 at the Ontario Motor Speedway in California in late November. Petty put the STP Dodge on the pole, with fellow Dodge driver Neil Bonnett starting alongside him. Though at times the race was led by many other contenders, the final shoot-out came down to the two front row starters. Petty took the lead temporarily from Bonnett with five laps remaining, but he could not hold the young charger at bay. Bonnett reassumed the lead from Petty and led the rest of the way to the flag. It was Bonnett's second career win and his second of the 1977 season.

The 1977 season concluded with

A classic Pearson/Petty battle for the lead. Note the large size of the STP logo on the hood of the Charger. Richard Petty Private Collection

Cale Yarborough and Richard Petty battling for the crown for the second straight year. Unfortunately for Petty, the Chevy driver enjoyed greater consistency and fewer mechanical ills along the way. Both drivers started all 30 events. Yarborough had nine wins, 25 top-five finishes, and 27 top-ten finishes for the season. Petty by contrast had only five first-place finishes, 20 top-five finishes, and 23 top-ten

finishes during 1977. Clearly the tide in Grand National racing was turning toward the Chevrolet effort. Something would need to be done quickly for the Mopar teams and especially the Pettys to ensure their competitiveness for the 1978 season. It was becoming more evident that forces outside racing were profoundly affecting the destiny of Chrysler and Richard Petty's racing fortunes.

The Chrysler replacement for the Charger fizzles leaving Petty Enterprises to search for a replacement and speed

The Magnum Misfires

I t was apparent in the latter half of 1977 that the Pettys had gotten about as much out of their faithful old Chargers that they were going to get. After they won five of the first 16 races, the well finally went dry after the Firecracker 400 at Daytona in July. As successful as the car had been, time was running out on it. As Richard put it, "The car was used up. We had extended it about as far as it would go."

To be successful in auto racing, many things must mesh. The driver has to be sharp and aggressive. The team has to work well together as a unit and work with its driver. The equipment has to be well-prepared and built so that it's competitive. Fall behind in any area, from engine development to chassis set-up to the speed of pit stops and the health of the driver, and you will be playing a nasty game of catch-up. Even the most experienced team will endlessly chase getting the car right — and possibly never succeed. Such was the case with the Magnum.

Richard was actually looking forward to running the new Magnum. It looked as if the car could develop into a real winner. Based on its shape, the car looked fast, though admittedly not as sleek as the Charger. Compared to the Charger, the Magnum seemed boxy or even bulky, but even the new Fords appeared to have the same problem. Chevy's Monte Carlo didn't

The Dodge Magnum turned out to be a huge disappointment for Petty Enterprises and a real puzzle to figure out. While not as sleek as the Charger, the new Dodge should have been a better car. Richard Petty Private Collection

look as sleek as the Magnum, although it and the rest of the GM bunch had proved reliable the year before. The Magnum should have been a good race car. But the Magnum had problems that defied solution. There was another problem developing as well that proved to be the Magnum's — and Chrysler's — ultimate undoing in NASCAR's premier racing division.

The first hint of trouble came while testing the car at Daytona. "The Dodge Magnum is undrivable at 190 mph," Richard said after his first runs in the car at high speed. Petty Enterprises spent more time testing the new Magnum than it did with any

other car in the history of the team. Yet getting "the handle" still eluded them.

If you're wondering why the Pettys didn't see that the Magnum wouldn't be competitive, you have to keep in mind that with the overall dimensions of the cars changing, stability on the track at speed had become the critical issue and had everyone guessing how to find it. Many other drivers felt the same way about the GM and Ford cars. Donnie Allison, one of the Olds drivers, said, "I can't drive the Olds. It moves around too much."

When the tangible stuff doesn't seem to do the trick, even the best of us start thinking about the intangible things in life, such as luck. In thinking

It took time for the Petty crew to get used to the Chevy. Here Richard drops out of the National 500 at Charlotte. The experience gained in the last half of the season helped the crew mount a successful bid for the championship the following year. Elmer Kappell

about the end of 1977 and the beginning of 1978 Richard was wondering if his luck had finally run out. "Ain't nobody been luckier than I've been. I had to be [lucky] to get as many wins as I have. Then suddenly everything went sour. Everybody in his lifetime — this is the way I was thinking in '78 — has so much good that's going to happen to him. I believed I had used up mine."

What didn't help matters and probably contributed to those feelings was an accident Richard had in the final race of the IROC V series at Daytona two days before the Daytona 500. The accident knocked Richard out and left him dazed for nearly an hour. Hospitalized overnight for observations, the doctors didn't want to let Richard race the following day. He went racing anyway.

The first outing of the new Petty Enterprises Magnum left the team with the impression that the car might be competitive. A blown tire in the Daytona 500 took Richard's Magnum and two other leaders out early in the race while he was leading. A rear end failed a week later at Richmond. Combined with the DNF at the season opener at Riverside in January, which was the final outing for the Charger, the team had a third DNF by the third race of the season.

March started off better for the Petty team with a fourth-place finish at Rockingham, but the Magnum overheated in the Atlanta 500 two weeks later, and a crash ended the day at the Southern 500 in Bristol. In the first six races the team had five DNFs. The other Dodge teams weren't doing much better, with the exception of the pair fielded by Jim Stacey and driven by Neil Bonnett and Ferrell Harris. Still, those two cars could manage no better than fifth in any race, and the

cars were usually a few laps down to the leaders.

Though the statistics show a marked improvement for Petty in the stretch starting at Darlington in April and ending at the Firecracker 400 back at Daytona in July, the team managed no better than a pair of seconds and a pair of thirds — all on short tracks or the road course at Riverside. On the superspeedways you could count on the Magnums, regardless of who was driving them, to finish laps down to the leaders. Richard finished five laps down at Talladega, six down at Dover, and two off the pace at the World 600 in Charlotte.

The Magnum's real problem didn't seem to be handling as much as power. Powerplant development, as we've seen, is a constant in racing. If there is no real development, the competition will leave you in the dust. This time, however, the power prob-

The Magnum Misfires

NUGGETS

Kyle decides to go racing

When Richard decided he wanted to become a race car driver, he simply walked up to his father and started to ask the question. Lee was way ahead of him and said "no" before he even had a chance to get it out. Lee told him to wait and come back a few years later. Kyle, however, took a somewhat different approach. He decided to first express his desire to become a race car driver to Ken Squire — in an interview on national TV. Richard didn't know anything about the interview until he saw it broadcast. Then they talked about it. By Richard's own admission, it wasn't much of a talk — Kyle's mind was made up.

In the months that followed, Kyle learned the ropes by literally following his father around the race track. By driving behind his father on the racetrack, Kyle was able to learn by doing, knowing where to turn, what line to take, and what not to do. The same technique is used today at the Richard Petty Driving Experience driving schools at Charlotte, Atlanta, and Las Vegas.

Kyle's decision to go racing opened a whole new can of worms for the family operation. It would be the event that would eventually affect the events and decisions in the years to follow.

The Magnum in a turn at Nashville in May. Grille and air duct openings changed constantly on the car.
Elmer Kappell

The interior of the Magnum was typical of stock cars of that day. Note the early type of drum fan used on the oil pump and Richard's headrest.
Richard Petty Private Collection

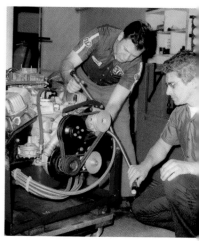

Parts were getting harder and harder to find for the 340 wedge. That combined with the speed parts suppliers shying away from Chrysler products made keeping the Mopar racing next to impossible.
Richard Petty Private Collection

In mid-season, Richard opted to buy a Chevy Monte Carlo from Cecil Gordon. It was reworked at the Petty shops and run for the first time at Michigan. This is Richard on his first-qualifying run in the car. Elmer Kappell

The first Magnum as it was being built at the Petty Shops. Note the Charger in the background.
Richard Petty Private Collection

lem was a symptom of something much bigger. As well as the Stacey Dodges were running, crew chief Harry Hyde said, "We've been running out of a junkyard for three years. Trying to run these Dodge engine blocks we get from the junkyard is like taking a mule to the Kentucky Derby."

Why would a NASCAR team be picking through junkyards for parts? Consider the state of things at Chrysler in 1978. Chrysler was in complete disarray — and the Mopar parts supply lines with it. Lee Iacocca said in his autobiography that his first discovery after joining the company in November was that Chrysler in the late 1970s was being run much the way Italy was in the 1860s: "Nobody knew what anybody else was doing. Each area was like a little empire run by its own prima donna."

Regular dealerships couldn't get parts. Chrysler couldn't pay for them. The situation was even worse for a team attempting to race Chrysler products. As a result, maintaining the engines was tough, and gaining ground with new development was next to impossible. "It just got harder and harder to get people to build pistons, rods, cranks, for that particular Chrysler engine [the 340 Wedge]," Petty recalled. "It was a good engine. All you needed was to keep improving the thing — but you couldn't get the pieces."

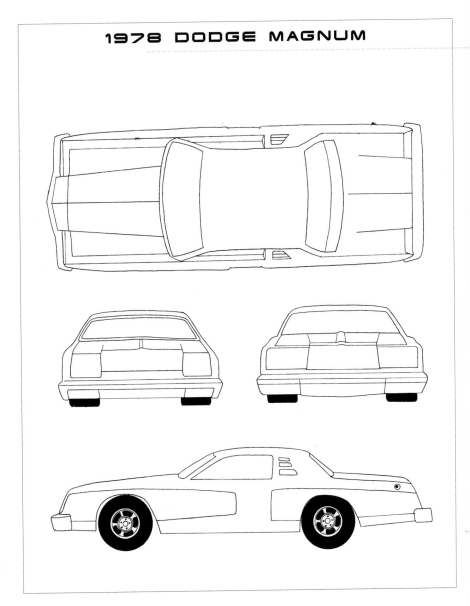

1978 DODGE MAGNUM

The tail end of the Magnum was decorated differently than had been the usual practice on Petty cars. Note how the bumper sweeps up to the bottom of the trunk lid. The car is parked in front of the Dodge tractor and converted lowboy trailer used to haul the car and equipment to the track. Richard Petty Private Collection

By midyear, few insiders bet that Chrysler would even be around the next year. Even if it was, publicly announced plans called for smaller four-cylinder powerplants — a completely new approach to building American cars that left anyone racing the company's stuff out in the cold. At the time, it looked as if the sun was setting on both the Wedge and on Chrysler.

After half a season back in the pack, the Pettys' time and patience with the Dodges finally ran out. On July 17, as a matter of survival and staying competitive, Richard purchased a Chevy Monte Carlo from Cecil Gordon. "We decided to get ready for the 1979 season and start

right away. We decided to go ahead and spend our money and get our experience with the Chevy." The car was then overhauled and rebuilt for its debut in Petty Blue at the Champion Spark Plug 500 in Brooklyn, Michigan. The Dodge dynasty at Petty Enterprises was, for all practical purposes, over.

The switch to Chevys didn't solve all Petty's problems instantly. Though Chrysler's support wasn't much, it was something, and all the Chevys and the parts to go with them had to be paid for out of the Petty Enterprises coffers. Also, in spite of the problems, the development of Chrysler engines and heads was far ahead of the GM products, and it

would take awhile for the team and its driver to get used to the new equipment and running gear.

At least there wasn't the parts supply problem to worry about. And despite its swoopy shape, the Monte Carlo turned out to be an excellent race car. Though the team didn't manage a victory in the closing races of the regular season, "the handle" — that combination of car, mechanicals, teamwork, and driving — was obviously coming together.

In the season's closing race at California's Ontario Motor Speedway, the Chevy blew an engine on lap 83. The car was still in good shape, and there was a spare engine on the truck. Somewhere between loading up all

The spacious nose of the Magnum housed both the oil cooler and radiator, shown being installed here.
Richard Petty Private Collection

SIGNIFICATA

- Because the hood is so long on the Monte Carlos, giving them a weight distribution advantage, engine mounts must be moved forward 2.5 inches to keep Ford happy.
- NASCAR bans the Laguna S-3 nose.
- Fiberglass seats with steel frames are now allowed.
- Driving an Olds Cutlass, Cale Yarborough wins his third Grand National Championship over the course of 30 races. Richard Petty finishes sixth in points.

Unlike the Fords he ran nearly ten years before, Richard's use of the Chevys came out of his own pocket with almost no support from Chevrolet. Times were different then as were the circumstances. Richard Petty Private Collection

the equipment and heading for home, someone suggested that Phoenix was on the way. The Western Division 250 mile race, held in Phoenix, was a NASCAR event that didn't count toward championship points — and therefore doesn't show up on the record books. Nonetheless, Richard entered the race and won, his first victory in the Chevy. The win closed out the team's efforts for the year on a high note and forecast what was to come. It was just a matter of time.

Petty and his Magnum race against Richard Childress and his Oldsmobile early in the May race at Dover. Petty finished 7th in this race. Ray Masser

1976 CHEVY MONTE CARLO

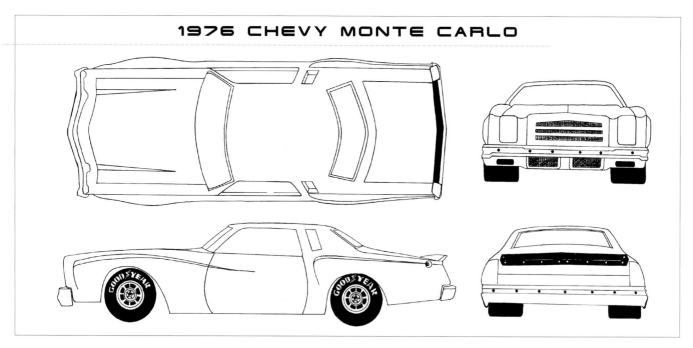

Telling the '76 Monte Carlo run in the last half of the '78 season from the '77 Monte Carlo run later on is easy if you can see the headlights. The '76 model had round headlight covers and a smaller grille, while the '77 had rectangular-stacked headlight covers. Ray Masser

Richard at Riverside in June for the NAPA 400. The Magnum looked pretty good on the race track, especially when compared to cars of the same era. Nonetheless, it wasn't remotely competitive. Bob Tronolone

Side view of the Monte Carlo. The paint schemes differ slightly between the Dodge and the Chevy. Elmer Kappell

At Talladega the Magnum couldn't even keep Richard in the hunt. Aside from puzzling aerodynamic qualities, powerplant problems kept the car from getting up to speed. Elmer Kappell

Back in the lead. With the Monte Carlo, Petty was able to get back up front and run with the best of them again. Here he leads the National 500 at Charlotte in October. Compare the front-end profiles of these cars to the Magnum and it's easy to understand why everyone thought the Dodge should have been a slick car. Elmer Kappell

Richard and Kyle discuss some details at the back of one of the Magnums. Norman DeHaven

As seen in this photo of a pit stop at Michigan, the Magnum sports an opera window divided into three horizontal sections. It was the only Petty car to run that way.
Elmer Kappell

*A Cutlass, a Monte Carlo and a Caprice power Petty
to his 7th championship*

Speed Found

The 1979 race season stands out in the history of Petty Enterprises for what both the team and Richard were able to achieve. The 1978 season had been a nightmare for Richard. Richard had been a consistent winner, and it was hard to go a season and a half without any wins. Racing was quickly changing. Both the team and Richard needed to prove they were still among the best, and there is only one way of proving that — winning races.

There was some measure of relief when the 1978 season ended. The second half had offered promise with some close races and the team getting a handle on the new equipment. They had proved that the Pettys didn't need a Plymouth or a Dodge to go fast.

However, not all was well with Richard. On December 5, during the winter break, Richard entered the hospital to have surgery for an ongoing problem with ulcers. Richard thought it would be something simple, but doctors removed 40 percent of his stomach and he was hospitalized for 12 days. His recovery was slow and Linda, worried about her husband's health, told him that unless he was feeling better by the end of the month he would go back to the hospital. Somehow, he felt better.

Despite doctors' advice to lay off racing for a while, Richard was back in the driver's seat for the season opener at Riverside on January 14, 1979. The Monte Carlo's engine lasted

Richard's last pole came at Bristol in this unusual car. It's a Chevy Caprice that is painted in the reverse of normal. The car was painted that way as an experiment in anticipation of the team fielding a car for Kyle. Note the slanted backglass and the unusual position of the rear spoiler. Steve & Gloria Dilts via the Richard Petty Private Collection

A Magnum in 1979? Look carefully and you will notice the car carries the number 42 and has the nose painted red. This was the car Kyle drove at Michigan at the Champion Spark Plug 400 in his second Winston Cup start. He finished 13th.
Richard Petty Private Collection

By the first Bristol race, the Olds had grown a set of red roof stripes so that it would match the rest of the fleet.
Bill Coulter

only 13 laps and Richard once again started the season with a DNF. This wasn't the best way to get things going, but remember this: Richard is one determined cat.

Work continued in the shops to prepare new race cars for the season. It had been decided that perhaps some makes and models were better on some tracks than on others and that it would be a good idea to get whatever would do the job, regardless of what make or model it was. After so many years of watching Petty Enterprises faithfully campaign with one make and model per year, it was strange to see the Petty colors on anything that would run fast.

The team wanted to run a 1977 Olds Cutlass "S" on the superspeedways, but how they got one has to be one of the stranger stories we can tell you. With a sloping nose and rear window, the Olds Cutlass sliced through the air better than the Monte Carlo at high speeds, giving it a slight competitive edge. The problem was where to get one. Nobody wanted to sell one, so the team had to build one. At the time, a family member had a street version of the car. Dale and Richard asked to borrow the car for a day in order to make a set of templates to use in building a race version of the car. Sheet metal was bought and shaped and within a week or so, Petty Enterprises had an Olds Cutlass "S" on a standard, but highly tweaked, stock car racing chassis.

The Monte Carlo remained as the main weapon in the Pettys' on-track arsenal, but its other drawback was its overall size. In the late '70s, the Monte Carlo was a big car — actually bigger than the Chevy Caprice. By the '80s and '90s this would be reversed, but in 1979 the Caprice had less bulk than the Monte Carlo. Bulk is certainly no

Dale Inman on the radio with Richard. Dale's strategy often was the key in getting Richard in victory lane. Richard Petty Private Collection

Richard starts on the front row beside Neil Bonnett at the World 600 in Charlotte. While it was the dominant car at the time, the Chevy seems to have a much bigger snout than its competitors. Elmer Kappell

The 1979 Daytona 500 winner was the home-built Olds Cutlass of Petty Enterprises. Note the absence of red stripes on the roof of the car. Bill Coulter

The '77 Monte Carlo had a slightly different front end than the '76 version run by Petty Enterprises the year before. Note the rectangular headlight covers — the Chevy sported two rectangular headlights stacked on top of each other — and the segmented front grille. Elmer Kappell

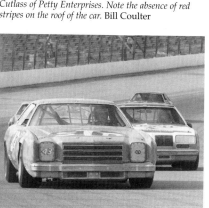

At speed at the Ontario Motor Speedway in the L.A. Times 500 in his trusty Monte Carlo. Bob Tronolone

The season turned into a battle for the title between Richard and the DiGard entry of Darrell Waltrip. DiGard was a powerhouse team at the time, although many didn't approve of their methods. Richard Petty Private Collection

1977 CHEVROLET MONTE CARLO

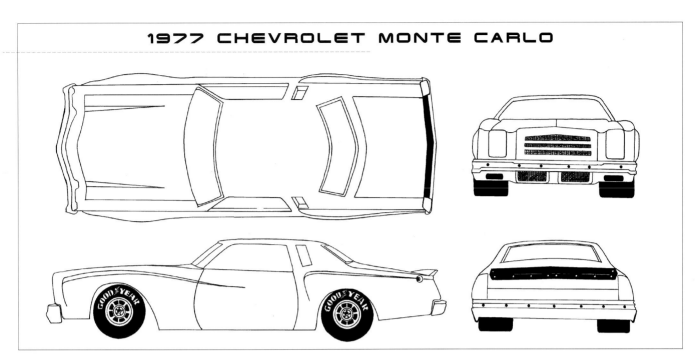

The Monte Carlo during practice at Michigan in June. Note the rear bumper fairings, the rear window straps, and the clean appearance of the car. Elmer Kappell

SIGNIFICATA

- Air shocks and rubber coil spring inserts are now allowed.
- Using three different makes and models of cars, Richard Petty wins his seventh Grand National Championship over the course of 31 races.

Richard shows off his new cowboy boots.
Bryant McMurray

asset on short tracks, so the Caprice got the nod there.

All in all, it didn't seem like a bad idea. The Olds would run at the larger superspeedways or places where its slick body would give it an edge. The Chevy Caprice would cover the other end of the spectrum by running on the smallest tracks, and the Chevy Monte Carlo would run everywhere else.

The season itself showcased the fact that it didn't take long for the team to adjust to a few new makes of cars, although a bit of good luck always helps. For instance, the Daytona 500 was won because the team was able to keep Richard and his Olds Cutlass in the hunt. Late in the race, Richard was half a lap down to the leaders, Donnie Allison and Cale

1977 OLDS CUTLASS 'S'

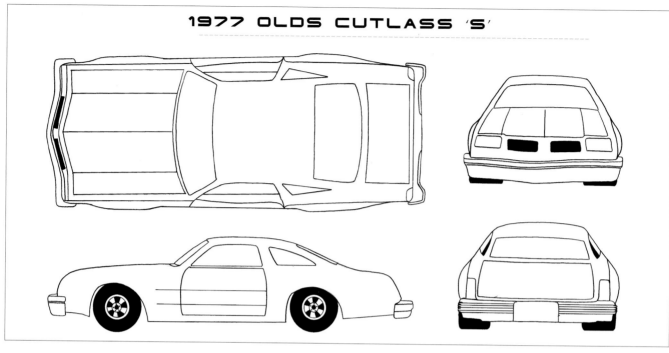

The Olds being unloaded from the lowboy hauler. Note the STP utility van in the background. Richard Petty Private Collection

The STP Chevy gets serviced by the Petty Enterprises crew. Note that the roof number doesn't have a drop shadow yet as it does nowadays. Bryant McMurray

Richard's Monte Carlo in for a four-tire stop at Michigan International Speedway. Bill Coulter

Yarborough, and battling with A.J. Foyt and Darrell Waltrip for third place. Richard was convinced he had a fourth-place car — maybe third at best. Donnie and Cale, however, were banging on one another hard enough that they eventually wrecked each other, coming to rest in the infield on the backstretch. When the yellow flag and warning lights came on due to the fracas, Foyt momentarily slowed, allowing Petty and Waltrip to scoot by — since passing is allowed until the cars actually take the yellow flag. A few moments later Richard was stunned to discover that the yellow was caused by the race leaders, leaving him to inherit the lead with Waltrip right on his heels. Richard succeeded in holding Darrell off to take the checkered flag and then was surprised again, on his victory lap. He passed the point where the former leaders had come to rest, only to find Cale, and Bobby and Donnie Allison involved in a good old-fashioned fist fight. All this took place in front of a national TV audience, since CBS had decided to broadcast the entire race — and the fisticuffs that followed — live on its network.

The Carolina 500 was next on March 4, a race in which the team was quickly eliminated on lap nine in a wreck caused by Donnie Allison and Cale Yarborough colliding again while racing for the lead. Both denied that it was a continuation of the battle fought at Daytona a few weeks before, but that was little solace for Richard and the other drivers caught in the scrap.

Fortunes changed after that. The team failed in the Monte Carlo at Richmond and ran fifth. The Olds was run at the Atlanta race and finished 11th. The Caprice then ran at North Wilkesboro, taking a second, followed by a fourth at Bristol in the Olds. Richard drove the Monte Carlo next at Darlington to gain another second and finally broke through with another win in the car at Martinsville two weeks later. The drive continued with a fourth in the Olds at Talladega, followed by another second in the Caprice at Nashville.

Richard's race at Dover in the Olds ended on lap two with a crash that involved Richard Childress and Jimmy Means, but that proved to be the last DNF and the last bit of bad luck for the season. Over the next eight races, Richard never finished lower than sixth and always ran up front. A win at Brooklyn in the Monte Carlo was followed by a second in the Caprice at Bristol. (It's interesting to note that though the Caprice is not considered one of Richard's more significant cars, he did win his final pole

at this race in one.) The gap between Richard and points leader Darrell Waltrip began to close. Before Brooklyn the gap was 229 points — and it was fading fast.

Richard and the Monte Carlo finished ninth at Darlington in the Southern 500, followed by a sixth at

On the way to his surprise Daytona 500 win, Richard and his '77 Olds Cutlass receive service from the Petty Enterprises crew. The Cutlass was one of three different cars run by Richard that year.
Richard Petty Private Collection

At the end of the 1979 season, Richard had prevailed to win his 7th Winston Cup Championship. He is pictured here with the race queen at the L.A. Times 500 at Ontario, California. Bob Tronolone

Richmond in the Caprice and a first at Dover on August 16, this time in a Monte Carlo. A second was next scored at Martinsville in a Monte Carlo, followed by a fourth at Charlotte. The Caprice was run in the

second North Wilkesboro race, where the Pettys finished third, followed by a first at Rockingham in the Monte Carlo. Waltrip's point lead was gone and Richard had taken the lead.

The next two races were simply exercises in "cool." Richard and the team were proven champions who had been through these fights before. Waltrip and the DiGard team did their best to try psyching out their rivals, but it only served to psych themselves out. When Waltrip finished fifth in the Dixie 500 at Atlanta, Richard finished a position behind him in sixth. Going into the closing race, Waltrip held the points lead by two points. "That means I'll have to beat him by just one position," Richard said when told by reporters that he was two points behind Darrell. But Richard also declared that he was going to Ontario to win the race — the only right way to win the championship. Waltrip, on the other hand, said he was going to race Petty.

In the race itself, Richard finished in a mad five-car dash to the finish, ending up fifth in the process. Waltrip finished a lap down in eighth, making the margin of victory for the championship a scant 11 points.

Of the 31 races run in 1979, Petty dropped out of only three, once from an engine failure and twice from crashes. Except for an eleventh-place finish in the Atlanta 500 and a ninth-place finish in the Southern 500, Richard never finished lower than sixth all year. However, not until the 29th race of the year did Richard finally take the points lead from Darrell Waltrip, for a seventh championship.

Richard remembers 1979 as one of the high points of his career, and with a special amount of pride. The team had come from behind, overcome a disheartening season the year before, and done so with brand-new equipment and all on their own. Hard work and consistency won the title, but if there was any one quality that brought Richard and the team out of the dark valley it had experienced, it was simply this: don't ever give up.

Dale Inman removes a tarp from the Monte Carlo prior to the start of a race at Dover. Paul Collins via the Richard Petty Private Collection

By 1979 there were a few small changes to the interiors of the cars. This is the interior of the Olds on display at the Petty Museum. Note the sheet metal cover over the side bars of the roll cage, the steering column supports, window bracing, and the dash panel. Tim Bongard

One of the rare times that Richard didn't finish a race in 1979. He wrecked only twice, but each time the damage was severe enough to prevent him from continuing. Richard Petty Private Collection

The crew checks the damage on Richard's Monte Carlo. The puddle from the wiped out front end gives you an idea of how bad the damage is. Richard Petty Private Collection

The slope-nosed Olds Cutlass was one of the slicker cars on the circuit. Note how the big front bumper has been cleanly reworked to smooth it into the rest of the body work on the car. It is on display at the Petty Museum. Tim Bongard

This blue and white Magnum seen here in the shops at Level Cross was the car Kyle used to win the ARCA race at Daytona. Richard Petty Private Collection

In a little pre-race fun for the press, Richard climbs from the Monte Carlo of Darrell Waltrip before the last race of the season. That's Waltrip in the window on the passenger side. Bob Josephson via the Richard Petty Private Collection

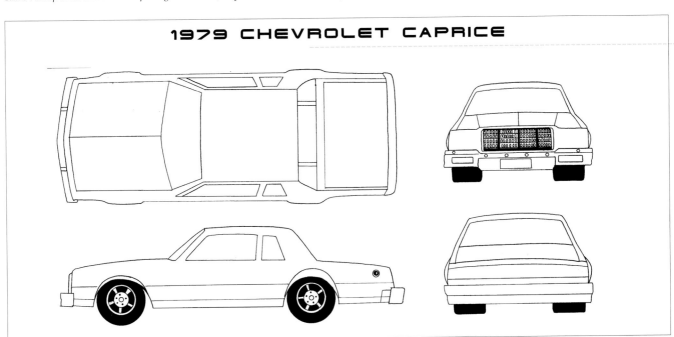

1979 CHEVROLET CAPRICE

Richard has two wins and two horrific wrecks as NASCAR prepares to downsize the cars

At Break Neck Speed

When you're on a roll, the idea is to keep it going. The Petty Enterprises team had found a successful combination in 1979 with its brace of race cars, so the plan was to keep doing what was working. However, there would be a few changes for the 1980 season. Rumors of downsizing the cars continued, leaving teams to wonder which way to go with the development of their equipment. The arrival of Kyle as a team driver also added to the mix. The team had to find and prepare cars suitable for the younger Petty. With no factory support, it was up to the Pettys to pay the bills for building their cars. The right decisions could save the team thousands of dollars in building costs. The wrong decisions could cause the team to buy much equipment that might be unusable the next year.

There were also some adjustments that seemed to come as an outgrowth of the previous year. Kyle had worn out or wrecked the remaining Magnums, so some of the other cars Richard had run would have to go to Kyle. The obvious thing to do was to give Kyle cars that Richard felt were expendable — and the first of those was the Chevy Caprice. Though Richard had done well with the car, even qualifying on the pole with it in Bristol, it would never remotely be considered one of his favorites. In fact, when Richard won that pole, the car was painted in a "reverse" paint scheme — experimenting with a flip-flopped version of Richard's STP colors for Kyle. Aside from the paint, however, Richard wasn't exactly cutting Kyle any breaks by giving him that car — a point that all involved chuckle about in hindsight.

The Olds would be the next to go: its performance had been good but not fantastic.

New and better parts are part of the ongoing development in stock car racing, so changing a detail here or there would seem positive. Careful observers noticed during the 1980 season, that the team had begun using a "wagon wheel" — a type of white mag wheel — with round holes as opposed to the oval slots. Changing a wheel style shouldn't have been a big deal, but as we will see, it did have a major impact on the race car, Richard, and the team.

The team picked up where it left off the year before. Richard scored a third-place finish in the season-opening Winston-Western 500 at the road course at Riverside. The race itself, begun on January 13, had to be halted due to rain after 26 laps. The race was finished almost a week later on the 19th in order to make it official.

The team then switched to the Olds to run the Daytona 500, but its luck in 1980 was not what it had been the year before. Buddy Baker set a blistering pace that was hard on his competitors. Though Richard led briefly on two occasions, he retired after 157 laps with a blown clutch.

At Richmond, Richard and Darrell Waltrip engaged in some heavy fender rubbing late in the race. At one point, Waltrip spun Petty trying to pass him, and after winning he apologized to Richard over the PA system. Petty finished third. The race at Rockingham was delayed a week due to inclement weather; when it was finally run it was a two-car battle between Richard and Cale Yarborough. Petty's Chevrolet was better on gas than the rest of the field; Yarborough's Olds, a bit faster. That, combined with other cars getting caught in the pits when a caution came out, ensured a two-way battle in which Cale prevailed.

The Atlanta 500 was next on the tour and the day ended early for Richard with a blown engine. His Chevy was awarded 33rd in the season's second DNF. The team then moved on to Bristol two weeks later, where the STP Chevy finished eighth after Richard was relieved by Richard Childress. In another two weeks, the poor luck continued when Ricky Rudd spun right in front of Richard and a few others on the first lap. Richard, who was able to keep his slightly damaged car going, eventually finished ninth in the rain-shortened event.

The first win of the season finally came at North Wilkesboro. Richard was able to stay in front, swapping the lead with Benny Parsons for most of the race. When Parsons fell out due to mechanical problems, Richard ended

I wouldn't stand there if I were you . . . A Winston Cup official attempts to hold a thundering herd of cars including Richard's Monte Carlo on pit road at Bristol. Bill Coulter

up winning with a full lap on the rest of the field. Kyle also managed a career-high finish of eighth in the old Caprice despite spinning out on three separate occasions. Of Kyle's efforts, Richard said, "He'd a-finished fourth or fifth if he hadn't a-been goin' in the wrong direction so much of the time."

At Martinsville, Richard had his hands full with Darrell Waltrip, Benny Parsons, and Buddy Baker. After the race was red-flagged for rain and then re-started, Richard was able to come home with a third-place finish. From the short track at Martinsville, the tour moved to the superspeedway at Talladega. Again, Richard opted to use the Olds in favor of the Monte Carlo, but the selection of the body type was rendered moot when the

engine let go on lap 57, handing the team another DNF and placing it 31st in the finishing order.

After that, the team started clicking off top finishes in rapid succession. Richard finished first at the short track at Nashville on May 10. A week later, he hung on to second despite running on only seven cylinders — a sure sign things were starting to go the team's way. The World 600 at Charlotte followed with Richard coming home fourth. It was then on to Texas World Speedway at College Station, for the NASCAR 400. Richard trailed Cale Yarborough by four seconds at the end to take another strong second-place finish. The tour then moved farther west to Riverside's road course, where Richard hung on to finish

eighth, two laps down to the leaders. As the racing headed back east at midseason, Richard recorded three fifth-place finishes in a row — at Brooklyn, Michigan; the Firecracker 400 at Daytona; and the second race of the season at Nashville.

While the team was starting to get things back together again, it was involved the entire time in a heated points battle with young Dale Earnhardt, the rookie of the year in 1979. When the teams arrived at Pocono for the Coca-Cola 500, Petty trailed Earnhardt by a mere 48 points. Unfortunately, the gap wasn't going to close and the run of good luck was about to end because of one of those little changes we mentioned earlier.

SIGNIFICATA

- The "NGN" (NASCAR Grand National) frame is officially established. Teams are now allowed to fully fabricate their own frames in accordance with NASCAR specs. Sheet metal is now hung on these frames instead of their stock counterparts.
- Doors no longer need to be removable.
- Minimum weight is set at 3700 pounds.
- Driving a Chevrolet Monte Carlo, Dale Earnhardt wins his first Grand National Championship over the course of 31 races. Richard Petty finishes fourth in points. Kyle Petty finishes 28th after running a partial schedule.

1977 CHEVROLET MONTE CARLO

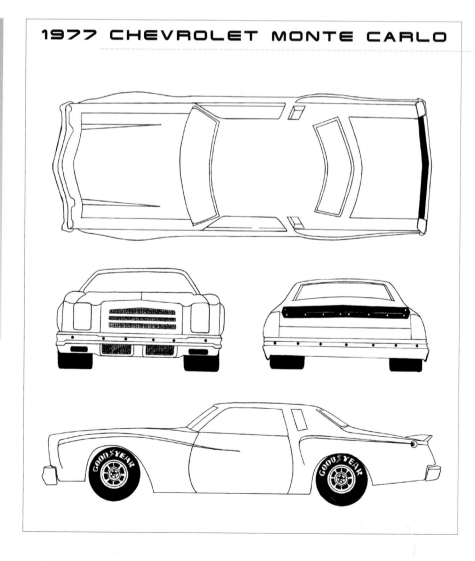

Richard and the Monte Carlo on the high banks of Bristol. Most of the grille has been taped over with duct tape. Elmer Kappell

At speed at Pocono. Two types of wheels were being used at this time. The slotted wheels in this photo were one type. Ray Masser

Dale Inman revealed that a second wheel failure later in the year at Rockingham (shown here) proved what the team feared was the cause of the Pocono wreck. You can clearly see that the welds holding the center of the wheel to the rim have broken causing the wheel to come apart. Again, it was the round-hole type that failed. Thankfully, the results weren't harmful to Richard although it tore up another car. Elmer Kappell

After qualifying a strong third, Richard was racing at the front and had led three times. Leading on lap 57, Richard suddenly felt the right front of the car drop, but he didn't hear a tire explode — leading him to think he had broken a wheel or some other front end part. He was headed into the tunnel turn, the second of the three turns at Pocono, and cranked the wheel hard to the left. Nothing happened, and the car plowed straight into the steel boilerplate retaining wall, then flipped high into the air before crashing back onto the race track. Chuck Bown and Darrell Waltrip tangled trying to avoid Richard. Waltrip actually got out of his car to check on Richard before driving his battered Gatorade Chevy back to the pits. Richard complained

that he thought he broke his neck. Though initial reports said it was only severely sprained, it was indeed broken. Petty was hospitalized for two days before being released and sent home.

The crash hurt Richard's ability to compete at full tilt for the remainder of the season. "My neck gave me a lot of trouble," he says. "In the August race at Bristol my right arm fell asleep, then in the September race at Dover my left arm went to sleep. I was wearing a neck brace. Undoubtedly, it was cutting off the circulation to my arms. Really, I wasn't capable of running the race car to the extent it could have been run."

The race after Pocono was the Talladega 500 at Talladega. Joe Millikan relieved Richard after just one

lap and ran well, actually leading for a few laps before having to retire with a blown engine on lap 154, which was good enough for an 18th-place finish.

Millikan was ready to relieve Richard again at the second race at Michigan International Speedway, but Petty drove the entire 400 miles, finishing fifth. A week later, Millikan again stood ready as Petty circled the high banks of the Bristol short track. After lap 214, Richard finally surrendered to the fatigue generated by the centrifugal forces and came in for a driver change. Joe finished the race in a respectable fourth place, just one lap down. At Darlington, Millikan again relieved Richard and brought the STP Chevy home ninth.

At Richmond, Richard drove the STP Chevy the entire distance while Millikan stood by. While he finished second, two seconds behind Bobby Allison, he said, "My neck is killing me."

At Dover on September 14, Millikan again relieved Richard and ran well until the engine let go on lap 468, still good enough for a 17th-place finish. A week later, and two months after his accident, Richard went the entire distance at North Wilkesboro on a track that started disintegrating even before qualifying began. In the atrocious conditions, Richard wrecked twice before finishing the race in 18th place.

At Martinsville, Richard was able to go the distance after a wild race with a record 17 cautions. The long day was good enough for 15th place, 57 laps down to the leaders. A blown

1977 OLDS CUTLASS 'S'

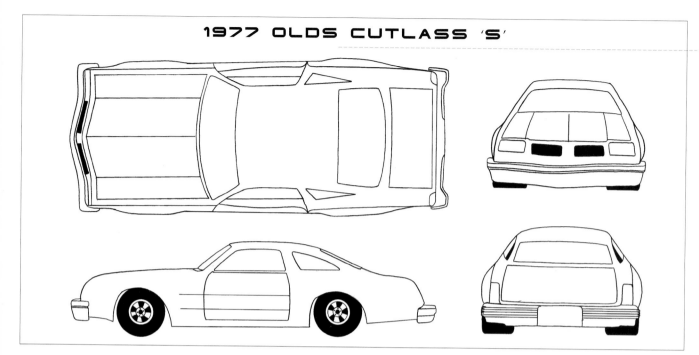

engine at Charlotte on October 5 handed the team another DNF after 252 laps and a 27th-place finish. Kyle didn't fare much better, losing his engine after only 10 laps for 35th place.

Rockingham finally showed the team the culprit of the Pocono wreck. During the race, Richard collided with Neil Bonnett after Bonnett wrecked trying to pass Richard and Joe Millikan, who was driving the RahMoc entry. It was during this race that another wheel break finally explained what had happened to the car at Pocono. The team realized that the wheel had caused the crash — not a blown tire or spindle, as some had suggested. Richard still managed a 14th-place finish in that race.

In the last two races, engine trouble yielded Richard 21st place at Atlanta and 30th place at Ontario Motor Speedway in Ontario, California. It was the last time the tour would race at the track that was a virtual copy of the Indianapolis Motor Speedway.

The last few races of 1980 didn't reflect how Richard was actually feeling. He thought he was back to 100 percent by the National 500 at Charlotte on October 5. Unfortunately,

blown engines and collisions didn't allow Richard the opportunity to show it. He did get his chance a week after the regular season was concluded. At the Winston West race at Phoenix, Richard finished first, leaving the team feeling much as it did at the end of 1978 — that the bad luck can't last forever.

Earnhardt won the championship by a slim 19 points over Cale Yarborough, while Petty slipped to fourth in the points as his neck healed. The Earnhardt team had experienced some incredible racing luck, as any team on a roll will. Recalling his apparent bad luck for 1980, Richard summed up his sentiments about the season in an interview with Gene Grainger: "You've got to be prepared. You've got to have a good crew, a good car and a good driver, and you've got to work for it. These boys [Earnhardt's team] really did work for it. On the other hand, if everything is going right for you, you can make these mistakes and get away with 'em. But when things start going bad it doesn't make any difference what you have. It's going to be bad. Everybody has good years and bad years."

Maurice tunes one of his engines. He was considered one of the best engine builders of his time, so much so that when it was announced that he would be building the engines for Richard's SuperTruck team in 1996, there was a collective groan from other competitors. Richard Petty Private Collection

Richard rests after being relieved by Joe Millikan at Dover in September. Richard's neck bothered him for most of the last half of the season. It wasn't until November that he felt strong enough to drive long and hard. Ray Masser

The worst part about the Pocono wreck was the length of time it took to finally hit the wall — and Richard knew it was coming. Richard broke his neck in the accident, although it was first reported as a severe sprain. Note the tire bounding across the track as Richard continues to skid after hitting the wall. Ray Masser

Richard finally comes to rest near the infield. Note the round-hole wheel on the right rear of his car and the center of the front wheel (still connected to the spindle assembly) laying on the track at the far left of the photo. The accident was caused by a wheel coming apart. Ray Masser

KYLE'S 1979 CHEVY CAPRICE

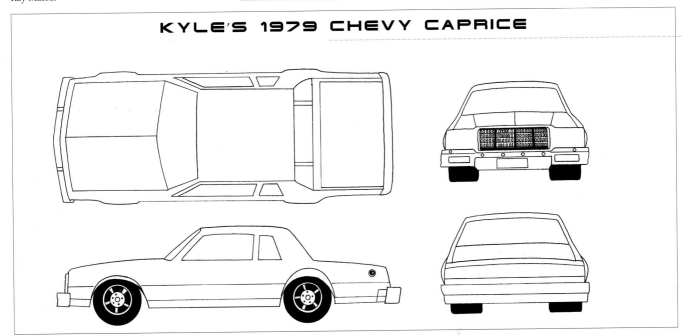

Richard waiting to qualify at Michigan in June. Note that the number shadow has changed from black to dark blue; also note the dark grey-colored wheels. Elmer Kappell

Petty leads Harry Gant at Nashville in May. Gant is in a Caprice.
Elmer Kappell

The Monte Carlo at Rockingham in October prior to the wheel failure that put the car into the wall. Elmer Kappell

The slant nose of the Olds Cutlass proved to be almost as slick as the special Laguna S-3 nose that NASCAR eventually outlawed. Bryant McMurray

David Pearson in his Mercury drafts behind Richard's Olds.
Bryant McMurray

This photo of the Monte Carlo on pit road shows the crew doing a four-tire change. It also shows the split tinting on the windshield that Richard used from time to time. The driver's side was clear, while the other side was deeply tinted blue. Richard Petty Private Collection

The Olds was used by Richard only at Daytona and Talladega in 1980 before being given to Kyle to use. Elmer Kappell

The Buick Regal dominates the first year of racing the downsized cars

The King's Regal Ride

T he year 1981 was one of changes for NASCAR. The Winston Western 500 at Riverside had been the opening race of the season with its mid-January date since 1970 (it was known as the Motor Trend 500 back then.) And though the 1981 season began the same way, it would also end in November at the famous road course, effectively moving the race to the end of the schedule. The change would make the Daytona 500 and its support and qualifying races during the annual Daytona Speed Weeks the beginning of the schedule.

In addition to the schedule change, NASCAR finally decided to take action on the size of the cars. NASCAR had been talking about reducing the size of the Winston Cup stock car since 1976 when Detroit began downsizing its cars. The standard race car had had a wheel base of 115 inches; the newer cars rolling off assembly lines were closer to 110 inches. It was the effect on the rest of the car body that had everyone worried. The cars were significantly smaller. In the vital deck areas where downforce was generated, they were downright tiny compared to the old cars.

Though it was obvious that sooner or later stock cars would have to follow suit and accept the new 110-inch standard, few teams were in a mad rush to embrace the smaller cars. As a result, NASCAR set a deadline of the 1981 Daytona 500 as the deadline for switching to the new short wheel base

Kyle on the low side of Neil Bonnett in the #21 Wood Brothers' Ford and Joe Millikan in the #75 RahMoc Buick. Richard Petty Private Collection

cars. It was like sailing into uncharted waters for everybody. After running the big cars for so long, no one knew how the new cars would handle, let alone how to set them up.

The faithful Monte Carlo was run one final time at Riverside at the Winston Western 500 on January 11, 1981. It was the last race for any of the "big" cars, and Richard was awarded fifth place when the checkered flag flew. From there, it was back to the drawing boards for everyone.

Petty Enterprises took a hard look at the options and decided to try running a Dodge Mirada. Things at

Chrysler weren't as bleak as they had been just a few years before: the Mirada looked as if it could be a fast race car. Besides, if anyone could still wring a few more horsepower from the old 340 Wedge engine, it ought to be the Pettys — or so the line of thought went. "We were still Chrysler people deep down inside," said Richard about the attempt. So the team set about building a new Dodge Mirada and took it to Daytona for testing.

Once at the track, Dale instructed Richard to take it easy until he had the car figured out. After a few tentative laps, Richard brought the car in. Pleased that Richard had apparently done as he had asked, Dale told him, "Okay, Richard, you can open her up." Richard simply looked at him and said, "I was opened up." Uh-oh.

The car was so bad that later on Richard shut the car off on the back-

Richard and Bobby Allison race to the line at Michigan International Speedway. Bill Coulter

stretch to do a plug check. Usually the cars coast around the third and fourth turns and down pit lane with no problem. The Mirada, however, ground to a halt between the third and fourth turns. Not a good sign. The team loaded the car back on the hauler and dragged it back to Level Cross. Having been down this road before with the Magnum, Richard and the team wasted no time in stripping the car of its Mirada sheet metal and Chrysler powerplant. According to Richard and Dale, the car was a Buick Regal 24 hours later.

To add to the confusion and folly of it all, the inspectors at NASCAR expected the team to be running a Chrysler when it showed up at Daytona with a pair of Regals. According to Dale Inman, it took a bit of convincing to get them to use the Buick template on the car — they still wanted to use the Mirada's.

The plan, on top of everything else, was to let Kyle run the entire season, so right from the start some additional money was needed to help the team field two cars. At the time, Winner's Circle money, a bonus paid to a select number of winning teams for the period of a year from the time they won, was based on the car number. Richard, perceiving a loophole in the rules, planned to drive the number 42 car right through it. So at Riverside in January 1981, the last race for the big cars, the famous number 43 was driven by Kyle instead of Richard, and Richard piloted #42 around the old Riverside road course. To a certain degree, the ploy got Kyle credit for the Winner's Circle money for his finish in number 43, but it was a 20th-place finish produced by a blown engine on lap 96. Richard managed a fifth-place finish, running on the lead lap. NASCAR didn't take too kindly to Richard's interpretation of the rules and advised the team that he and Kyle would have to revert to their respective numbers.

By the time the Daytona 500 rolled around, the team had two new Regals, painted in similar but reversed col-

ored STP paint schemes, prepared for Richard and Kyle. Kyle ended his day early with a blown engine on lap 128. Richard, however, was able to run up front with the leaders again all day. As the race came down to the final laps, Richard was in fifth place behind Bobby Allison, Buddy Baker, Ricky Rudd, and Dale Earnhardt. As each of the leaders stopped for green flag pit stops, each took on tires and gas. Petty was the last to pit, but Dale Inman had already decided to give Richard only a quick splash of gas and forgo changing tires. The STP Buick ran as well on old ones as it did on new ones. The move shocked the other teams and put Richard out front of everyone. He finished the race 3 1/2 seconds in front of second-place finisher Bobby Allison.

Days later, Dale Inman announced that he was leaving Petty Enterprises to join the Rod Osterlund team. He stayed on through Rockingham and then left to join Dale Earnhardt's team. Richard named Wade Thornburg and a young Steve Hmiel as co-crew chiefs to take his place, but by Petty's own admission, it was the first event in a series that would eventually lead to the closing of racing's most famous family operation.

At Richmond, Richard finished third and took the Winston Cup points lead. Kyle, on the other hand, had another DNF with a faulty rear end, finishing 24th. Rockingham was next and produced another third-place finish for Richard after he ran out of gas trying to stay in the lead three laps from the end. While disappointing, the run turned out to be a good one for Kyle with an eighth-place finish.

At Atlanta on March 15, the team experienced a bit of what was to come for the rest of the season. Richard started the day 14th on the grid, with Kyle starting ahead of him at 9th. Unfortunately, Kyle's day would end quickly with his engine expiring on lap 17. Richard was able to get his car to the front and lead on two separate occasions for 35 laps when his engine

The King's Regal Ride

Kyle raced a full schedule in 1981. Here his car sweeps around a turn at Nashville. Bill Coulter

1981 BUICK REGAL

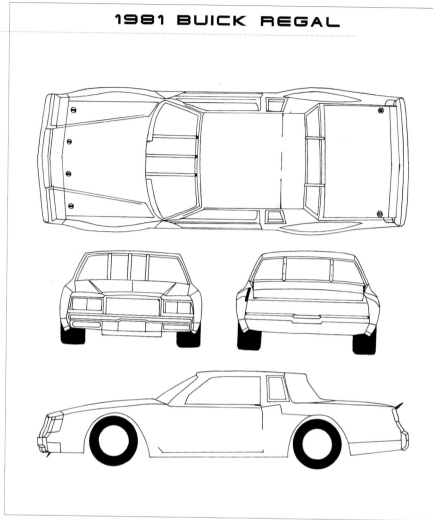

Richard heads into the first turn at Nashville in May. Note how the Buicks worked their bumpers into the bodywork; also note the duct tape on the grille. Elmer Kappell

Richard at Bristol in the spring of 1981. Bill Coulter

Kyle's #42 Buick receiving service from his crew. Bryant McMurray

failed as well on lap 113. The blown motor cost Richard the points lead, as he finished in 38th place.

Bristol was next two weeks later. Again, Richard had his engine fail, this time on lap 116, dropping him to a 29th-place finish. Kyle, on the other hand, fared better, finishing the race in 11th place.

Fortunes were better at North Wilkesboro, where Richard won on a slick track, while Kyle finished 22nd, crashing out of the race after spinning his car on three occasions. For the next three races — Darlington, Martinsville, and Talladega — neither car was able to finish a race. Each engine failed at Darlington. A crash eliminated Richard at Martinsville and Talladega: another engine failure

and an ignition problem knocked Kyle out of both races.

Nashville brought some relief to the team with a fourth-place finish for Richard and a seventh-place finish for Kyle. But with things looking up, Dover was a disappointment a week later. Both cars were eliminated within 30 laps when Kyle's engine failed on lap 342 and Richard's rear end seized on lap 368. The team lost another engine a week later at Charlotte, when Richard's motor quit on lap 296. Kyle, on the other hand, came home a surprising fifth.

In the very next race at Texas World Speedway, Kyle and Richard swapped places. Kyle's engine failed on lap 34, while Richard came home in fourth. Aside from the dismal number of engine failures, there was a problem with how the cars ran when the engines held together. Richard had led only a handful of laps since North Wilkesboro, and it appeared the handle on the cars had gone away.

The engines held up for the next few races, but there still was a haunting feeling about the way the cars

Racing has a way of aging a man. Kyle at Bristol already has that serious racing look about him. Bill Coulter

Richard is joined by his mother, Elizabeth, and his father, Lee, in victory lane. Bryant McMurray

Richard spins in front of Kyle at Bristol. Kyle had already tagged someone else and is missing the right front corner of his car. This shot shows the reversed color patterns on the two Petty cars. Elmer Kappell

were handling. At Riverside, Richard finished third and Kyle in sixth, with both of them leading a number of laps. At Brooklyn, Michigan, Kyle lost an engine on the final lap and scattered engine parts and oil all through the first and second turns. He was several laps down, and was about to be lapped again by the leaders, when the engine let go. A mad scramble ensued as the leaders charged into the corners, and Kyle's debris, racing for a last-lap win. Bobby Allison survived the mayhem to take the win, while Richard managed to tiptoe through for a sixth-place finish.

The July 4 Firecracker 400 at Daytona was next and turned out to be a good day for the team. Richard was competitive and finished third while Kyle finished a respectable sixth. Kyle repeated his sixth-place finish a week later at Nashville, and Richard finished in ninth place, a few laps down. At Pocono two weeks later, Richard almost had the win but was passed on the last lap by Cale Yarborough, who was a lap down. In that drafting move, Cale towed Darrell Waltrip past Richard, allowing Waltrip to slip into the lead. Cale thought he had won the race until the scorecards proved that he was indeed a lap down. Kyle finished eighth.

On the second visit to Talladega on August 2 for the Talladega 500, Richard had no better luck than he did the first time. By lap 12 the STP Buick was dead with more engine-related problems, this time being the oil pan.

Kyle managed a seventh-place finish, just one lap down to the leaders.

Victory finally came again in the Champion Spark Plug 400 at Michigan International Speedway. In a wild race that saw 14 different drivers swap the lead 63 times, Richard prevailed for the last five laps and beat Darrell Waltrip and Ricky Rudd to the line. Kyle, who managed a nineteenth-place finish, was still running at the end of the race. But that would be the end of the long run of finishes for both cars.

In the last ten races of the season, Richard failed to finish six and managed only an 11th at Richmond, a 10th at Dover, a 4th at Rockingham, and a 7th at Riverside in the season-ending race. During that entire spell, Richard led only a handful of green-flag laps. Only at Rockingham did he lead a serious number of laps. The last ten races were no picnic for Kyle,

SIGNIFICATA

- Winston Cup cars now required to conform to a down-sized 110 inch wheelbase from 115 inch wheelbase.
- Stock hood and trunk hinges no longer have to be used. Exposed hinges are required as is a NASCAR approved hold open device.
- Big-block engines are dropped from the rules. Small-blocks are the only accepted engines.
- Three steel straps now required to hold the front windshield in place.
- Contingency decal placement is now regulated by NASCAR.
- Ontario Motorspeedway closes after the last Winston Cup race of the season.
- Driving a Buick Regal, Darrell Waltrip wins his first Winston Cup Championship over the course of 31 races. Richard Petty finishes eighth in points, while Kyle finishes 12th.

Richard at speed in his Buick Regal on his way to victory at Michigan in August. When the Petty Buicks held together they were as competitive as anything else. Elmer Kappell

Richard poses with his wife Linda in victory lane at Michigan International Speedway. Bill Coulter

1981 was one of the rare years that the team used white wheels to help set off the paint scheme.
Bryant McMurray

Richard's car at Martinsville in September. Elmer Kappell

Kyle's and Richard's crews prepare the cars for the fall race at Martinsville. Note that while the cars had reversed paint schemes on the outside, they were both painted Petty Blue on the inside as had been the practice for many years. Elmer Kappell

either. Kyle dropped out of seven of those races, finishing 22nd at Richmond, 7th at Dover, and 8th at Atlanta. In the Atlanta race Kyle led several laps under the green, but most of those ten races involved drivetrain-related failures.

Between them, Richard and Kyle raced 62 times, with 3 wins, 13 top fives, and 26 top tens —not too bad a year by today's standards. But it's the other side of the balance sheet, 32 DNFs, that killed the efforts of the team. Twenty-two of those DNFs were directly related to engine failures, only five being related to crashes.

Though Kyle had unfairly gained a reputation for bending up equipment, he wrecked out of races fewer times in 1981 than his father did.

The combination of Dale Inman's departure and Maurice Petty trying to supply the team with enough quality engines to keep the team running was taking its toll. Things had to be changed to restore the team to real competitiveness. Switching to a different car the next year might do the trick. That and a bit of racing luck certainly would help. After all, Lee always did say he'd rather be lucky than good. Then again . . .

Johnny Cline removes some of the masking on one of Richard's Regals after application of the two tone paint scheme.
Richard Petty Private Collection

KYLE'S FLIP-FLOP 1981 BUICK REGAL

Richard's Regal early in the 1981 season at Bristol. Note the absence of glass in the opera windows and the lack of chrome trim on the windshield. Elmer Kappell

Richard climbs from his car in victory lane in Michigan in August. Note the split tinting on the windshield with 2/3rds of it heavily tinted. Only the portion directly in front of Richard was clear.
Richard Petty Private Collection

On the line at Michigan in August. By then the team had switched the type of windshield that was being used and was using black windshield molding instead of chrome. That's a rag stuffed into the header pipe. Elmer Kappell

One of the first Petty Regals being built in the shops at Level Cross. Note the stock door panel and the spliced covers over the locations of the door handle and side mirror. Richard Petty Private Collection

Power by Pontiac

While other teams were using the Buick Regal with great success, Petty Enterprises was struggling with the car. When the engines held together, the Pettys struggled with the car's handling. This meant that they were usually close to the front, but not actually in the lead pack. Far too frequently they were sidelined with something terminal, very frustrating for a two-car team.

On the other hand, Pontiac was more than willing to lend greater support on several fronts. After some negotiations with Dick Emerick, then the Motorsports Coordinator of Pontiac, Richard signed an agreement to run Pontiacs for the 1982 season.

Kyle runs ahead of the #44 Buick Regal of Terry Labonte and the #90 Ford Thunderbird of Jody Ridley. From this angle it's easy to confuse Kyle's '82 Pontiac with the paint scheme on Richard's '83 Grand Prix. Dave Chobat via the Richard Petty Private Collection

In 1982 Petty Enterprises again fielded two cars painted in flip-flop schemes, but this time they were Pontiacs. Here they run at Martinsville. David Chobat via the Richard Petty Private Collection

The car was based on the same body shell as the Buick's, although its front-end design did not appear to be as aerodynamic. Nonetheless, the Grand Prix was an attractive car, especially in the new flip-flop scheme created for Richard and Kyle for 1982.

If 1982 was supposed to bring a certain amount of relief to the bad luck Kyle and Richard had experienced the year before, Daytona proved to be a bad way to start. While running close to the front, Richard became involved in an eight-car wreck when Benny Parsons cut down a tire and hit the wall after running through debris scattered on the track on lap 103 by Bobby Wawak's exploding engine. Richard was not only put out of the race, but suffered a fractured right foot and torn ligaments in the leg. That resulted in a 27th-place finish; Kyle placed 23rd with a blown engine. It was not an encouraging start.

Richard and Kyle pose by their new Pontiacs at the start of the 1982 season. Behind them is one of the most famous car haulers of all time. David Chobat via the Richard Petty Private Collection

The interior of the '82 Grand Prix. Note the dash panel and the footrest below the steering column. The Richard Petty Private Collection

Richard's injury was initially diagnosed as a severe sprain, although it was later discovered that the foot had a hairline fracture. A week later Richard showed up in Richmond in a fiberglass cast from just below the knee, down to and including the entire foot. Most folks with a cast on the foot that mashes the go and stop pedals would have sat on the sidelines, but then again, this man had raced at Bristol with his neck in a brace. About driving with a broken foot, Richard said, "I really didn't know what the foot would feel like when I tried to drive the car. Then I found out after practice that I didn't have any pain when I mashed the gas and only some when I hit the brake because there was more tension involved."

The 400-lap race was shortened by rain after just 250 laps, but even so, Richard drove the entire race — and took second place. Kyle didn't have as lucky a day, but finished the race in 20th place. At Bristol Richard finished 7th and Kyle 11th. At one point just past the halfway mark Richard was running in the lead, but he slipped back in the later stages of the race.

It seemed as if the team once again had a good setup on the Pontiacs that they lacked on the Buicks. Running in the lead was the thing that proved it. Such was the case at Atlanta when rain again curtailed the event some 40 laps shy of completion. This time Richard was in the lead being chased down by Darrell Waltrip. As a yellow

flag came out for rain, Petty and Waltrip raced back to the flagstand for the lead and possible win in case the race were stopped and could not be restarted. As they closed on the third corner, Petty drifted high to go around some slower traffic. Waltrip watched from behind and prepared to dive under Petty. "I drove into that third corner up there and the rain hit my windshield like somebody had thrown a cup of water on it," said Petty. "I didn't know whether turn four would be wet or not, so I let up a bit." Waltrip took the chance, dove under Richard, and beat him to the line by less than a foot. When the race was officially halted for rain an hour later, Waltrip was awarded first with Petty being shown in second. Kyle's day had ended much earlier with another blown engine on lap 216, placing him 26th in the finishing order.

On April 18, the tour was at North Wilkesboro, where Richard finished fifth and Kyle finished 14th. Kyle wasn't finishing as well as he had the year before, and he wondered if his car was being prepared as well as Richard's. Maurice and the rest of the crew worked hard to ensure that no one was favored over the other. On the other hand, Richard's car was the one earning the Winner's Circle money, and the team did need to make sure that at least one of the cars stayed on that program — otherwise the money would really get tight.

Failures again knocked both cars from the Martinsville event on April

25. A fuel pump failure knocked Richard out of the Winston 500 at Talladega, handing him a 27th-place finish. However, Kyle had a banner day, finishing fourth in the lead pack. "We were tickled with the finish, even though we would have liked to have won. Hey, we were in a position to do that today," said the younger Petty.

Nashville was the next event. Richard finished ninth in a race dominated by Darrell Waltrip leading all but one lap. Kyle lost his transmission on lap 265 and had to park his car for

Richard waits patiently for his turn to qualify at Martinsville. Bobby Saunders via the Richard Petty Private Collection

The Grand Prix at Talladega in May. Depending on the track and the climatic conditions the chrome panel at the center of the bumper could be removed to let more air in. This also gave the car its distinctive "chin." Elmer Kappell

A Grand Prix under construction at the shops in Level Cross. The Richard Petty Private Collection

Richard's Grand Prix at Martinsville in September sported the extra chin grilles. Note also that the window trim reverted back to chrome. Elmer Kappell

the night. Engine failures took out both cars at Dover Downs and took out Kyle's car again at Charlotte for the World 600 on Memorial Day weekend. Richard had to be relieved, at first by Lennie Pond and then by Donnie Allison. Donnie was able to bring Richard's car home in eighth place.

For the next three races, the team struggled to get both cars to run well. Richard finished seventh at Pocono on June 6, while Kyle finished eleventh, with Richard showing enough strength to run up front and lead on numerous occasions. But at the next two races, Richard's day ended early when he blew motors. Kyle, on the other hand, followed up his Pocono finish with a 12th at Riverside and a 6th at the Brooklyn, Michigan track.

At the Firecracker 400, Kyle's clutch failed in the Ellington Buick after just 41 circuits. Richard's day ended on lap 136 when he was caught in between Geoff Bodine and a spinning Harry Gant. Gant had tangled with Tim Richmond in front of Petty. When Petty backed off to avoid the wreck, Geoff Bodine rammed him from behind and shoved him into Gant. So much for the Firecracker 400.

The next few races were a virtual potpourri of results. At Nashville, no one could even touch Darrell Waltrip, who was on an absolute tear. Kyle had a rear end fail after 241 laps, placing him 23rd at the finish. Richard finished 7th, two laps off Waltrip's pace.

At the Mountain Dew 500 at Pocono on July 25, Richard, Darrell Waltrip, and Bobby Allison battled for the lead in the closing stages of a race that saw 46 lead changes among 11 drivers. Petty took the lead on lap 187 but dove into the pits on lap 194, having run his tank dry. Waltrip led for three more laps when he too ran out of fuel. That left Allison to inherit the lead, finishing 17 seconds ahead of Petty, who was able to claim second after his splash for gas. Kyle meantime finished 15th in his Hoss Ellington ride.

The Talladega 500 was the following week, again with mixed results. After breaking a camshaft on the seventh lap, Kyle was classified 39th finisher of the day in his UNO Buick. But Richard ran at the front for most of the day and was in the lead when he was passed by Buddy Baker and Darrell Waltrip on lap 171. Baker led that lap and then fell to second as Waltrip took the lead. Petty explained the end of the race by saying, "I was in the position I wanted to be [third on the last

lap], but Buddy never made a move. The guy in second has to make the first move, but Buddy never pulled out. It was a heckuva race and I ran wide open all day. For us to run this good at Talladega is almost like winning. That's the only thing missing — winning."

At Brooklyn, Michigan for the Champion Spark Plug 400 newly erected concrete retaining walls had the effect of keeping all the racing debris on the track, instead of blowing it out under the guardrails. With all the junk and small debris in the track, a number of competitors ran over things that damaged both their cars and their efforts for the day. Kyle was one of them: he ran over something that punctured his right rear tire. "We had a good day going there for a while," said Kyle. "Then we cut down a right rear coming off the fourth turn. I couldn't slow it down in time to pit, and by the time I got to the first turn, the tire was in many pieces." He finished 15th in the only run he had in

Richard at speed at Talladega in May. Elmer Kappell

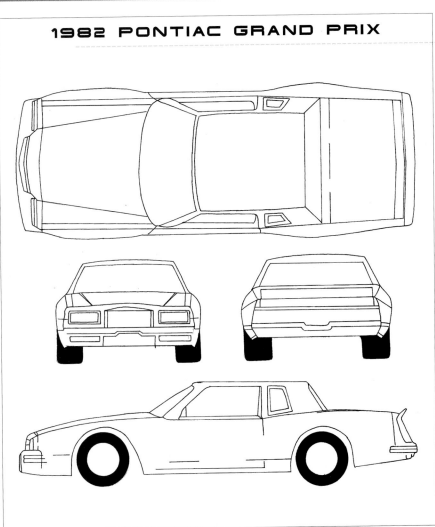

1982 PONTIAC GRAND PRIX

Ellington's Pontiac. Richard meanwhile chased down Bobby Allison in the last 20 laps and was ready to pass him on the last lap. Then a slight move to the inside on both the backstretch and the last turn prevented Petty from moving around Allison. Richard settled for second.

Things didn't go nearly so well at Bristol a week later. Kyle finished 30th in his STP Pontiac with another failed engine, this time on the second lap. Richard dropped out on lap 50 with a failed steering box — not a good thing at Bristol. At Darlington a week later on September 6, Kyle was once again in the Hoss Ellington Buick and finished 14th, and again, his father was engaged in another titanic battle at the end of the race for a win. With 18 laps to go, Cale Yarborough and Richard raced past Dale Earnhardt to take the first two places. Cale and Richard then dove under one another several times and traded places. Yarborough finally prevailed over Richard by a mere 0.79 seconds at the finish line.

Kyle poses with his #1 UNO/STP Buick from the Hoss Ellington stables as part of the deal he ran during the 1982 season. The Buick was painted just like the Pontiacs and ran only once.
Richard Petty Private Collection

Kyle's #42 STP Pontiac. Note how this differs from the markings on the #1 car in the photo above.
Bryant McMurray

In some ways the finish foreshadowed future events as well. M.C. Anderson, Yarborough's car owner, wanted Cale to run a full schedule for the championship. Yarborough had already had enough of that and wanted no part of running every race again. In the end he told Anderson he would not run. Anderson then surprised everyone by stating he would close his front-running operation at the end of the season. Petty's timing was off by just a hair. Still looking for a way to solve the financial problems at Petty Enterprises, Richard approached Anderson about taking over Cale's ride, and running the whole schedule to boot, but it was too late. "He had already made his commitment," said Petty. "I admire him for that."

At Richmond, Richard managed a 13th-place finish while Kyle finished 14th. At Dover a week later, Richard had another steering box fail, which put him in the 30th finishing spot after leading 40 laps in the contest. Kyle, on the other hand, almost won the race, running in his #42 STP Pontiac on the heels of Waltrip's Mountain Dew Buick for the last 150 laps. Of Kyle's

run, Waltrip said, "My hat's off to him. He drove like a pro. In fact, I thought Richard had gotten in the car." Like father, like son.

The month of October saw a few strong finishes for Richard, but more trouble for Kyle. At North Wilkesboro Richard finished fourth in a race that was basically another Allison-Waltrip duel. Kyle finished tenth. At

Charlotte, Dale Earnhardt ruined a good run for Richard when the former spun the latter causing a multicar melee. Earnhardt claimed it was Petty's own fault. Richard, in a rare display of anger, pointed to the yellow paint on his car as evidence of who did what to whom. In spite of the spin, he managed an eighth-place finish. Kyle, in his last ride in the Hoss

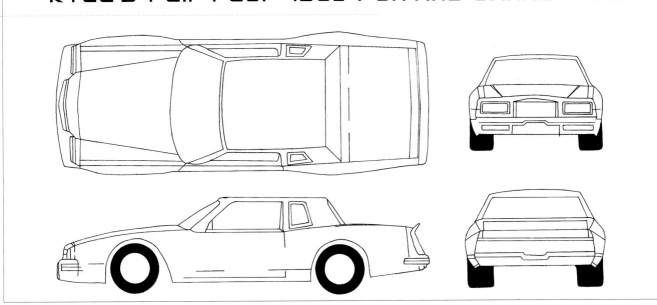

The flip-flop scheme worked well because it simply reversed the colors. That made it easy to tell the cars apart, yet they looked so similar it was easy to think they were identical. Bryant McMurray

Ellington Buick, finished 29th with another blown engine.

At Martinsville, Kyle again dropped out early when his rear axle failed on lap 241. Richard charged from 17th qualifying spot to finish 3rd, but never was able to put the car in the lead all day. The month ended at Rockingham on Halloween. Engine gremlins took Kyle out of the running yet again on lap 208, dropping him to 29th place, while Richard finished 6th after a few sorties to the front of the lead pack in the last half of the race.

At the Atlanta Journal 500 those gremlins were still busy at work. Kyle's day ended on lap 156 with another bad engine, a malady that struck his father on lap 312. Kyle was classified 31st, with Richard getting 15th after leading 54 laps of a race that saw 14 different drivers swap the lead 45 times.

The season came to an end at Riverside on November 21 at the Winston Western 500. Kyle didn't race in that event and Richard's day ended on lap 87 with the clutch gone out of the STP Pontiac. Nonetheless, Richard managed a fifth-place finish in the points race for the championship,

This isn't a potential wreck on pit road — the absence of gear in the pits indicates this is during practice. The cars show the two wheel types that were dominant at the time. Petty's car sports five-hole wheels while the #2 Stacy Buick of Joe Ruttman has the nine-hole variety. Bill Coulter

Kyle's version of the flip-flop paint scheme. Bryant McMurray

while Kyle finished 15th. While still having far too many DNFs and engine failures, Richard had enough top-ten finishes to place well at the end of the season. The only thing that was missing was winning.

Richard gets some fast attention from his pit crew. Bryant McMurray

Richard occasionally used a plain, untinted windshield as demonstrated by this photo. The split-tinted windshields were used at tracks where bright sunlight and glare were a problem. Bryant McMurray

Richard celebrates 25 years of racing by notching 3 more wins

Transitions

The two cars fielded by Petty Enterprises are shown with their transporters in front of the Level Cross shops. Kyle's #7 7-Eleven-sponsored car ran with this colorful scheme for a short time before being simplified. Kyle's transporter was the old converted lowboy with a new paint scheme. (see chapter on Haulers and Transporters)
Richard Petty Private Collection

The 1982 season had seen a number of improvements and the team was able to try a few new things out with mixed results. The team ran better than the year before, but there were no wins during the '82 season and that was always a reason for disappointment. The main issue and concern, however, was the ever present need for proper funding of the operation. It would take sponsor money, money from the Winner's Circle program and other award programs and pools. There also was the concern to make sure all was fair for both Richard and Kyle — something that sounded easy but wasn't.

Both Kyle and Richard had taken steps to relieve the strains that the two-car team was creating. Kyle's floating deal with Hoss Ellington certainly tested the waters to see if Kyle could find a ride and other sponsorship with another competitive team. Richard, seemingly by moments, missed a number of good opportunities with some front-running teams. So the Pettys stuck together and made the best with what they had.

In an effort to make things work better for Kyle and perhaps keep things more segregated than in the previous couple of years, Kyle's cars would operate out of the buildings at the back of the Petty Enterprises com-

plex. In addition, Kyle was able to secure sponsorship for his car from the 7-Eleven Convenience Store chain. With that change, he would run his cars with the number 7 instead of 42 and they would be painted to reflect his new sponsor's colors instead of the familiar Petty Blue and STP Red.

Richard's STP Pontiacs would still be housed in the main shops at the front of the facility. Both teams would still be provided with motors from Maurice's engine room and all the funds were still going into and coming out of one pot. Kyle would have more autonomy — at least that was the idea. But as time would show, things didn't pan out exactly as followed Baker, nipping Foyt for third. Petty fans were thrilled.

In the second twin, Richard battled with Neil Bonnett in a close race for the win. Richard had been strong throughout the race and had led for a total of 20 out of the 50 laps. After taking the white flag, Neil sling-shot past Richard on the backstretch. Richard was going to return the favor coming off turn four, but was prevented from doing so by slower traffic low on the race track. "I didn't have any help. That slower car hurt me and helped Bonnett. I knew what he was going to do on that last lap, and I knew what I was going to come back with. The deal was, I didn't get a chance to do it. It was almost enough. I didn't win, but I did the next best thing."

At the Daytona 500, the race started with Richard in 6th position on the grid and Kyle in 7th. Richard took command of the race on lap 3 and, to the delight of the Petty fans watching, Richard and Kyle both battled for the lead with Dale Earnhardt, Dick Brooks, Geoff Bodine, and Joe Ruttman. Most folks expected this of Richard, but Kyle was finally asserting himself and doing well. Unfortunately, these high hopes were dashed as Richard blew an engine while leading the race on lap 47. Kyle was forced to retire 52 laps later with the same problem.

The race at Richmond a week later marked another significant milestone in Richard's career. Ralph Salvino, the vice president in charge of STP's racing programs, was on hand to act as grand marshal over a celebration of Richard's 900th career start. STP gave away hundreds of T-shirts and comic books to celebrate. Richard celebrated by thrashing his way to a hard fought 8th-place finish that left his car without a smooth or undented panel on it. Even Dale Earnhardt said, "He drove the hell out of that race car, didn't he?" Kyle finished 14th.

March 13th turned out to be a lucky day for Richard. At Rockingham, a week later than originally scheduled for the rain-delayed Warner Hodgdon

Kyle at speed at Daytona in his '83 Pontiac Grand Prix. Note that the bumper openings were not always symmetrical.
David Chobat via the Richard Petty Private Collection

At speed during the Daytona 500. Note again the split tinted windshield that Richard frequently used; see how the spoiler is painted on this car. Elmer Kappell

planned. Richard later reflected that one of the real problems during that time was "there were just too many Pettys trying to run things."

The season started off showing some promise to the new arrangement. Both cars did well in their respective twin 125-mile qualifying races. Kyle ran in the first one and surprised everyone, not the least of which was A.J. Foyt. In the closing laps of the race, Dale Earnhardt took the lead with Buddy Baker sweeping past Foyt to take second. Kyle then

SIGNIFICATA

- Ford introduces a newly designed Thunderbird with greatly improved aerodynamic performance.
- Chevy brings out a new aerodynamic nose for the Monte Carlo and calls the model the Monte Carlo SS.
- Cale Yarborough breaks the 200 mph qualifying barrier at Talladega in May with a speed of 201.744 mph. He ran a lap of 200.503 at Daytona in February, but lost control of the car and flipped on the next lap.
- All electrical switches are required to be on the dash panel.
- Header dump pipe size is reduced from four to three and a half inches.
- NASCAR finally drops the cubic inch markings for the hood as an option in the rule book.
- Driving a Buick Regal, Bobby Allison wins the Winston Cup Championship over the course of 30 races. Richard Petty finishes fourth in points, while Kyle finishes 13th.

Richard runs with Cale Yarborough at Talladega in August. The Chevy and Pontiac shared the same basic notch-back body, but the Monte Carlo benefited from a more aerodynamic nose. Elmer Kappell

Carolina 500, Richard won his first race in, appropriately enough, 43 tries. He was running third behind Cale Yarborough and Neil Bonnett who were dominating the race when a collision between Cale and Neil eliminated them both. From then on, Richard only had to worry about a strong Bill Elliott. Elliott almost managed to pass Petty on the last lap. "He really came off that last corner," said Petty. He admitted he didn't come off the last corner as hard as he could and it gave the Melling driver a chance to almost take the win. Kyle managed a 15th-place finish.

Over the next few races the team struggled to put the cars in the top ten, succeeding only twice with Richard: a fifth at the Coca-Cola 500 at Atlanta and a tenth at North Wilkesboro. The teams seemed to be loosing momentum.

It was also apparent that all the work involved in running a two-car effort like Petty Enterprises was doing, took its toll on Maurice Petty — physically. Maurice's leg problems from his bout with polio were starting to affect him — he was now using crutches more and more to help him get around.

Richard poses in front of his Grand Prix during the 1983 Speed Weeks at Daytona. The new paint scheme altered the look of the car dramatically. Elmer Kappell

Things came back together again at Talladega on May 1st. On lap 71, a tire blew out on Darrell Waltrip's Pepsi Challenger; he then collected Phil Parsons. In the ensuing melee, a number of cars were damaged and put out of the race. Unfortunately, Kyle's was one of them. He could take comfort in his 30th place DNF knowing that his father won the race. Richard managed to avoid the massive wreck and then outran Benny Parsons for the check-

ered flag. After pitting on lap 165 for a splash and dash stop for gas, Petty elected to stay in front of Benny Parsons and Lake Speed instead of trying to slingshot past them later on. Instead, he simply anticipated each of Parsons' moves and prevented him from passing on the last lap. "He was always right in front of me," said Parsons. "When I went high, so did he. When I went low, so did he. I would have done the same thing in

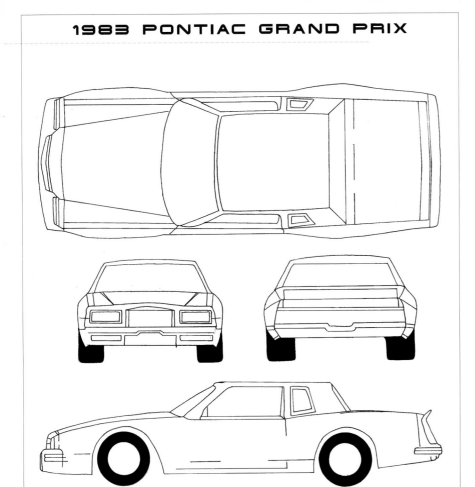

Richard discusses lap times and set-up with a young Larry Pollard and Robin Pemberton at Nashville in May. Elmer Kappell

Richard at Charlotte in October. Note that the STP product on the rear fender has changed from STP's Son of a Gun Cleaner/Protector to their Oil Treatment. Elmer Kappell

his shoes. It was like he was turning my own steering wheel."

The Talladega win seemed to set the team back on fire. At Nashville a week later, Richard finished in 6th. At Dover on May 15th, Richard and Kyle finished 7th and 11th respectively. At Bristol a week later, Kyle repeated his 11th place finish, while Richard placed 5th. The World 600 at Charlotte kept things rolling for both drivers with Richard finishing 2nd and Kyle finishing 8th, 5 laps down.

Riverside was the sight of the Budweiser 400 on June 5th, where a mid-race tangle dinged up the front end of Richard's car. He finished the day 2 laps down and in 10th place. Kyle, on the other hand, had a good day. He finished with the leaders in 6th place. At Pocono, Richard came home in 3rd despite having problems with his brakes and running out of fuel on lap 191. Kyle finished 13th.

The next few races weren't so kind and the team ended each race mired in the middle of the pack. The single bright spot was back at Talladega where Richard came home in 4th after leading only 3 laps in a race that had only 2 caution periods.

Things might have improved at Brooklyn, Michigan if it weren't for Richard hitting a pot hole in the track coming out of turn four on lap 175 while leading the race. Cale Yarborough was in second to pounce on the bobble that followed, took the lead, and held on to it as Petty faded to 6th. Kyle finished 3 laps down in 14th spot. From there though, the mid-pack blues continued, with Richard managing a 9th at Bristol, Dover, and Martinsville, with a 6th at Richmond thrown in for good measure. Short tracks had always been a strong suit of Richard's and mid-pack was not where the team should have been. The frustration seemed to be

building and the rumor mill at North Wilkesboro buzzed about changes brewing at Petty Enterprises with either Richard leaving the team or new people being brought in.

Then came Charlotte and the Miller High Life 500 on October 9th. It was probably one of those moments in the history of Petty Enterprises that everyone involved would rather forget. Many teams at the time were occasionally cheating by running engines that were larger than the maximum 358 cubic-inch limit. It was rampant in the sport and Richard knew he had been beaten to the front-running spots by big engines a number of times. The trick was not to win with one of those whoppers in your car, but run a good second or third.

KYLE'S 7-ELEVEN 1983 PONTIAC GRAND PRIX

In June at Michigan International Speedway, the Grand Prix had a number of changes on it since the car ran earlier in the year. Note the grille on the front bumper, the black metalwork around the windshield, and the natural metal spoiler on the tail. Elmer Kappell

The STP crew pushes Richard's car on to pit road at Pocono for qualifying. Note the white wheels and the taped-over lower grille on the front bumper. Richard Petty Private Collection

During this period in NASCAR history, NASCAR only inspected the winner of the race and not the second or third place car. As long as you weren't inspected, or didn't put yourself in a position that you would be, you would likely get away with running a big engine. No one would deliberately win knowing he had a monster engine under the hood.

Tim Richmond qualified on the pole for the race in his Pontiac. The race was run in just over three and a half hours and saw 30 lead changes among 13 different drivers. As a caution came out for a spin on lap 294, all the leaders headed for the pits. When the green flag flew again, Waltrip took the lead. Richard then stormed through the front-runners and blew by Darrell Waltrip coming off turn two on lap 312. From there, it seemed like Waltrip simply conceded the race to Petty, allowing Richard to cruise to a 3-second lead and win the race. The nearly 120,000 fans went wild as Petty claimed his 198th win. But this would be a win Richard wouldn't be able to enjoy. Instead it would underscore the state of things in the team and how the NASCAR inspection system needed to be revamped.

First, Richard learned as he pulled into victory lane that the crew had put left side scuffs on the right side of the car — a definite no-no as far as NASCAR was concerned. Left side tires have a softer and therefore grippier rubber compound than right side tires and will make the car go much faster, although they will wear out much faster. NASCAR restricts those compounds on the outsides of the cars for obvious safety purposes. A NASCAR inspector noticed the errant serial numbers on the tires and radioed that there was a problem even as the car sat in victory lane.

Then, after the celebration, the car was brought to the garage area for the post-race inspection of the winner. It was here that NASCAR officials also became aware that the car was running an engine that was almost 25 cubic inches too big, measuring out at 381.983 cubic inches. Wax had been used to seal some of the valves to slide the big engine past the inspectors during the pre-race inspection.

Later that night NASCAR announced that they would fine Petty Enterprises a whopping $35,000 and strip the team of 104 points won in that race. This kept Petty from gaining any ground on Harry Gant, who trailed Petty by 84 points prior to the race. NASCAR also allowed the win to stand.

Howls of protest followed in the media barrage that ensued. Many felt that NASCAR was wrong for allowing Richard to keep the win, but from NASCAR's point of view, they had no other choice. Waltrip and his team, along with the 2nd-place car, had already packed up and left the track by the time Petty's car went for post-race inspection. If NASCAR had stripped Petty of the win, there would have been complaints (even possible lawsuits) that Waltrip's car hadn't been inspected.

Everybody had something to learn from the incident. NASCAR's pre-race and post-race inspection procedures changed almost immediately. NASCAR also implemented a number of regulations that made running an oversized engine — regardless of your finishing position — downright crazy. Engines were also required to warm-up for two to three minutes prior to the pre-race inspection, making the wax gambit a thing of the past. Finally, NASCAR instituted a rule that impounds the first three finishers and two others at random for post-race inspection, thus allowing NASCAR the option of stripping a winner of his finish if circumstances warranted such action.

The night of the Charlotte race, Richard spent a few hours talking to Harry Hyde and Rick Hendrick about the new team they were forming and possibly running for them. He also continued talks with Mike Curb about the new team he was forming. Finally on October 31st, Richard held a press conference in Greensboro to announce that he would be leaving Petty Enterprises and would run with Mike Curb in 1984 with STP as his sponsor. Buddy Parrott was named as the crew chief and Kyle would be left in charge at Petty Enterprises.

Somehow, the last two races didn't really seem to matter. Kyle lost another engine at Atlanta and finished 13th at Riverside. Richard placed 5th at Atlanta, 2 laps down and 10th at Riverside, one lap back. A dynasty had ended, or so it seemed.

At Atlanta in November, Richard ran with an in-car remote television camera. *Elmer Kappell*

The right side and back of the 1983 version of the Pontiac Grand Prix. Note the double row of bolts holding the rear spoiler in place and the window straps and clips. Bill Coulter

The left side details on the Grand Prix. Note the brake rotors used on the rear wheels, the dashboard layout, and the missing glass in the opera windows. Bill Coulter

The Grand Prix had to deal with the likes of Ford's newly sculpted Thunderbird. Compare the Wrangler T-Bird to the STP Pontiac for an idea of the aerodynamic advantage the Fords enjoyed. Bryant McMurray

A shot of Kyle's new 7-Eleven car just after it was painted. Note the orange wheels. Richard Petty Private Collection

Kyle receives service at Rockingham from his crew. He also has a split-tint windshield like the ones used by his father on the #43 car. David Chobat via the Richard Petty Private Collection

Record Season

By the end of 1981, Richard had begun to consider driving for someone outside the family operation. Over the next couple of years he quietly followed up a number of leads, but potential deals just wouldn't come together or Richard would miss a good deal by a week or so. The key was finding a good ride with an organization that had the ability to field equipment at least as good as what he had back home in Level Cross — not an easy set of requirements to fill. At one time or another, potential rides of that caliber were discussed with car owners Harry Ranier and later M.C. Anderson, but in both cases things just never panned out.

Nonetheless, driving for someone else seemed to be a good solution to the problems that Richard and the rest of the Petty clan had experienced in the previous few years. Richard could be a driver only and not have to worry about running a racing team or paying the bills or chasing down parts. Since STP was his sponsor, any team that hired Richard would get only a share of his money from STP, in addition to having to pay him as the driver. It would mean more income that could go back to Petty Enterprises.

The change was supposed to give Kyle a chance to run things economically back at Petty Enterprises, concentrating on one car. It would also take some of the pressure off Maurice and Lee. All in all, it would give everyone

The most famous stock car in history parked in front of Ponce de Leon Inlet Lighthouse south of Daytona Beach.
Richard Petty Private Collection

some badly needed space. So Richard kept looking for that quality ride.

At the end of 1983, Richard began talking to Butch Mock and Bob Rahilly of Rahmoc Racing. They were in the middle of putting a deal together with Mike Curb, of Curb Records. Rahmoc was well-known for putting together powerful race cars, and Curb had sponsored Dale Earnhardt during his first championship run in 1980. After several false starts, it appeared that Curb would set up a deal with Rahmoc and Richard. Richard then agreed verbally at a meeting at the Riverside race in November to run for Rahmoc. Everything was set in Richard's mind. Announcements were made, equipment and cars were moved, and it seemed as if the new alliance would work. Rahmoc was going to build the engines for the cars, while Buddy Parrot would head up a small group brought from Petty Enterprises, which had even taken a car to Daytona for testing.

But while the racers were busy racing, the business folks were having some troubles. Curb, Rahilly, and Mock couldn't come to a final agreement. The tug of war raged until the beginning of January. At one point, Mock confessed that he felt no agreement would be reached and asked Richard to come drive for Rahmoc. That was all well and good, but Richard — thinking that everything was going to be worked out between the parties — had already signed a contract with Curb. Parrot and Petty packed up all their cars and equipment at the Rahmoc shops and headed back temporarily to Level Cross. The Rahmoc connection was gone along with their stout engines — Rahilly wouldn't be building them for Petty or Curb.

To solve the powerplant problem, Curb went to DiGard racing and arranged with their chief engine builder, Robert Yates, to supply the new team with engines. They then used the shops at Level Cross until new Curb Motorsports Shops were ready in Kannapolis.

With the changes and adjustments having to be made, it's not too surprising that it took a little while for things to get back on track. At the Daytona 500, Richard retired on lap 92 with a broken camshaft, placing 31st in the big race. A week later, he finished 15th, four laps down at Richmond. However, as time gave the team a chance to get its act together, it started to run well with the Yates engines under the hood.

In March, Richard finished fourth at Rockingham and fourth in Atlanta in the Coca-Cola 500. He followed this up with a number of competitive runs placing as high as sixth at the Winston 500 at Talladega. The breakthrough finally came with Richard posting his 199th win of his career at the Budweiser 500 at Dover's Monster Mile. Once again the racing team was hitting its stride.

And once again the business folks were having some troubles.

What a difference a few stripes can make! The Grand Prix remained essentially unchanged for 1984, but the STP paint scheme was refined by adding some dark blue stripes, changing the center stripes slightly, and placing the roof number in an oval. Throw in some chrome wheels and the results were amazing! Elmer Kappell

Curb and DiGard were having problems in their dealings with one another, and Richard and Buddy Parrot never knew what to expect next. Bluntly, the relations between Curb and DiGard were a fiasco. Curb was slow in paying his obligations to DiGard, and the Gardener brothers, who owned DiGard, never had the reputation of being easy to deal with. To keep the business side of things

Richard and a crew member work under the car to make an adjustment at Nashville. Clearly evident is the blue pinstriping that edges the broad white stripes. Elmer Kappell

The STP Crew hustles through a green flag stop.
Bryant McMurray

Air Force One comes in for a landing at the Daytona Beach Airport as Richard races down the backstretch of the Daytona International Speedway during the Firecracker 400. President Reagan arrived in time to see Richard beat Cale Yarborough to the finish line and win his 200th career victory.
Richard Petty Private Collection

A celebration banquet complete with Kentucky Fried Chicken was shared by all, including the president.

Richard and Bobby Allison pose with President Reagan after the Firecracker 400 as Richard presents him with an STP crew member shirt as a momento of Richard's 200th win. Eagle Valley Studio via the Richard Petty Private Collection

from interfering with the racing, Richard told Robert Yates to keep the engines coming and that he would cover anything Curb didn't pay for. Richard believed that took care of things, but he was unaware that Curb and DiGard had agreed to part company after the Firecracker 400 at the beginning of July.

It turned out to be a race that they almost didn't get to run. The DiGard group tried to collect its engine right out of the STP Pontiac, apparently because Curb was late in paying for several of engines. At the last minute, some agreement was finally reached, the engine stayed where it was needed, and everyone went racing.

It turned out to be a big day for Richard and the team. Not only was

the race being televised live nationwide, but the command to start engines was given by President Reagan from Air Force One. The president's jet was en route to the race so that he could be on hand for the finish of the race, and what a finish it turned out to be! With only three laps left, Doug Heveron's Chevy wrecked in turn one. Petty was leading Cale Yarborough going into the backstretch and both drivers knew the race back to the yellow would also end the race, since there was no way it could be restarted with so few laps remaining.

Yarborough drafted Petty and used a slingshot move to pass him on the backstretch, but Petty did the same thing through the last turn and edged Cale out to win by less than a foot.

The celebration was something else. Winning his 200th race with the President in attendance was about as good as it gets, almost impossible to top under the best of circumstances. It even had a way of camouflaging the problems the team faced for the rest of the year.

On the day after the Firecracker 400, Curb Motorsports not only didn't have an engine program, but it didn't even have a racing engine. There was nothing to work with. No engine room, no tools, no parts. Everything would have to be farmed out and then assembled at the shop in Kannapolis, which would take a lot of time to get right — if ever.

It was all downhill from there. The rest of the season reflects the team's hardware problems, but it doesn't even begin to reflect the personal strain on the team members. Richard's best finish in the last half of the year was a fifth at Richmond in September and four other top tens sprinkled throughout the rest of the year. By the

Richard straps on his helmet. Note the Pontiac name across the back valance panel inside the car — an often forgotten detail. Bryant McMurray

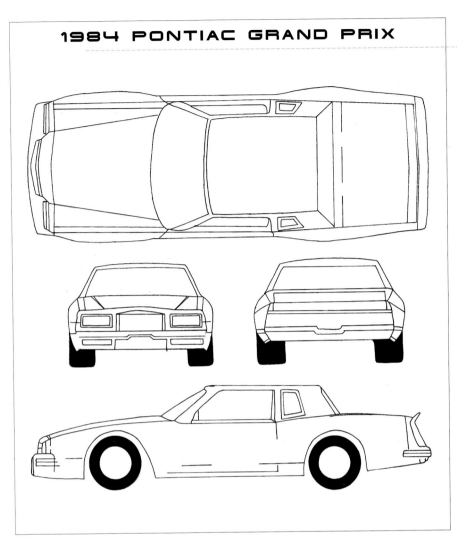

1984 PONTIAC GRAND PRIX

Relaxed, cool, and unruffled, Richard waits his turn to qualify. Bryant McMurray

time it was over, Buddy and Richard were blaming one another for the troubles they weren't even wholly responsible for. Parrot left at the end of the season, but Richard stayed on for the very same reason he had stuck with Curb in the first place — he had given his word.

Buddy Parrott poses beside the STP Pontiac. Note the brake rotor and cooling-duct work on the front end of the car. Richard Petty Private Collection

Richard's 200th win came as a result of beating Cale Yarborough to the start/finish line by mere inches as seen here in this amazing photo. Bryant McMurray

Richard holds his 200th victory trophy aloft in a rather soggy victory lane. Bryant McMurray

Oops! The crew works on the car at Nashville after it sustained some damage during practice. Note the single row of bolts holding the spoiler on. Bill Coulter

Regardless of the angle, the changes to the paint scheme made the Grand Prix look sleeker. Bill Coulter

*Richard fields a question at a press conference after his
200th win. Bryant McMurray*

The STP Pontiac is being prepared for the November race at Atlanta.
Elmer Kappell

*Note the number of openings between the grille and headlamp covers,
designed to get enough cool air to the equipment. Bryant McMurray*

A good idea gone bad

Like being
Parked
at the Curb

Compare the STP Pontiac's front end to Neil Bonnett's Budweiser Monte Carlo SS. The Chevy's cleaner front end gave it a distinct advantage over its Pontiac cousin. Bryant McMurray

A famous passage from <u>The Tale of Two Cities</u> says, "It was the best of times. It was the worst of times . . . ." In Richard Petty's case, most of his fans would consider any season when you win your 200th race — in front of the President of the United States, to boot — at least something to write home to Mama about. From Richard's perspective, 1984 had been an exercise in watching bad business mess up some pretty good racing.

The question now was: what could possibly be worse than Richard's experience in 1984? Unfortunately, the answer in 1985 turned out to be more of the same. If you have a rough time imagining Richard getting into such a mess, remember that the King of Stock Car Racing is a person just like you and me — although blessed with the ability to drive a lot faster.

With Buddy Parrott gone, Richard brought in Mike Beam as crew chief. For all the changes Richard hoped to make, he found his hands tied again and again by business decisions. Mike Curb owned part of Dan Gurney's racing operation. With no real equipment to work with and unable to get anyone to sign on, Curb was forced to have his California connection build engines in California and ship them east for Petty to use. As a result, there were never enough engines to go around and the team was never sure there would even be one to use. Gurney's group built engines for a different type of race car than the folks back in stock car land. If control was a problem with farmed-out parts, just imagine the problems with farmed-out engines. The team was so unsure of the Gurney engines that it frequently practiced with other engines in order to save the Gurneys for the race. Even so, the team fell out

At first glance, the STP Pontiac appears to have the same paint scheme for 1985 as it did in 1984. It's the striping that has been reversed — dark blue where it had been white and white where it had been dark blue. The Richard Petty Private Collection

SIGNIFICATA

- For the first time, NASCAR allows aluminum or fiberglass replacement parts for certain standard parts.

- No weight reducing holes of any kind are allowed.

- Cars have a required minimum weight of 3700 pounds.

- NASCAR institutes a "big engine" policy that can result in the suspension of the driver and car owner for no less than 12 weeks if an engine is found to be in excess of 358 cubic inches.

- Internal polishing, porting, altering, and/or relieving of engine parts is now permitted.

- Dual master cylinders now required.

- Bill Elliott sets a new record at Daytona of 205.114 mph. In May he raises the Talladega record to 209.398 mph. The summer races have records set with 201.523 mph at Daytona and 207.578 mph at Talladega.

- Driving a Chevy Monte Carlo, Darrell Waltrip wins his third Winston Cup Championship over the course of 28 races. Richard Petty finishes 14th in points.

of eight races in the season with engine failures.

At the Daytona 500 in February, Richard was forced to retire early, in 34th place with a blown clutch. A week later at Richmond a wreck put him out of the race; he took 26th place for his efforts. He then finished 8th at Rockingham and 13th in the Coca-Cola 500 at Atlanta, followed by another 8th-place finish at Bristol. Through the beginning of April, the frustration began to build.

By the end of June, things only became worse. The bright spots were three seventh-place finishes at the

short track at Martinsville, the one-mile Dover track, and the road course at Riverside. But Richard was also handed four more DNFs in that time at Talladega, Charlotte, Long Pond, and Brooklyn, all due to engine failures. It seemed as if the Gurney group couldn't put a strong enough engine together that would last, especially at the big tracks.

The situation got so frustrating that in June Richard hired some help to build engines using the Petty Enterprises shops that had been vacated earlier in the year by Kyle and then Maurice. With Richard footing the bill

for the parts and help, they quickly assembled and tested race engines that looked more promising than what was coming out of California. "I paid the help and bought all the pieces out of my pocket," Richard said. "I didn't ask Curb for anything. That's how much I wanted to win. I was willing to spend my own money to make it work."

At Daytona for the Firecracker 400 — a year after his last victory — the team showed up with two Gurney engines and one of Petty's. Richard was ready to race and ready to try anything to win.

Curb wasn't. He wouldn't even let Richard try one of his own engines. That was it for Richard. Seeing that this operation wasn't headed anywhere positive, he decided to set his sights on the next season

1985 PONTIAC GRAND PRIX

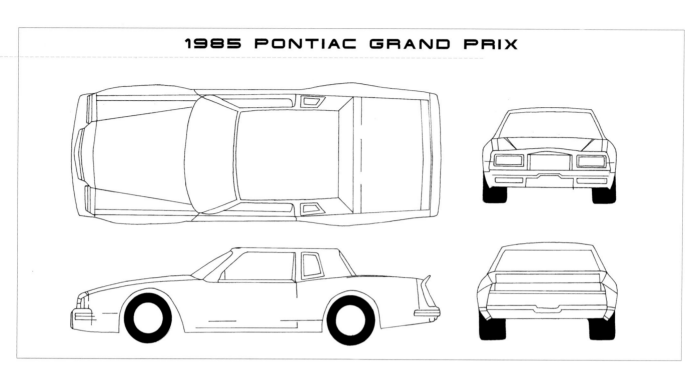

Shots of the front end of the car such as this one at Daytona make the color scheme changes more apparent. The team started the year with small STP ovals on the hood as seen here. The red stripe on the grille is colored tape.
Elmer Kappell

and start getting his own ducks back in a row.

It's important to note, however, that Richard didn't storm out of Curb Motorsports screaming foul or even walk out on his contract. He finished out his contract there with a determination that still earned him eight top-ten finishes and a third place at Richmond in September.

These two years — with the exception of his 200th win — might seem like years to forget, but in a strange way they also show the character of the man named Richard Petty better than all the races and other

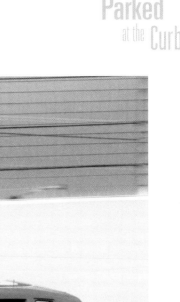

By the time the team got to Charlotte, the car was running with a much larger STP logo on the hood. The car also occasionally showed up with black wheels instead of the chrome ones. NASCAR eventually banned the wheels with plated finishes because they would shed wheel weights too easily. Elmer Kappell

records combined. Through the entire experience with Curb Motorsports, Richard displayed poise, patience, and determination to hang in there and hunt for a solution to make it work right. He demonstrated a level of patience and poise with a bad situation that most folks would have walked out on.

During the last half of the season, Richard made arrangements to reopen Petty Enterprises and asked Dale Inman to return to run the operation so that they could go racing as a team again in 1986. Whoever wrote "You can never go home again" was wrong. Sometimes it's exactly the thing you need to do.

Strapped into his seat as he waits to head out onto the track, this shot gives you a good idea of what the interior of a Winston Cup car looked like by 1985. Bryant McMurray

Richard re-opens Petty Enterprises with Pontiac's odd looking aerocoupe

The Pontiac Droop Snoot

As the 1985 season wound down, preparations began to breathe life back into Petty Enterprises. In addition to the engine men Richard had assembled in June, he asked Dale Inman to return and run the operation. When Inman was released from the Hagan team in September, he returned immediately to Level Cross to begin working on the new race cars for the upcoming season.

For 1986, Ford introduced its restyled Thunderbird body, which took the previous model's good looks and race worthiness to the next step. Olds and Buick were working with two equally clean body designs in the Cutlass and LeSabre, which also held promise as slick race cars. The second war of the aerocoupes had arrived.

In the Chevy camp, it can be argued that when Chevrolet introduced the SS version of the Monte Carlo, it actually improved the looks of the car. Even with the addition of the glass fastback, which changed the designation to Monte Carlo SS Aerocoupe for 1986, the car was still a great-looking car and wickedly fast.

Would that the Pontiac Grand Prix had been so lucky. The aero version of that car called the Grand Prix 2+2 was, in the view of most folks, downright ugly. In some ways it did have a no-nonsense look to it, but from most angles the old notchback simply looked like a hunchback with a drooping nose and a body that had been

At Watkins Glen. This shot compares the front-end profiles of three of the GM cars well. Petty's Pontiac leads the Olds 88 of Terry Labonte and the Chevy Monte Carlo SS of Dave Marcis. It looked as if the Pontiac should have worked. Bill Coulter

The Pontiac Grand Prix 2+2 featured a revised nose and rear window bubble in an attempt to make the car more aerodynamic. Bill Coulter

pumped up with steroids. The engineers at Pontiac told the Petty team that the car would be thirteen mph faster than the boxy standard version of the standard coupe, according to wind-tunnel calculations and other scientific estimates. How the car would really perform on the racetrack was another matter. One thing was for sure: with the changes made to the shape of the car, it wasn't going to handle anything like the old version. The first challenge of the reborn Petty Enterprises team was to sort out an essentially brand-new race car.

They also faced two additional challenges. In the time that Dale had been away from the team, the cars had switched from a "front steer" type front-end setup to a "rear steer" setup. The difference is in the steering box's position in relation to the arms that actually cause the wheels to turn right or left. It took him time to learn the setup and what Richard had become accustomed to.

The other challenge was, once again, the engine program. Granted, Richard's boys were much closer to hitting the mark on stock car engines than what had been experienced the previous year. At least they had the right tools and equipment to work with in order to give the team competitive engines. The problem was all the lost time and lost wisdom and knowledge. With Maurice out of the picture, the vast engine-related knowledge he had acquired over the years was gone. And while the shops had been closed, the rest of the teams on the circuit had continually modernized. It proved to be a challenge that would shadow the team for a long time.

The Daytona 500 was a disappointment once again as a crash on lap 63 placed Richard 36th with his first DNF of the season. The team struggled with the car the following week at Richmond, finishing 20th, some 37 laps down. The good news at Richmond was that Kyle won his first Winston Cup race after surviving a last lap melee that eliminated the rest of the cars still on the lead

Sleight of hand. At first glance it looks as if there is a great deal of open grille area on the nose of the Pontiac 2+2, but the team has taped much of the nose and the headlamp cover openings off with black tape. Elmer Kappell

lap. More good news came a week later at Rockingham when the new Petty 2+2 came home in a very competitive third place. Development of the car continued with a seventh-place finish at Darlington in April, another seventh at Talladega on May 4, and a sixth at Dover two weeks later.

One of the more unusual cars of the King turned out to be a loaner. In practice two days before the Coca-Cola 600 at Charlotte, Richard totaled his Pontiac after qualifying. The heavy crash made the car unrepairable and sent Richard to the hospital overnight for observation of a concussion and a bruised leg. As Richard recuperated, NASCAR enforced its ruling that no back-up cars would be allowed — leaving Richard without a car. Independent driver D.K. Ulrich then offered his Monte Carlo for Richard's use during the race. As odd as it looked, D.K.'s lime-and-white colored number 6 rolled out into the field adorned with STP stickers and Richard Petty at the helm. A blown engine on lap 123 put him out of the race, but the car remains an interesting oddity in Richard's driving history.

The next race was at the Riverside road course, where Richard did well and finished sixth for the day. This was followed by a disappointing 19th at Pocono a week later and a 13th at the Miller American 400 at Brooklyn, Michigan. The Brooklyn race was sig-

Dale Inman and the crew wait to see their car on the front stretch at Watkins Glen. Bill Coulter

The nose section itself was Pontiac's version of the Chevrolet Monte Carlo SS's aero nose. Here the crew works on the car during practice at Bristol. Bill Coulter

1986 PONTIAC GRAND PRIX 2+2

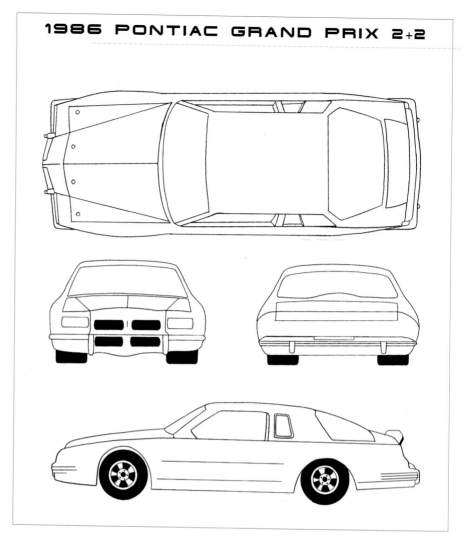

Inman and Petty watch other drivers at Bristol late in the afternoon in the closing moments of practice.
Bill Coulter

nificant for a special pre-race celebration that marked Richard's 1,000th start. His daughters issued the command — "Daddy, start your engine!" — and Richard's car alone rumbled to life. The rest of the field started moments later. Richard later said he was glad he wears those dark sunglasses all the time — it let his eyes get watery without anyone else being the wiser. For him, it was one of the most memorable moments in his career.

That having been said, there was a small controversy over whether the start was his 1,000th or actually his 999th. Record keeping and some statistical procedures had changed over the years, but in the long run, it really didn't matter. If it wasn't at Michigan, then it was certainly at the Firecracker 400 on July 4.

The results during the second half of the season were either good or fairly bad depending upon the event. He

finished 22nd at the Firecracker 400 after a hard run. Crashes at Pocono and Talladega handed the team two DNFs.

NASCAR returned to the famed Watkins Glen road course in Watkins Glen, New York, which had been home to the U.S. Grand Prix many years before. Richard did well and finished tenth.

As the season headed into its closing weeks, the team finished with a seventh at Bristol, a fourth at Richmond, a third at North Wilkesboro, an eighth at Rockingham, and a strong second at the Atlanta Journal 500. Those strong finishes allowed the team to finish 14th in the standings — the same position as the previous year. But two important things had changed. The team had finished closer to the front in most races than the year before and most importantly, it was in charge of its own destiny.

Ouch! Pocono has a way of tearing up race cars and Petty has had his share. Here the 2+2 limps into the pits missing a good part of its sheet metal. Jim Juka

SIGNIFICATA

- Plexiglass is now allowed in the rear quarter windows and must be mounted flush with the body work.

- NASCAR changes the battery location rules to state that the location has to be approved by NASCAR, although it doesn't say where.

- All drive shafts are now required to be painted white.

- No electric blower or pump motors are permitted in the trunk of the car.

- Chevy and Pontiac answer Ford's Thunderbird with aero packages for the Monte Carlo and Grand Prix. The Monte Carlo has a glass fastback added to smooth the notchback and call it the Aerocoupe. The Pontiac has a new nose and bubble back added and call the combination the 2+2.

- Elliott runs 212.229 mph at Talladega in May and 209.005 mph later in the summer.

- Watkins Glen returns to remain on the Winston Cup schedule.

- Driving a Chevy Monte Carlo, Dale Earnhardt wins his second Winston Cup Championship over the course of 29 races. Richard Petty finishes 14th in points.

At Michigan International Speedway, Richard poses with a special decal that commemorated his landmark 1000th start. Bryant McMurray

A pit stop at Michigan in August shows the Pontiac now sporting a full wrap-around chin spoiler on the front end. It helped keep the nose on the ground at speed. Note all the black trim work that was carried throughout the season. Elmer Kappell

1985 rookie of the year Ken Schrader receives some personal instruction on the finer points of the STP Pontiac from the King himself. Bill Coulter

Kyle Petty in the Wood Brothers' Ford Thunderbird drives beside Richard in his Pontiac Grand Prix 2+2. It was the Thunderbird that capitalized best on the push towards more refined aerodynamics. Wayne Moyer

The most unusual car of the King has to be D.K. Ulrich's rented Monte Carlo SS Aerocoupe with STP markings on it. D.K. offered it to Richard after his crash in practice that eliminated the STP Pontiac. Elmer Kappell

At Daytona in February. The huge rear window was larger than the one used on the Chevy Monte Carlo SS Aerocoupes, giving the car a hunchbacked appearance from some angles. Elmer Kappell

A side shot of the car at Talladega. Note the absence of a thin dark blue pin-stripe separating the Rocket Red and Petty Blue areas of the car. This is one of the few ways to differentiate the 1986 version of the car from the 1987 version because the paint schemes were essentially identical. Elmer Kappell

Richard races side-by-side with Cale Yarborough and his Hardee's Thunderbird. This is a good study in the attempt by Pontiac to make the Grand Prix slip through the air more easily. Bryant McMurray

Two of the best ways to go fast on planet Earth. Richard and his Pontiac pose with the Space Shuttle Enterprise. Bryant McMurray

Richard completely trashed his 2+2 during practice at Charlotte for the Coca-Cola 600. The damage was so severe that the car couldn't be repaired. Elmer Kappell

As the Monte Carlo flies, the 2+2 struggles to find the same combination

Searching for Speed

By the beginning of the 1987 season, it had become apparent that the Pontiac Grand Prix 2+2 still needed a lot of work. Not nearly as fast or stable as the Pontiac engineers originally predicted, the street version was far from a raging success in the dealerships, either. Work had begun on Pontiac's successor to the current body style, and everyone was looking forward to it — anything would be better than the 2+2. Still, it was all they had for 1987, so Petty Enterprises knew it had to make the best of things and keep improving on the car.

And the Pettys did improve the car. Though there were no obvious differences between the 1986 and 1987 cars on the outside — the STP paint scheme remained the same except for adding a dark blue pin stripe between the Petty Blue and STP Red sections of the car — Dale Inman and the boys had fiddled with the thing enough to improve the handling. At least the front end didn't want to lift off the ground as much as before. Still the problem was how to get the proper balance on the car.

At Daytona, it seemed as if all their hard work had indeed paid off. For the first time in a long time, the Daytona 500 was kind to Richard and the crew. Richard stayed in the hunt most of the day, finally taking the lead on lap 190. He kept it for only one more lap before being drafted by Bill

The 1987 version of the Pontiac at Bristol. In addition to the almost invisible dark blue pinstripe separating the main colors of the car, it also carries an endorsement for political candidate John Carrington for the 1988 elections. Elmer Kappell

Elliott and Benny Parsons, but managed to hang on to third place for his strongest finish there in years.

Rockingham's Goodwrench 500 followed the Daytona 500 on March 1. In an event dominated by Dale Earnhardt, Richard managed only a 15th-place finish. The following week at Richmond, Earnhardt won again. This time, Richard was caught up in a 10-car pile-up a third of the way through the race. Though he was able to continue, his heavily damaged STP Pontiac ended up finishing 83 laps down in the 23rd spot —the last of the cars running when the checkers fell.

Atlanta hosted the Motorcraft 500 on March 15, and again ill fortune claimed Richard. On lap 283, he and Cale Yarborough collided, spinning both cars and ending their chances at a win for the day. After some quick repairs, Richard was again able to continue, eventually finishing 14th, three laps down.

Richard's fortunes improved, though, for the next few races. At Darlington near the end of March, Richard finished third and followed that finish with a sixth at North Wilkesboro a week later. From there the tour went to the high banks of

Allison in his Miller-sponsored Buick. On lap 21, Bobby felt his car hit some debris on the front stretch and immediately cut down his right rear tire. As the car slid sideways, it became airborne and tore into the catch fence along the main grandstands. There was no escape for anyone. It was simply an act of divine intervention that kept the 3,700-pound car from getting into the stands — at nearly 200 miles per hour — or from taking out the flagstand. As it was, the back of Allison's car dragged the tall catch fence onto the main straightaway and required more than 2 1/2 hours to repair. The race was stopped as those repairs were made. Fortunately, neither Allison nor any spectators were seriously hurt. Bobby's son Davey went on to win the race after it was resumed.

Charlotte Motor Speedway hosted the next race, the Coca-Cola 600, and it too turned into another father-son story. Kyle Petty outlasted all the other leaders and cruised home a lap ahead of the field in his Wood Brothers' Thunderbird. Richard followed in fourth place, two laps down. Watching both their cars circle the track together was something to see.

At Dover, fortunes turned south again. Richard broke a couple of ribs in an accident on lap 69 when a cut tire sent him into the wall. He was hurt significantly enough that he was only able to start the next two races and run the pace lap. At Pocono and then again at Riverside, Joe Ruttman qualified the STP Pontiac and drove it for both races, finishing 29th at Pocono after another wreck ended his day, and sixth at Riverside.

Richard was feeling strong enough to race by the time they got to Brooklyn, Michigan, for the Miller American 400, where he finished 12th. The tour then returned to Daytona for the Pepsi Firecracker 400 on the July 4th holiday. Once again, Richard had to be relieved, this time by Lake Speed. He was able to bring the STP Pontiac home in 26th place. The see-

saw year continued through the next couple of races. At Pocono, two weeks after the Firecracker, Richard finished eighth in a race that saw 35 lead changes among 15 drivers. At Talladega a week after that, Richard's engine blew on lap 47, ending his day with a DNF good for 37th position.

Watkins Glen hosted the Budweiser at the Glen on August 10. The race was originally scheduled for Sunday the 9th, but rain forced a postponement — and a chance to test NASCAR's new "next clear day" rule, prompted by the rain-soaked 1986 season. So on the 10th, the race got under way and was eventually won by fellow Pontiac driver Rusty Wallace. Richard came home in 14th place. The following Sunday, it appeared that Richard was finally going to break out of the slump at the Champion Spark Plug 400 at Michigan. He was pulling away from the field late in the race when a caution came out for a pair of spinning cars elsewhere on the track. Having forsaken a tire change to gain track position on the previous caution, Richard was forced to pit. He rejoined the field in sixth place as the green flag came out again. On the last lap, a pack of 11 cars diced for the lead as Richard traded paint with Davey Allison. On the backstretch, the two cars came together and Petty spun out, getting credit for 11th place in the process. That disappointment, however, foretold a renewed strength that would carry the team through the rest of the season.

At Bristol on August 22, Richard finished fifth in a race once again dominated by Earnhardt. Two weeks later, Earnhardt took another win in a rain-shortened event that saw Richard take a strong third. At Richmond a week later, Richard finished fifth, and he followed it up with a ninth at Dover a week after that. At Martinsville on September 27, he finished 13th and followed that up with a ninth at North Wilkesboro in the Holly Farms 400.

Bristol where Dale Earnhardt, after another day of redefining the term "aggressive," edged Richard for the win by less than a second.

When the team got to Martinsville, its luck changed yet again. Richard was forced to take his first DNF of the season when a timing chain broke on lap 347, handing him a 22nd-place finish. Richard didn't fare too well at Talladega in the Winston 500 either. Relieved halfway through the race by Greg Sacks, he saw the STP Pontiac come home in 16th place. The day would be remembered, however, for the horrifying flight taken by Bobby

The Oakwood Homes 500 at Charlotte Motor Speedway turned into a demolition derby that Richard somehow survived, taking fifth place in the process. Usually a magnet for such things in recent years, Richard avoided several major wrecks that eliminated 11 cars and left Neil Bonnett with a broken hip after his car cut a tire and creamed the fourth-turn wall.

At Rockingham, Richard was able to finish in 17th place after fighting his car all day. Riverside followed on November 8 and once again served up another of those father-son moments. Kyle came home in third while Richard followed him for fourth. Finally, as the season ended at Atlanta, Richard's day ended early

when he and Geoff Bodine collided coming off the fourth turn. The lap 154 accident not only knocked two principals out — literally — but eliminated Rick Wilson and J.D. McDuffie, driving in relief of Charlie Baker, as well. Petty was credited with a 30th-place finish for the day.

With the close of the season, Richard and the team had managed to finish eighth in the point standings after an up-and-down year. But for a team that finished only four times in the top five with ten DNFs the previous year, this was a definite improvement. Certainly things were still better than the last 18 months with Curb Motorsports. "The year was not up to our expectations," Petty said, "but if you look at it both ways it was better than the last couple of years, so at least we're not going downhill."

Then too, there were obvious high hopes for the new Pontiac Grand Prix . . . .

A crew member brushes rubber from the lower front grilles. Tire rubber and other debris can clog the cooling inlets and create major mechanical headaches unless it's constantly cleared away. Bryant McMurray

Just about the time that the crew finally got most of the 2+2 figured out, it was time to retire the car and begin work on the new version of the Grand Prix. Bryant McMurray

1987 PONTIAC GRAND PRIX 2+2

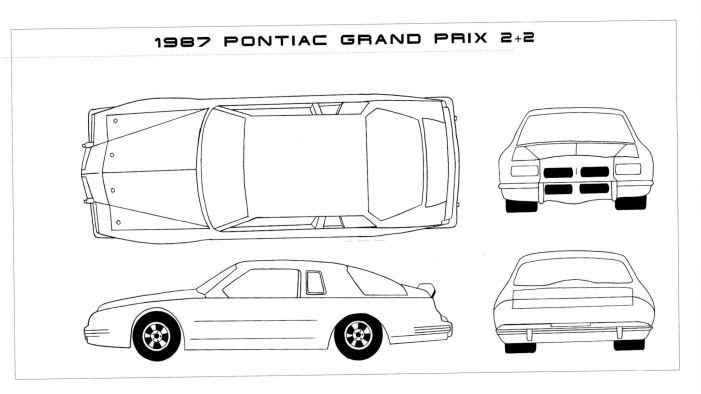

Bad luck strikes again. This time the 2+2 is shown wrecked after a close encounter at Atlanta in November.
Elmer Kappell

1988

Baptism of the New Grand Prix

When Pontiac announced in 1987 that it would be releasing a new body style for the Grand Prix the following year, there was a collective sigh of relief among most of the Pontiac teams. The 2+2, a difficult car to get a handle on, had never even approached the promises and hopes the engineers had for the car. Then too, it had been intended as an interim car until a new Pontiac was ready to go racing.

When race fans saw the new Grand Prix, most assumed that this would be a much better race car. Once again, it looked like what a fast race car should look like. Its aggressive stance and clean body looked as if it would slice through the air better than anything else out there. It simply looked sharp. What the 2+2 had lacked in good looks, the new Grand Prix more than made up for.

While race fans and the public were oohhing and aahhhing over the new car's good looks, the reaction from most race teams was a big "Uh-oh." The rear trunk deck lid was so small that the car had difficulty finding enough downforce at the rear to run safely at high speeds. NASCAR's response was to allow the Pontiac teams to run with larger rear spoilers. By the time of the Daytona 500 the cars were a bit more stable, but there was still a lot of concern among the teams.

Things did not bode well from the start with the new car. Richard wrecked early in the first 125-mile qualifier for Daytona, but he was still able to make the field for the 500, starting 34th.

No one remembers that wreck. The wreck they remember is the one in the Daytona 500. On lap 106 Phil Barkdoll bumped into the back of Richard's Pontiac coming out of the fourth turn. The Grand Prix, which was already light in the rear end to start with, started to swap ends despite Richard's best efforts to stall the spin. A.J. Foyt, following close behind, then caught up to Barkdoll and Petty as they slowed. Foyt clipped the nose of the STP Pontiac. As the noses of Petty's and Foyt's cars touched, the rear end

Richard leads Alan Kulwicki in the #7 Zerex Ford Thunderbird down pit road at Talladega during the July race. Elmer Kappell

The new Grand Prix race car was actually developed in Detroit in Pontiac's R&D center. At first glance it looks like it should be fast. Richard Petty Private Collection

An overhead shot clearly shows how short the rear deck lid was on the Grand Prix. This would be a problem that would haunt the car throughout its racing career. Richard Petty Private Collection

A good shot of the proposed front-air dam. The dam would become flatter as time passed. Richard Petty Private Collection

If you note where the hood ends and compare it to the 1995 version, it is easy to see how much the nose grew over the course of time.
Richard Petty Private Collection

of the Pontiac lifted until it virtually stood on its nose.

Momentum carried the car into the fence near the flag stand. The car tumbled and spun like some amusement park ride gone wild. The car shed parts in all directions as the force of the impact tore the car apart. Finally, as the STP Pontiac finally appeared to

come to rest, Brett Bodine punted the shattered remains with his Crisco Ford as he slid out of control trying to avoid the wild wreck.

By the time the accident was over, there was hardly anything left of the new Pontiac. Richard was mercifully spared any serious injury, with a badly sprained ankle and torn ligaments. Race fans were also spared serious injury as well, but for the second time in less than a year a 3,500-pound race car had come dangerously close to getting airborne and into the crowded stands. NASCAR had had enough of flying cars. It quickly decided to add two pieces of angle iron along the outside edges of the roof on cars racing at the bigger

tracks. These "roof rails," as they are now called, were installed in an effort to break up the airflow over the roof when the cars were no longer headed into the wind. These would later be required on cars for all tracks, but at the time NASCAR felt this might be enough to do the trick.

The team went from dealing with the 2+2, a race car that couldn't keep its nose on the ground, to a race car that couldn't keep its tail where it belonged. It was bad enough when it was on the track by itself, but in traffic the Pontiac lost air off its spoiler long before anything else. It made for a loose, squirrelly race car.

The results for the season seemed to confirm the worst. On the small tracks, the Pontiac could hold its own and actually run near the front. But the bigger the track, the worse the car handled.

After the dramatic crash at Daytona, Richard came back the next week with an impressive third at Richmond — at the time a half-mile oval. But at Rockingham two weeks later he crashed out of the race on lap 17. His engine blew at Atlanta in the Motorcraft Quality Parts 500 two weeks later, placing him 23rd.

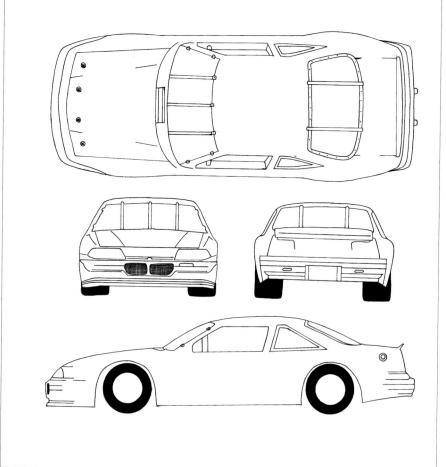

Another wreck followed a week later in the TranSouth 500 at Darlington.

Bristol and North Wilkesboro yielded a pair of sixth-place finishes in the first half of April, but a blown engine prevented the team from making a good showing at Martinsville at the end of the month. Richard posted a 20th-place finish at Talladega and followed that up with a pair of 15th-place finishes at Charlotte and Dover — each time proving the point that the car needed some serious help on the bigger speedways.

At Riverside, the team managed another sixth-place finish — but things became grimmer from that point on. Except for an eighth at Bristol in August and an 11th in Charlotte in October, the team never finished higher than 17th and had nine DNFs.

Not that the troubles with the new Grand Prix were universal. The Blue Max racing team, owned by Raymond Beadle with Rusty Wallace at the helm, managed six wins and 19 top-five finishes. The same was true for

The actual race version of the car as built by Petty Enterprises looked very similar to the prototype. The markings differ only slightly, with bigger STP ovals on the rear quarter panel and an all-red air dam. Elmer Kappell

With its tail pointed high in the air, the Grand Prix had an almost wedge-like appearance. Note the license plate. Richard Petty Private Collection

Sliding at Charlotte. The Grand Prix always wanted to swap ends due to the lack of downforce generated by the tiny rear deck. LaDon George

the RahMoc team with Neil Bonnett and Morgan Shepherd, with two wins and five top fives between them. The handle these teams found eluded the Petty Enterprises team. As if to underscore the point, at the Atlanta Journal 500 in November, Rusty Wallace had

his Pontiac dialed in enough to dominate the race while Richard was forced to retire on lap 84 after another wreck. At least with Rusty doing so well, there was hope for the new car. All the Petty team had to do was find it and mix it with a little luck.

The start of one of the most famous racing wrecks in history began when Phil Barkdoll got into the back of the STP Pontiac at the end of turn 4 at Daytona. LaDon George

As Petty tried to correct the front end of the car, Barkdoll's momentum continued to push the tail of the #43 car around. LaDon George

Petty's slide was causing him to slow more than Barkdoll, and A.J. Foyt in the #14 Copenhagen car was closing in on the pair with great haste. LaDon George

As Barkdoll backed off, Petty was still trying to save the STP Pontiac. Note the angle of the front wheels as Petty tries to steer into the slide. LaDon George

SIGNIFICATA

- Chrome wheels are no longer permitted.
- Pontiac introduces a new body style for the Grand Prix. While looking very sleek, the car has a very small rear deck and proves to be very squirrelly.
- Restrictor plates are reintroduced at Daytona and Talladega in an effort to slow the cars down. Qualifying speeds drop below 200 mph at both tracks.
- Richard Petty gets airborne at the Daytona 500. Following the frightful crash, NASCAR requires roof rails and side skirts on superspeedway cars for the rest of the season.
- Richmond is redesigned and expanded from .542 miles to .75 miles between the spring and fall races.
- Riverside in California finally closes after the June race.
- Phoenix in Arizona joins the schedule in the fall.
- Driving a Ford Thunderbird, Bill Elliott wins the Winston Cup Championship over the course of 29 races. Richard Petty finishes 22nd in points.

...for the rear end to begin to lift. And that's when all the fun started. LaDon George

The STP Pontiac might simply have looped if it hadn't bumped noses with Foyt's oncoming Oldsmobile. It left the Pontiac at a critical angle for just long enough . . . LaDon George

As the rear end of the Pontiac begins to get airborne, Barkdoll goes to the right while Foyt heads off to the left with Rick Wilson in the Kodak Olds close behind. Richard said he knew he was in serious trouble when he could look down and see A.J. looking up at him as he went by. LaDon George

With Barkdoll into the wall the STP Pontiac starts to go up on its nose. Jim Coleman via the Richard Petty Private Collection

Richard's car stands on its nose for a split second as it begins a tumbling pirouette towards the grandstands and all the fans. Richard Petty Private Collection

How close did Richard come to going into the stands? Too close! These shots show some amazing details and the force of the crash. Mel Stettler via the Richard Petty Private Collection

Sheet metal and parts went everywhere. Here the car sheds its front end as it barrel rolls down the front retaining wall. Mel Stettler via the Richard Petty Private Collection

As the tumble continues, both ends of the chassis are torn off by the force and momentum. Mel Stettler via the Richard Petty Private Collection

Near the end of the tumbling, you can already see how much damage the car has sustained. When the car finally came to rest it was then punted by Brett Bodine in Bud Moore's Crisco Ford Thunderbird who was trying to avoid the wreck. Mel Stettler via the Richard Petty Private Collection

Amazing! With hardly anything left intact on the STP Pontiac, the roll cage held its integrity and Richard survived with a few bumps and bruises. The Richard Petty Private Collection

The paint scheme sprouted headlamp covers around the season halfway mark. Here the car is shown on the grid at Darlington in September. Bobby Proctar via the Richard Petty Private Collection

Compared with other cars on the tour, the Pontiac appeared to be slicker and sleeker, especially when compared to a car like the #98 Curb Motorsports Buick of Brad Noffsinger. Al Steinberg via the Richard Petty Private Collection

Richard and Rick Wilson in the Kodak Olds battle for position at Michigan International Speedway. Bill Coulter

The STP Crew goes to work on Petty's Pontiac during a pit stop. Note that in this photo the cowl panel is painted black and the hood pins are taped over. Richard Petty Private Collection

Richard charges up the hill at Sears Point Raceway in Sonoma, California in June. The yellow dot on the windshield is an inspection sticker. Moto-Foto via the Richard Petty Private Collection

Suffering the battle scars of Bristol in April, note the absence of the painted headlamp covers. Elmer Kappell

The small addition of painting the headlight covers silver did a lot to improve the looks of the car as seen here at Michigan International Speedway in June. Elmer Kappell

Richard poses at Daytona with his fully-intact 1988 Grand Prix. It didn't stay that way for long. Richard Petty Private Collection

Some years are better forgotten

The Bottom Drops Out

A contemplative King sits quietly in his car during testing at Daytona. Yes, that's a gray car. LaDon George

If the Petty team's problems had affected the rest of the Pontiac teams, 1988 would have been easy to understand. Unfortunately, Rusty Wallace had almost won the championship in essentially the same car the Petty's had raced. With a little luck and some new tricks, the Petty team hoped to find what the Blue Max team had found and get back to the front.

Things didn't work out that way. A disappointing 17th-place finish at Daytona was followed by a 16th-place run at Rockingham three weeks later. At the Atlanta International Raceway two weeks after that, Richard actually led for nine laps, but the joy evaporated when Robert Callicutt, Petty's gasman, was severely burned in a pit stop fire. With second degree burns covering almost 40 percent of his body, Callicutt was transferred to a burn center in Augusta, Georgia. If that weren't enough, the engine on the STP Pontiac failed on lap 257, dropping Petty to 27th place.

Those disappointments, however, could not compare with what was to come. On March 24, Richard failed to qualify for the previously postponed Pontiac Excitement 400 at Richmond. A crash in practice squelched any hopes of a second-round qualifying run, and for the first time since November 1971, Richard and the team failed to make a race. This ended his string of 513 consecutive starts. Rodney Combs and Jim Sauter offered

to let Petty take their seats and run their cars in the race, but Richard declined the kind offers and returned home to Level Cross. It was a tough drive home. Linda said she cried all the way from Richmond to Randleman.

A week later, the team managed to place 15th in the TranSouth 500 at Darlington — the Lady in Black dealing Richard a kinder hand than Richmond did. However, a week later, Richard and the team again failed to make the

Richard leads Darrell Waltrip in the #17 Tide Chevy Lumina at the first Pocono race of the season. Note how the red paint on the front air dam of the STP Pontiac has been sandblasted off by track debris. Jim Juka

Petty poses with his 1989 Pontiac Grand Prix. The roof rails are now mandatory. Note the angle of the rear spoiler!
Elmer Kappell

32-car field as they tried to qualify for Bristol. The nightmare didn't end there either. Preparing for the North Wilkesboro race on April 16, Richard failed to make the starting grid.

This was almost too much to take. In years gone by, the short tracks had been Richard's personal possession. But now he had failed to make the race at three short tracks in a row. To make matters worse, this had been the only area of solace the previous year. If they couldn't get the car to run well at the big tracks, at least they had a chance at the smaller ones. Now they were having trouble getting into the field.

Things brightened up a smidgen for the next dozen races. Though never really in the running, at least the car was on the starting grid and Richard was out there turning laps — that is, until the second Bristol race of the season. Once again, Richard failed to make the field. From that point on, he made the starting grid for each of the remaining nine races, but finished none. The season ended with Richard and the team failing to score a single

top-ten finish in 25 starts. Adding insult to injury, Rusty Wallace did win the championship in his Pontiac.

The team had shown occasional flashes of promise in the previous years, but the team and Richard had simply struggled since the inception of the smaller Grand Prix. One of the credos a racer lives by is that there is always the next race, always the next season. Richard's brand of common sense made it logical to think that sooner or later things would get better, as long as the team kept doing its best. Besides, Richard, Dale, and the crew basically knew what they were dealing with.

However, Richard was content knowing he and the team had done their best and that would be good enough for today. That kind of confidence in self and those around you can carry an enterprise through until tomorrow, when your own best will be better than everyone else's. And, like every other team in NASCAR, Petty Enterprises had as much of tomorrow as anyone else. Why not press on?

RULES 89

- Goodyear introduces the radial to Winston Cup racing to counter Hoosier's bias-ply tires. First attempted at Daytona, the tire was withdrawn and later introduced at North Wilkesboro in April.
- Chevy introduces the Lumina to replace the Monte Carlo. The final race for the Monte Carlo was the Pannill Sweatshirts 500 at Martinsville, VA. The Lumina was introduced at the Winston 500 at Talladega.
- The size of restrictor plate openings are reduced to help slow speeds even more.
- Roof rails are now mandatory on all race tracks.
- Sears Point International Raceway in Sonoma, California replaces Riverside on the schedule.
- Alabama International Motor Speedway changes its name to Talladega Superspeedway.
- Driving a Pontiac Grand Prix, Rusty Wallace wins the Winston Cup Championship over the course of 29 races. Richard Petty finishes 29th in points.

The STP crew works on the left side of Richard's car during a green flag stop. Bryant McMurray

After a long hiatus, Richard returned to run in the 1989 IROC series which was running Camaros at the time. Bryant McMurray

When the STP Pontiac showed up at Michigan, the scheme had been adjusted with larger roof and hood ovals. Also, all the ovals were now bright red, including the ones on the rear quarter panels. Bill Coulter

1989 PONTIAC GRAND PRIX SE

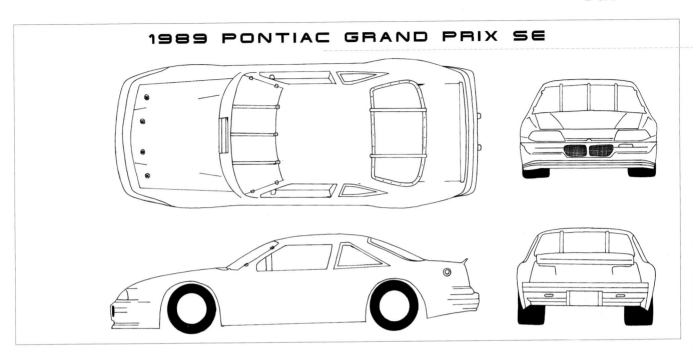

Richard straps on his helmet. Note the mask hanging from the right side of the helmet. Bryant McMurray

It was thought that Richard might be suffering from the heat and the effects of carbon monoxide poisoning in some of the races since the addition of side windows and other aerodynamic items to effectively seal the cars up. To counter this, Richard and his crew experimented with using a fighter-pilot style mask to channel fresh air to the King. LaDon George

The STP Pontiac showed up at Daytona with dark red STP ovals and a bright red oval around the roof number. Note the crease lines in the side body panels that would disappear in the years to follow. Elmer Kappell

The road back takes time

Back to Basics

Richard and the 1990 version of the Grand Prix at Daytona. The paint scheme was changed to add a broad red stripe that ran from the front all the way to the back. Breaking the red and Petty blue areas of the car was a white stripe edged with dark blue pin stripes. Elmer Kappell

The wrap around paint scheme was even applied to the spoiler. Note the size of the STP oval on the hood. Elmer Kappell

A competitor who finds himself far behind the leaders has few options. Giving up or giving in is the easiest to select, but it often comes with a high price tag. Reaching down deep inside to find the stuff to keep going, never easy, is even harder to do for a whole team. Nonetheless, this is the position the Petty organization found itself in at the beginning of the 1990 season.

Richard had vowed to get himself and his team competitive again. To underscore the point, Richard turned a lap of 193.590 mph with a special-development engine from Pontiac. For the regular season, the team would switch from building its own engines to those built by Peter Guild of Pro Motors. Other changes included moving Dale Inman into the role of team manager; he would train the rest of the crew. Richard himself started a physical-training regimen designed to help build his endurance. Asked if he intended to retire, Petty said, "The farther down they get me, the farther any retirement gets." He needed to get Petty Enterprises competitive again to keep the business going after he stopped driving.

In the first twin 125-mile qualifier for the Daytona 500, Richard not only ran well, but actually clawed his way through the field, leading strongly for several laps. However, Richard's run at the front slipped away when he smoked his tires exiting the pits on lap 43. He ultimately finished fifth. He had proved that he still had the right stuff and that the team was making good progress.

"It's more fun up front," Richard exuded. "I know more people up there. One on one we were as strong as anybody, but together they were better than me alone. The car ran really good, but we used our tires up on the pit stop getting back on the track. The car got loose then and that's when they beat me. But we've come further than anybody this year and it's got us excited." Everyone was pleased to see the team doing so well.

Richard hustles the STP Pontiac into a corner at the June Pocono race. Note the front air dam. Jim Juka

*Richard leads Derrick Cope through the turns at Charlotte in October. 1990 was one of the prettier
paint schemes the third generation Grand Prix carried.* LaDon George

He initially kept the car low in turn two as the tire went flat, but ended up skimming the wall while wrestling the steering wheel. After 12 laps' worth of repairs, Petty rejoined the field and finished 34th for the day.

Even though the new motors seemed to have as much as 60 more horsepower, they didn't last long. Engine failures took Richard out of eight races, including many of Richard's favorite tracks: Rockingham, Darlington (twice), Bristol (twice), Charlotte, Michigan, and Martinsville. Crashes eliminated him outright from four more: Richmond, North Wilkesboro, Pocono, and Daytona — the crash at Daytona's Pepsi 400 taking place on the very first lap. At others such as the Daytona 500, Atlanta, Talladega, and Dover, accidents and other mechanical gremlins seriously damaged the car and the run leaving the team many laps down after repairs were made. That was the bad news.

The good news was that a few items were worth writing home about. For example, even though his engine blew and ended his day at the Champion Spark Plug 400 in Brooklyn, Michigan, Richard had run close to the front, leading five laps under the green at one point. His 11th-place finish at the spring race in Michigan was another one of his better finishes. Also noteworthy was his ninth-place finish at the second Pocono race, his only top ten of the year.

Still, by year's end, the media began to wonder out loud when Richard would finally give it up and retire. But to Richard, the issue wasn't so much not winning. It was the chance that there was still one more win left inside him and his team somewhere. The thought of winning just one more was enough to keep him and the team going. "Nobody, and I mean nobody, wants Richard Petty to win number 201 more than I do," he said.

When Petty spoke with NASCAR President Bill France about threatening to win the qualifier, he said, "I didn't want the fans to tear the grandstands down. If I wait until Sunday [for the Daytona 500] to win, you'll have until July to rebuild them." His efforts placed him 11th on the grid for the Daytona 500.

If the season could have ended there, it would have been great. But though he started strong and stayed up front in the Daytona 500 itself, Richard had a tire go down on lap 26.

How the headlamp covers were treated was always an item in flux. At Daytona they were made to look like headlights. Later on they were painted dark blue. Richard Petty Private Collection

Richard and his trademark hat. LaDon George

Shown here is a detail often missed in photos of the 1990 car: the black panel just aft of the hood and immediately in front of the windshield. LaDon George

Richard leads a group of cars through the fourth turn at Charlotte. LaDon George

SIGNIFICATA

- With only GM and Ford cars running in the series, NASCAR specifies that the GM cars must run the Chevy "corporate" block.

- Wheels must have the number of the race car painted on the back side of the rim.

- Refueling and catch can crewmen are now required to where complete firesuits including gloves, shoes, head, and face shields.

- Restrictor plate bore is further reduced to 7/8ths of an inch.

- Driving a Chevy Lumina, Dale Earnhardt wins his fourth Winston Cup Championship over the course of 29 races. Richard Petty finishes 26th in points.

1990 PONTIAC GRAND PRIX SE

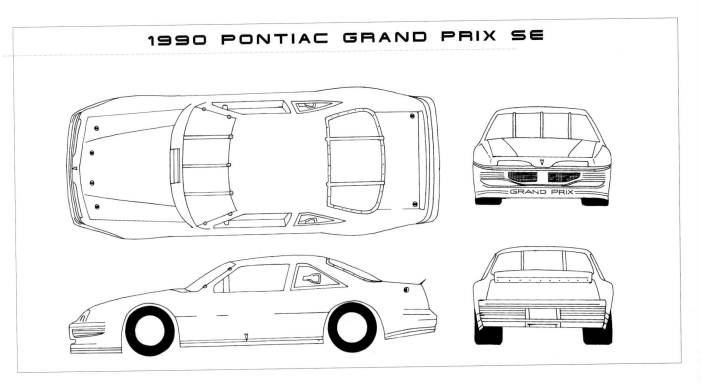

The STP crew gives some quick service to Richard and his Pontiac at North Wilkesboro in September. LaDon George

Shifting Gears

The STP Pontiac under the lights at Bristol shows a few battle scars obtained during the August race. In this case the stripes on the nose do not split the headlamp covers. Elmer Kappell

To the uninitiated race fan, two things are above all sources of confusion. The first is understanding how a car and its driver "get lapped" and then "get the lap back." For some fans — and occasionally a few teams and drivers — this is a constant source of confusion. The second is the concept of "cautions," or running under the yellow, and all the things you can do and can't do. Competitors are allowed to race back to the flagstand to "take the caution" when a caution flag comes out and the caution lights come on around the track. From there they slow down and follow the pace car in order. But prior to the flagstand it's every man for himself.

Nowadays, the pits are opened only after the pace car is actually pacing the field, and they are first opened only to those cars on the lead lap, followed by the rest of the field a lap or so later. Drivers are instructed and shown how fast they are allowed to travel on pit lanes; each has a different speed limit depending on the size of the track. But things haven't always been this way, and 1991 was the season when most of these rules came into play.

After the death of Mike Rich, a crew member killed on pit road in the final race of the 1990 season, NASCAR acted swiftly to change the procedures used on pit road, with an eye toward keeping the crews safe as they worked on the cars. Starting with

the 1991 Daytona 500, teams could no longer change tires under caution. Only green-flag tire changes would be allowed. Two pace cars would control the field, and one of them would actually lead cars into pit lane in small groups in order to control the number of cars at any given time. Most teams and drivers viewed the new rules with a wait-and-see attitude, but obviously the face of stock car racing would change.

For the 1991 season, NASCAR also added another provisional starting position to each race for former Winston Cup champions. Thus, in the case of Daytona, any former champ who failed to make the Daytona field would be awarded the 43rd starting spot in the field. The rule quickly earned the handle of "The Petty Rule." Richard, for his part, proved he didn't need it by running a strong second behind Davey Allison in one of the Gatorade twin 125-mile qualifying races.

Richard straps on his helmet before the beginning of the Daytona 500. Bryant McMurray

The Daytona 500 itself was once again less kind to Richard, who finished 19th after a spin on lap 104 that collected Robbie Gordon in the process. "The way they have everything with the caution flags and green flag stops, you just go out there and run," said Richard. "You don't know where you are at." Aside from confusion over rule interpretation, the long stretches of green flag racing prompted spins and wrecks from worn tires in numbers unknown in recent years. "It might be all right in the pits, but not on the racetrack. They're going to have to make a tradeoff somewhere. We can't be tearing up $100,000 race cars. We need to make it better on the racetrack and come up with something different," Richard added.

the series for years. However, to prevent a wholesale dash of all competitors down pit road when a caution came out, NASCAR stipulated that though tire changes could now take place under the caution, the access to pit road would be based upon how a car had qualified. Odd-numbered spots on the starting grid could pit first once the pits were opened during a caution. On the following lap, even-numbered qualifiers could come down pit road for service. For the restart of the race, the drivers were

underscore Richard's original complaint that making pit road safer had made track conditions more dangerous, there were a record 19 cautions, in part due to fast cars in the back of the pack running over slower ones on restarts.

NASCAR adjusted the rules again for the race at North Wilkesboro. Instead of prohibiting tire changes during cautions, limiting access by qualifying position, and all the other schemes, the sanctioning body decided to create speed limits for every pit lane at every track. The speed limits would differ from one track to the next depending on the pit facilities and the size of the track. Because stock cars haven't had speedometers since the truly stock years, the drivers would determine the accepted speed by following the pace car and taking note of the gear they were in and the engine RPMs displayed on their tachometers. Drivers caught speeding would be penalized a lap or black flagged for a stop-and-go penalty.

To keep the mayhem on pit road to a minimum, yet safer than prior to the Atlanta accident, the pit road would open only after the entire field was under control of the pace car and to those cars on the lead lap first, followed by the rest of the lot a lap later. A flag man stationed at the entrance to pit road would signal if pit lane was opened or closed. Apparently the new and far less confusing rules set well with the team: Richard moved from 33rd starting spot to 16th by the end of the race.

The 1991 paint scheme was a variation of the 1990 scheme. The side stripes were widened and split by a dark blue stripe. This scheme was similar to the 1984 scheme. Note the treatment applied to the headlamp covers. Elmer Kappell

For the Richmond race, NASCAR revised the new pit rules to allow changing spotted or flat tires during cautions without being penalized. Bill Elliott had experienced the problem in the Daytona 500 and pointed out how seriously Bobby Allison was injured years before at Pocono attempting to limp around the track on a flat tire.

Even with that modification, however, the rules had turned the usual exciting, door-handle-to-door-handle races into endurance contests in which the cautious and shrewd could win by guessing the tire strategy right.

At Bristol, NASCAR tweaked the pit rules again to restore the classic racing that had been the hallmark of

required to line up with the odd-numbered qualifiers on the bottom and the even-numbered qualifiers on the top — in essence starting the race all over again.

Confused yet? Wait, it gets better. With 50 or fewer laps to go, the race leaders could finally move to the front of their respective columns. Until this point, Darrell Waltrip really hadn't objected strongly to the new rules, but this variation promoted Darrell to say, "The new pit rules have got everyone so frustrated that you have to do stupid things." Rusty Wallace won the race from two laps down by craftily using the rules and the confusing restarts to his advantage. And as if to

It was racing back to usual, then, by the time the series got to Talladega — well, almost back to usual. In what appeared to be great haste and a severe lack of common sense, drivers raced three and four abreast through the tri-oval. Ernie Irvan tried slipping between Kyle Petty, who was high on the track, and Mark Martin, who was low. The wreck that quickly followed involved 20 cars by the time it played out. The race had to be red-flagged for 34 minutes while the track was cleaned up. Richard was spared that

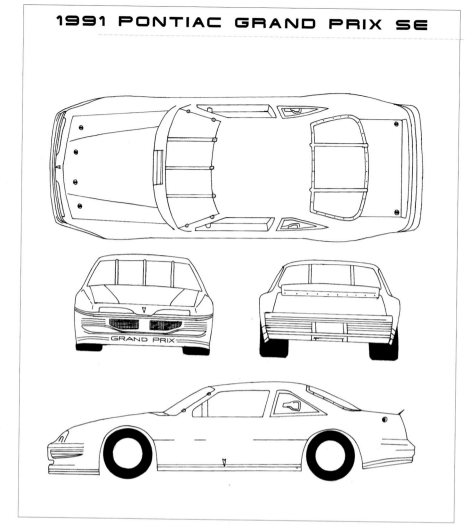

1991 PONTIAC GRAND PRIX SE

GRAND PRIX

catastrophe only because he had been hit likewise on lap two, eliminating him and the car from the race.

The Winston and its companion race, the Winston Open, was run two weeks later at Charlotte Motor Speedway. Richard ran in the Winston Open and finished sixth after starting tenth among 30 drivers. A week later at the Coca-Cola 600, Richard was running well when a late-race accident ended the day on lap 383, relegating him to 20th place.

At the Sears Point Raceway in Sonoma, the STP Pontiac slid off the track with 11 laps to go and careened into a tire barrier with enough force to spray tires in every direction and nearly stand the car on its nose. Richard was first taken to Sonoma County Hospital for precautionary x-rays. He was later released, but he would be on crutches for some weeks to come.

As crazy as it seems, it was as if the accident made Richard more determined than ever to do well. A week after the wreck at Sonoma, Richard qualified 23rd at Pocono and finished a strong 11th, as if to quietly say, "Hey, don't write me off yet." All this came after an early incident damaged a number of the leaders' cars — Richard included — and the event was shortened by one of Pocono's inevitable June rainstorms. At Michigan a week later, a faulty valve spring broke on lap 166 and handed the team another DNF. With so many teams running

strong that day, the effort earned only 35th place in a 41-car field.

At the Pepsi 400, Richard qualified 21st and finished just one lap off the pace in 22nd, which was encouraging after the visit to Michigan. The second Pocono race, held two weeks later, again gave the team some hope with Richard's strong performance the month before. He backed this up with a 17th-place qualifying effort, and things looked good until an accident ended Richard's day on lap 97 and relegated him to 31st. July ended with an 18th-place run at Talladega, finishing a lap down to the leaders — but at least finishing.

August 11 was the date of the Bud at the Glen, held at the road course at Watkins Glen, New York. For a guy who really doesn't like road courses — even though he had done well on them in the past — this one produced the ironic finish of the year. After qualifying 31st on the grid, Richard

carefully marched through the field and into the top ten — and what would be his best finish all year. It was overshadowed, however, by a racing accident that took the life of a popular independent driver. J.D. McDuffie was killed when his Pontiac's brakes failed at the end of the back straight going into turn five. His car collected that of Jimmy Means and then flipped on its roof before striking the barrier in the turn, apparently killing McDuffie instantly. Though never a front-runner, J.D. had been around for a long time and was liked by many of the folks in the garage area.

The tour moved back to Brooklyn, Michigan, where Richard scored a 23rd-place finish. This was followed a week later on the short track at Bristol with a solid 12th-place run and a week after with a 16th-place finish after starting in 30th at Darlington, South Carolina. At Richmond on September 8, the STP team finished

Richard plows off the course and into a rubber tire barrier at Sears Point Raceway in Sonoma, California as Rusty Wallace goes by on the track.
The Richard Petty Private Collection

The STP Pontiac comes to rest after the hard lick. The severity of the hit is seen by the damage the front end has taken. Note how the tires are being scattered by the impact. The Richard Petty Private Collection

Would you mess with this man? Richard's air mask gives him a rather fearsome countenance.
Bryant McMurray

24th. The race at Dover a week later was more of an endurance event than a race: only 17 of 40 cars were still running at the end of the race. Unfortunately, Richard wasn't in one of them; his engine expired 389 laps into the event. Proving that racing can sometimes be just plain weird, it gave Richard 20th place nonetheless. At Martinsville a week later, Richard experienced the other side of the coin by racing some 348 laps at the half-mile track until he was retired by an accident. This time, most of the field survived to see the end, which left the team in 30th place. North Wilkesboro finished out the month of September and the short track season, with Richard finishing 19th.

On October 1, Richard held a press conference at the shops at Level Cross. It had been speculated widely that he would be announcing his retirement. As if the poor performance of the past few years were reasons for him to go into retirement, Richard, self-effacing as ever, said, "I think when Richard Petty came along, God said, 'OK, you've got 25 years of good luck.' I just tried to stretch it into 35." Then he chuckled at himself.

Instead of announcing his retirement at the end of the year, Richard would run for one more year. That final circuit of races, called the Richard Petty Fan Appreciation Tour, would give Richard a chance to say good-bye to all his friends and fans in

his last season as a driver. "I'm doing a fan appreciation tour next year. It's not a farewell tour, because I'm not going anywhere," he said. It was toward the end of the 1990 racing season that Richard first started talking to his sponsors about plans for retiring. "Age has something to do with it," Richard explained. "Not winning races has something to do with it. While racing, I still think, 'I really love driving this race car.' But I also started asking myself, 'Do I really have to do this?'"

As if it were some sort of relief to have that finally out of the way, Richard finished 12th at Charlotte on October 6 and 16th at Rockingham two weeks later. A wreck relegated Richard to 41st place at Phoenix at the beginning of November in the next-to-last race. In Atlanta, Richard ran a good race and finished 22nd for the day.

The last few years of Richard's career teach a few lessons each of us could learn from. Some said he should have quit racing years before. He even has said the same thing, but he has also said he loved what he was doing. He stuck with it when the going was tough. He kept at it when things were bad, but he also kept his wits about him. No fool he, Richard knew the day would come for him to quit driving, and the trick would be to do it with some class and not just walk away. So he and his sponsors carefully prepared a plan — and there is the lesson: when the time comes to finally put a thing down or lay it to rest, think it through, follow it through, and then let it rest.

The last dance that lasted a whole year

The Fan Appreciation Tour

A special logo was created to mark the celebration and it could be found just about everywhere. Steve Mohlenkamp

aring about his fans has always been a hallmark of Richard Petty. There are endless stories of Richard signing autograph after autograph at a track following a grueling race, long after the other competitors had packed up and gone home. Where other racers feel the fans break their concentration and get in the way, Richard has maintained a love affair with them since he first started winning races. "I wouldn't be where I am now if it weren't for the fans," Petty has said in the past.

Jerry Kellar, sports columnist for the Wilkes-Barre Times Leader, tells of an incident in the garage area of Pocono International Raceway in 1990. An elderly man slowly limped up toward Petty as Friday morning practice began. Richard and the man spoke together for some time and when they finally finished, Richard took him by the arm and walked him gently to the garage area gate down the long road adjacent to the trailers. There they shook hands and bid one another farewell. The whole process lasted almost 20 minutes. During practice on Friday before a race that might as well be 20 hours.

Kellar, figuring that the two had to be family or at least long-time friends, decided to find out in an interview he had with Richard later that day. "Was he a relative of yours?" Kellar asked. "Never saw him before in my life," Petty answered easily. He noticed the incredulous look on Kellar's face and

Coming or going, it was a very pretty car. The Richard Petty Private Collection

went on, saying, "That guy told me he watched me race for 30 years. That's a long deal. He just wanted to talk. I figure the least I can do is spend some time with him." It's easy to see why folks believe that Richard not only likes his fans, but actually cares about them — whether he's having a good year or not.

Unsurprisingly, when Richard finally decided it was time to quit driving he thought of the fans and the

sport that he feels have given him so much. On October 1, 1991, Richard announced what was to become the Fan Appreciation Tour as his final season as an active Winston Cup driver. Packed with appearances and special fan activities, Richard would have a chance to say good-bye to all the folks he cared so much about.

The festivities began with the Daytona 500. Richard was asked to be the grand marshal over all the activi-

Probably one of the most famous of Richard's cars is the 1992 version of the Grand Prix driven during the Fan Appreciation Tour as seen here with Richard on the lawn at Level Cross. The Richard Petty Private Collection

This overhead shot shows the wrap around paint scheme and the various aerodynamic fences that were used in 1992. Note the way the fences on the rear window channel air to the fences on the rear deck lid. Elmer Kappell

This angle also shows how the fences were set up. These were used only at Daytona and Talladega. The fin at the front edge of the roof is a TV camera pod. Elmer Kappell

Richard was mobbed by photographers wanting to catch the moment he climbed into the famed STP Pontiac for his last Daytona 500. Elmer Kappell

ties of Speed Weeks, and it set the stage for the whole year. With the Winston Cup tour essentially making two stops at almost every track, everyone on the team felt that things probably wouldn't get emotional until the last half of the season. But as the fans greeted Richard with a standing ovation during driver introductions, no one could help getting choked up — Richard included.

Bill France, Jr. put an unusual twist on the traditional command to the field to start its engines for the 500 by asking, "Will the gentleman representing the kingdom of Randleman, North Carolina, please start his engine?" Alone, Richard cranked and started the STP Pontiac's engine. As grand marshal, Richard then put his own twist on the traditional command: "Okay, guys, let's go. Crank 'em up." It was pure Richard Petty.

Richard led the field around the track during the parade lap and then fell back to his starting position as the pace car brought the field up to speed to go racing. Throughout the year, this tribute was played and replayed at every NASCAR Winston Cup race. It became more touching each time. During the Daytona 500 itself, Richard was moving up through the pack from his 31st starting position until he was swept up in a wreck on the backstretch. In spite of the car damage, the crew was able to get him back out fast enough to allow a respectable 16th-place finish.

At Rockingham the first week of March, Richard again ran well and finished 16th. Attention was focused on Kyle too, who qualified on the pole. His hopes for the day were high,

but the Sabco team struggled with the car's set-up until the camshaft broke, ending Kyle's day early.

Linda Petty was the grand marshal at the Pontiac Excitement 400 at Richmond a week later, giving the traditional command to start engines. And once again, Richard had a good run going until the team was caught in the pits on a green flag stop as the yellow came out. Caught in the pits until the pace car brought the field around, Richard fell a lap behind and was never able to make up the difference, finishing 21st.

The downright cold temperatures encountered at Atlanta Motor Speedway a week later played havoc with the Goodyear Eagle tires. Never able to work up to the usual temperatures, the tire compound blistered and chunked off the tires at a horrifying rate. Nonetheless, Richard once again came home with a respectable 16th-place finish.

Darlington yielded the first DNF of the season when the engine went sour, ending the day early with a 32nd-place finish. Bristol a week later looked more promising for a while. After qualifying 14th, Richard was able to keep pace until Ricky Rudd hit the wall. Rudd slid right into the path of Richard and the STP Pontiac. The car was damaged badly enough to put Richard toward the back of the field, and he ended the day classed as the 27th finisher.

If the family was concerned about wrecks, especially after Richard's shunt the previous year at Sears Point, then the next two races made everyone just a bit nervous. On lap seven at North Wilkesboro on April 12, Richard was again caught up in a wreck that ruined the handling on the car. He eventually had to park the car and take a 31st-place finish and his second DNF. Two weeks later, a wreck on lap two at Martinsville

again ended his day early, this time in 29th place.

Talladega was the next race and Richard ran well, finishing 15th in an encouraging run. He followed this up at The Winston All-Star Race in Charlotte with another strong run. The unusual format of the Winston allows the race to be run in two parts with a break in between. During the break, the fans were allowed to decide if the field would be inverted for the restart or maintain the finishing order from the first half. The fans elected the latter, and when the green flag fell, Richard followed Geoff Bodine and was threatening to take the lead when the rest of the pack caught up to them. Kyle eventually took the lead until the last lap, when he and Davey Allison battled all the way down to the finish line. Davey prevailed, but wrecked in the process. It

The crew hustles through a pit stop at Phoenix in the last half of the season. Steve Mohlenkamp

Richard races with his son Kyle who is driving the #42 Sabco Mellow Yellow Pontiac at the Pepsi 400. Elmer Kappell

Another scene that would repeat itself was Richard leading the parade lap at each race. Steve Mohlenkamp

was, however, one of those great moments in racing.

At the Coca-Cola 600 a week later at Charlotte, Richard again had a good run going until the car got up into the "marbles" (the little globs of tire rubber and other debris on the track) and slid into the wall at turn three. The damage took out his front brakes, which made continuing difficult. It finally caught up with him when he was swept up in a wreck in front of him. The King was relegated to 42nd place and another DNF.

At Dover for Memorial Day, the team took a 20th and followed it up with a safely run 21st at Sears Point a week later. The team was happy just to finish the day with no damage to the driver or car in spite of a minor spin. The tour then moved to Pocono on June 14 for the Champion Spark Plug 500, where Richard once again

finished 16th. Then, a week later at Michigan, Richard again did well, finishing 15th in spite of the cooler-than-usual track conditions.

Back at Daytona for the Fourth of July holiday and the Pepsi 400, Richard appeared to have qualified for the pole. Sterling Marlin upset that with a blistering run late in the day, but Richard was on the front row for the start of the race. If that weren't enough, the celebrations took on an almost frenzied level. Richard's 55th birthday was celebrated with a giant cake that resembled his race car. A city bus, similarly decorated, was unveiled at a ceremony at the track. And to top it off, President Bush was grand marshal of this race and introduced Richard at the driver's pre-race introductions.

For Petty fans, it was a dream day. Richard, jumping ahead on the first

lap, beat Marlin and the rest of the field to the strip to lead the first lap. It was almost as good as winning to many fans, and the numbers that were on their feet cheering the King proved it. Unfortunately, that would have to do, for the heat caught up with Richard early. As Eddie Bierschwale circled the track as his substitute, Richard retreated to his motor home to recover. For most folks, that would have been it for the day, but Richard was soon back outside signing autographs for the fans.

At the second race at Pocono, Richard again qualified well, putting him seventh on the grid. He finished a decent 20th in spite of Davey Allison's horrible spill down the backstretch. Once again the aeromonster had reared its ugly head. Lucky to be alive, Davey sustained a broken forearm and shoulder, but he too would keep on racing.

1992 PONTIAC GRAND PRIX SE

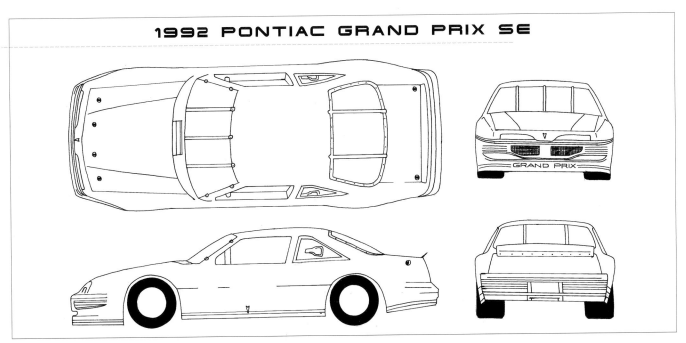

Looking rather stylish in his driving suit, hat, and sunglasses, Richard relaxes perched on the back of the STP Pontiac in the Charlotte garages. Note the gray interior of the car. Elmer Kappell

Occasionally the STP Pontiac fell victim to some bad racing luck. Here, at Bristol, the damage was fairly heavy, but Richard kept the car running. Note the black cowl panel. Elmer Kappell

Pavement grit, sand, and rubber can sandblast the finish off a car in no time. The famous #43 was no exception as this photo of the car at Atlanta Motor Speedway testifies. Note the gold colored wheels. Elmer Kappell

At Pocono the Grand Prix used a different grille on the lower half of the air dam. Jim Juka

Back at Talladega, the team worked to control Richard's exposure to the heat, and the strategy paid off. In withering temperatures and humidity, Richard ran all day and finished 15th.

The road course at Watkins Glen on August 9 hosted the Budweiser at the Glen. Rain ended the race just beyond the halfway point, handing Petty a 28th-place finish for the day. Michigan a week later was kinder and yielded 18th place for his efforts. From there, the tour returned to Bristol, Tennessee, where Richard's grandson, Austin, was grand marshal. Again, Richard finished 16th. The team was starting to joke about running well or

running badly; they always seemed to finish 15th or 16th.

Rain interrupted the last Darlington race of Richard's career, again just after the halfway point. The race could not be restarted. The 20th-place finish there was followed by another 16th-place finish a week later in Richmond under the lights. Dover followed a week after that, but Richard's night ended early. A heavy crash took him and several other competitors out on lap 272 after Dick Trickle spun early in the backstretch.

Rain played a part in the next two races again. At Martinsville, the race ended early and Richard claimed 18th place. It rained again at North

Wilkesboro, forcing the event to be completed on Monday. Richard finished 27th.

At Charlotte, Richard did well for most of the race but ended up with a disappointing 27th-place finish. There was reason to celebrate though, with Kyle leading a good portion of the race and finishing third. Kyle continued up front at Rockingham and won the race. Richard finished 25th. A week later on November 1, he finished 22nd before a crowd of well-wishers and fans eager to see Richard racing in one of his last events.

Finally the day came for Richard to run his last race. At Atlanta for the Hooters 500, Richard could barely get in his car for the crush of photographers wanting to snap a piece of history. It was the emotional day everyone thought it would be. His daughters gave the command once again for their father to start his engine, the way they did on Father's Day in 1989 when they celebrated Richard's 1,000th start. The STP Pontiac paced the field again on the parade lap — slower than in the past, or so it seemed to fans looking on at the track and on TV, as they savored the moment to make it last just a little longer. Then it was time to go racing.

And race Richard did until he was caught in a wreck on the front straightaway on lap 96. The accident knocked the front oil cooler off the car and dumped the oil onto the headers. As flames erupted, Richard pulled the stricken car into the infield and right up to a fire truck parked in turn 1. Richard climbed out and waved to the crowd, showing that he was okay. By the end of the race, the team had rebuilt the car enough to get it around the track for one last time.

As Richard took this last lap around the Atlanta Motor Speedway, he waved to the crowd as they lined the fences three and four deep, with his thumb sticking out and middle and ring fingers curled into his palm. Most folks may have missed it, although the hearing impaired probably saw it right away because it's sign language. It was a fitting way for the King of Stock Car racing to say goodbye to all his fans and close out his career as a driver. It means simply "I love you."

As the car coasted to a stop, everyone held their breath, for the fire looked worse than it really was. Richard later joked that this wasn't exactly the blaze of glory he had in mind when he thought about his final drive. He was unhurt in the incident.
Richard Petty Private Collection

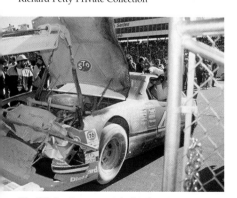

The STP Pontiac was carted off to the garage area covered with the powder used to extinguish the oil fire. The crew and Richard then decided that they could get the car rolling again for a final lap at the end of the race. So with nothing to gain besides giving Richard that final emotional moment, the crew went to work on the car.
Elmer Kappell

Part way through the final race at Atlanta, another accident collected Richard in a frightful way. After crushing the nose of the Pontiac, leaking oil ignited. Richard turned the flaming car towards the infield to a fire truck he knew was parked in turn one. Richard Petty Private Collection

Ouch! The STP Pontiac on the hook at Charlotte in May. Running mid-field left Richard in a position to get collected in some unfortunate wrecks. Elmer Kappell

Petty leads a gaggle of cars through turn four at Charlotte in May. Elmer Kappell

As the Fan Appreciation Tour reached the halfway point at Daytona for the Pepsi 400, the city of Daytona Beach unveiled a special city bus painted to honor Richard. Elmer Kappell

After having an accident during practice, Dale Inman and Robby Loomis work with the crew to get the car set back up. The suitcase and blocks are a set of computerized scales that show how much weight is on each wheel. Compare this deal with the "high tech" we saw earlier in the book. Elmer Kappell

Richard and the STP Pontiac on the road course at Sears Point Raceway, Sonoma, California. Note the size of the rear spoiler! Richard Petty Private Collection

Richard sits in his "office". The white cloth hanging from the front of his helmet is actually a white towel soaked in ice water. Richard used that to chew on and keep his mouth from getting dry. This was a habit of Richard's that dated back to his dirt track days.
Steve Mohlenkamp

The noseless STP Pontiac re-emerged from the garage area at the end of the race, a testimony to the dedication of Richard's crew. Elmer Kappell

Richard's last lap as a competitive driver. It didn't matter that Richard was not leaving the sport or that the car was battered. One look at the crowd in the background says it all. Elmer Kappell

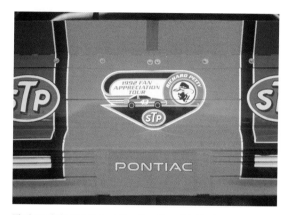

The logo of The Fan Appreciation Tour. Steve Mohlenkamp

Early in Richard's last race. Note the TV camera fin on the back edge of the roof. This was done to help the viewers see the field behind Richard as he led his final parade lap. The emotional moment was made for TV. Elmer Kappell

The 1992 Pontiac Grand Prix. Steve Mohlenkamp

The 1992 Pontiac Grand Prix Richard used in his last race is now housed in the Richard Petty Museum at the Level Cross facility. The car remains the same today as it ran on that final lap and it is an excellent study of recent stock car technology. Note that the wheels and suspension parts are painted "Equipment Blue" — not quite the dark blue used in the trim stripes, but obviously darker than "Petty Blue". Tim Bongard

Mark Martin's Valvoline T-Bird slips between Richard and son Kyle in the #42 Mellow Yellow Pontiac. Wayne Moyer

The front end as viewed from the driver's side. The use of single gas-filled shocks is evident here. Tim Bongard

The Fan Appreciation Tour car was one of the nicest-looking cars ever driven by Richard. Petty Enterprises has always been known for having equipment that was always well prepared. The STP Pontiac was a great-looking race car. Steve Mohlenkamp

Richard begins his career as a car owner

Lukewarm
Runs and Hot Laps

Retirement as a driver had a rather special beginning. Richard was honorary flagman at the beginning of the Daytona 500 with his son Kyle leading the field. Kyle had had earned the pole in the Mello Yellow Pontiac. Wilson is starting on the inside of the eighth row.
Richard Petty Private Collection

Have you ever gone on a vacation you thought would be interesting and had so dull a time that you couldn't even think of anything to fill up a postcard to Mom? Then you have a rough handle on how history views 1993 for Petty Enterprises.

Three things were rough for Petty fans to adjust to at the beginning of 1993. The first and most obvious was that Richard would no longer be at the wheel of the most famous stock car on the circuit. It was not only an adjustment for the fans, but it took some doing for the King as well. After all, he'd never seen the car race from the outside.

The second was that there wasn't going to be a #43 racing this year. The team decided that for at least the first year, the STP Pontiac from Level Cross would carry the number 44 instead of 43. The car would also carry the name of the driver on the car. Richard hadn't had his name on the car for many years, humbly contending that race fans should already recognize who was in the car and if they didn't, it didn't much matter.

The name that would be on the car came as a surprise. Rick Wilson, former driver of the #4 Kodak car prior to Ernie Irvan, was selected to drive. Though not regarded as a front-running driver, Wilson did have a reputation for bringing the equipment home in just about the same number of pieces he left with. That alone

would benefit a team trying to adjust to a new driver and Richard trying to adjust to his new role as an owner.

The season-opening Daytona 500 once again had a Petty in the headlines, although this time it turned out to be Kyle Petty. Kyle put the Mellow

Well, it looked like Richard's car, but there were a few other differences besides who was driving the car in 1993. LaDon George

Yellow Pontiac on the pole with a speed of 189.426 mph, saying, "If I knew I was going to run so good after he retired I would have had Momma lock him up in the house for the last seven or eight years."

The race began with Richard unfurling the green flag from the flag stand as his son led the cars to the start-finish line. Kyle, caught between

two lines of cars in the draft, was in tenth place before he could get back in line and work back toward the front. As the afternoon unfolded, Kyle's efforts were dashed when a hapless Bobby Hillin in the Helig-Meyers Thunderbird caught Kyle up in a wreck, ending Kyle's chances for his first Daytona win and placing him 31st.

Richard runs a hot lap around the Indianapolis Motor Speedway during the 1993 NASCAR test of the facility in anticipation of running the first Brickyard 400 scheduled in 1994. Wayne Moyer

Rick Wilson in the #44 STP Pontiac leads Dale Jarrett in the Interstate Chevy Lumina. LaDon George

Rick Wilson had driven for a number of other teams that included the #4 Kodak Oldsmobile before landing a ride with the King. LaDon George

Wilson on the other hand hadn't done too badly. He finished a respectable eighth in the first 125-mile qualifier, which gave him a 15th starting spot on the grid for the big race. He even led lap 51, although it was under caution. Unfortunately, his race ended early as well when he was involved in an accident in turn three on lap 140 — ironically, with Bobby Hamilton.

At Rockingham, Wilson finished the day roughly where he started, qualifying 15th and finishing three laps down in 17th. He did have the highest-placing Pontiac aside from Rusty Wallace, who was the race winner. That marginal distinction proved to be a high-water mark for many races to come. From the Pontiac Excitement 400 at Richmond on March 7 through the Hanes 500 at Martinsville at the end of April — six races in all — Wilson qualified no better than 18th and finished no better than 17th. Most of that early stretch found the STP Pontiac in the mid-twenties in both qualifying and finishing position.

For a time, though, it looked as if things were about to work themselves out and get the team moving to the front. A fourth-place qualifying effort at Talladega on May 2 was encouraging even though Wilson finished 16th — a season best. The SaveMart 300 two weeks later at Sears Point Raceway yielded an eighth-place finish after qualifying 20th. In Charlotte for the Coca-Cola 600, the team received its second DNF of the season, but came roaring back with a fifth-place qualifying run and an 11th-place

1993 PONTIAC GRAND PRIX SE

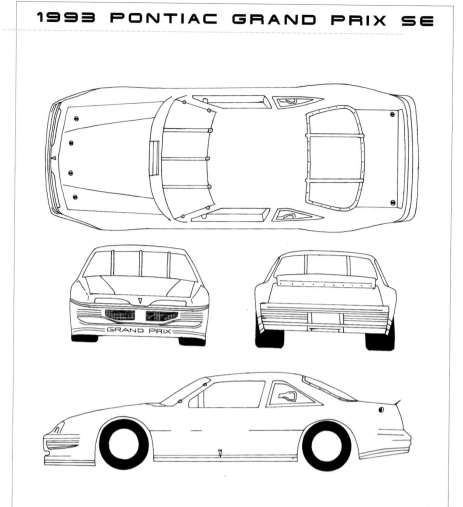

SIGNIFICATA

- New Hampshire International Speedway in Loudon, NH joins the schedule and hosts its first Winston Cup event.
- Passenger side glass and skirts are required on all tracks of 1 1/2 miles or longer in length. On shorter tracks, the cars must run without the side glass.
- Driving a Chevy Lumina, Dale Earnhardt wins his sixth Winston Cup Championship over the course of 30 races.

finish at Dover. It was something of a miracle: the Budweiser 500 was marred by 14 cautions in a horrendous wreckfest. "I've been in some pretty rough ones up here at Dover, but this is just about as bad as I've ever seen. Half the cars running had already been in the pits — some of them 20 laps and some of them for a hundred," Richard later said about the on-track carnage.

The stronger finishes continued a week later at Pocono, where Wilson finished 12th. While seemingly on the edge of cracking the top ten, the car was felled by an oil leak at the Michigan 400, handing the team another DNF for a 34th-place finish. Things were still looking up when the team arrived back at Daytona for the Pepsi 400 on July 3. Qualifying ninth on the grid, Wilson again hovered at the edge of the top ten with an 11th-place finish in the mid-season classic.

The Pepsi 400, however, was about it for the year's highlights. From that point on Wilson never finished higher than 21st; he almost seemed to slip further back in the field as the season rolled on. There were a few flashes of brilliance in qualifying: a sixth at Bristol in August and another sixth at Dover in September, but by then team members had become so disenchanted with Rick's performance that it was no secret they were looking for another driver. By the end of September they made an offer to Wally Dallenbach, Jr. to drive the STP Pontiac the following year.

Ironically, Wilson was injured in a wreck at Dover after qualifying so well. Jimmy Hensley substituted for him the following week at Martinsville and qualified eighth on the grid but his promising drive was cut short in an early wreck. While the team made repairs, the ensuing handling problems eventually forced Hensley and the team to retire the car early.

Wilson's performance and enthusiasm seemed to trail off after the Dallenbach announcement. The last half of the season simply slipped away like some foggy mist. The high point on the track came from the guy who wasn't supposed to take the wheel anymore. One of the more unusual events of the season for the Petty team took place at NASCAR's first full test for all teams at the famed Indianapolis Motor Speedway. The test was conducted to help teams find appropriate set-ups and to give NASCAR a chance to get operations ironed out for the first Brickyard 400

being held at the track the following year on August 6. During the test, Richard once again donned his driving suit and appeared on the track with a Pontiac bearing the STP logos and the #43 — to take a few ceremonial "hot laps" on the track.

Afterward, a 1992 STP Pontiac from the Fan Appreciation Tour, a car that was last run at Bristol, was presented to Speedway president Tony George and placed on display in the track museum. "I ran for 35 years and halfway dreamed of running Indianapolis with a stock car, not an Indy Car. The first thing they do when I retired is the Speedway cuts a deal with NASCAR," Richard said after his ride. "I really had second thoughts about it because I told everybody I wasn't going to get back out here after that last race in Atlanta. Hopefully, everybody knows it was just a P.R. deal and they will forget about it. I won't go back on my word on that part."

Looking back at 1993, however, a lot of folks probably wish he had.

When Wilson was injured, Jimmy Hensley got the nod to substitute for him. LaDon George

The car on display at the Speedway Hall of Fame Museum is one of Richard's 1992 Fan Appreciation Tour cars originally built in 1990 and is not the same car that he took laps in around the Speedway. Bill Coulter

At Martinsville Wilson got in trouble by getting the nose of his car shortened. He rejoined the field after repairs. LaDon George

It was odd to see the STP Pontiac with a number other than 43. Here Wilson races with Wally Dallenbach in the #16 Keystone Beer car. Dallenbach would replace Wilson behind the wheel of the STP car for 1994.
LaDon George

Richard and Indy President Tony George exchange some gracious words for the crowd. Richard donated one of his race cars to the Speedway Museum after the ceremonial hot laps.
Wayne Moyer

After a few quick circuits of the famous Indy oval, Richard brought the STP Pontiac back into the pits. It was the only time that the 1993 paint scheme appeared with the number 43 on it. Wayne Moyer

Looking a lot like Richard's final ride, Wilson limps the wounded STP Pontiac around the track.
LaDon George

1993 PONTIAC GRAND PRIX SE-INDY "HOT LAP" CAR

Dallenbach and Andretti show two very different levels of performance in STP Pontiac

A Tale of Two Drivers

When it was announced that Wally Dallenbach, Jr. would join the Petty organization for 1994, racing insiders thought that it would make the team more competitive immediately. Wally was coming to the Pettys from Roush Racing, where he had served as Mark Martin's teammate in the #16 Keystone Beers car. Though Wally did well in stock cars, his reputation as a racer came from a couple of impressive years running in the Trans-Am series in the SCCA. While running Roush-prepared Cougars in the mid-'80s, Wally clinched the Trans-Am championship and the runner-up spots. That, and the fact that his dad was a highly regarded driver in his own right, led one to believe that the boy could drive a car.

But the chemistry and personal dynamics that make racing teams gel is far from scientific. Often a "dream team," such as the Darrell Waltrip, Wadell Wilson, Hendrick Motorsports combo in 1987, never works out. On the other hand, stranger combinations, such as the Harry Hyde and Tim Richmond pairing in 1986, turn out better than anyone could ever imagine.

Things started off slowly at the Daytona 500 as Wally finished a lap down to the leaders in 17th. The following week at Rockingham, he made quite an impression — literally — on Jeff Gordon in turns one and two on lap 462, wrecking Jeff's car badly

enough to prevent Gordon from continuing the race.

If that alone didn't give fans a less than warm feeling for Wally, what happened next certainly didn't help. With the tire wars continuing in full song, qualifying had itself become a race just to get into the show — and there were a lot of losers! At the Pontiac Excitement 400, Dallenbach failed to get the car up to a qualifying speed. After the last attempt on Saturday failed, the team was forced to pack up and head for home. The team couldn't secure a provisional starting spot — one of three in the field — because two of them were determined by the point standings from the previous year, with the third spot reserved for a former champion. Because Rick Wilson's final points total had been so low in 1993, the team had to wait in line. Eight other drivers also went home unable to secure starting berths.

Not making the race a week later in Atlanta was even tougher on the team. Again the car failed to come up to the required speed, and again the team was too low on the list to get a provisional. The team was caught between a rock and a hard place. Now that the season was under way, the provisional starting spots were now being calculated on the points awarded thus far in the season. With a poor showing in the first two races and a complete no-show in the third, the team didn't have enough points to get

a provisional for Atlanta. By not making that race, the team sank even further down the list, with no points earned at all in the two races they didn't qualify for. Wally offered to resign, but Richard declined to accept. He took responsibility himself, saying he would have to put more time in with the team.

With so many teams struggling to make fields, NASCAR added provisional spots to most races and modified the system to determine provisionals so that teams like STP wouldn't face double jeopardy. The new system would allow for five provisional starters — the first two spots going to those drivers highest in the current year's points, the next two spots going to car owners from the previous year — again based on points — and the fifth spot reserved for a former Winston Cup champion who didn't make the field.

At Darlington at the end of March, Dallenbach made the field without the help of a provisional, but just barely. Qualifying next to last, the day ended early anyway with a failed engine on lap 131. Being the first car to retire, Dallenbach was awarded a 43rd-place finish — dead last.

The misery would have continued at Bristol, but by then the new provisional rules were in place and the team was able to take the first provisional spot in the field. Dallenbach salvaged a troubled run with a 17th-place finish, 36 laps down.

The nose of the '94 was also enhanced for racing purposes. Compare this to earlier versions.
Chuck Torrance

The 1994 Grand Prix was much smoother than in previous years. Note the flush fitting side windows.
Chuck Torrance

to the leaders.

North Wilkesboro was kinder and gentler to the STP team, with Dallenbach qualifying 27th and finishing 16th, only four laps down. Maybe things were starting to look up. Then again, maybe not. At Martinsville a week later, Dallenbach failed to qualify, and even the modified provisional rules didn't help. The team made the field at Talladega, but another crash ended their day and gave them a 34th-place finish.

On May 15, the tour moved west to Sonoma, California, and the road course at Sears Point Raceway. Dallenbach took to the track like a duck to water, qualifying seventh and finishing fourth. If that weren't enough on the good-news front, NASCAR had decided to help the Pontiac teams with the handling problems they had been experiencing. Starting with the Coca-Cola 600 at Charlotte, the Grand Prix would be allowed another two inches on the

front and four inches on the back, effectively giving the cars the downforce needed to match their Chevy and Ford rivals. Things were looking up again.

It came as a profound disappointment when Wally finished 25th in the Coca-Cola 600. His driving didn't show the sparkle of the week before. A week later, Wally finished tenth at Dover Downs after qualifying 27th. This was followed a week later on June 12 at Pocono with a 17th-place finish and a DNF following a late race crash that ruined a bid for a much higher finish in the top five.

Folks were starting to wonder about the hot-and-cold performance of the entire team. Was it the driver? Was it the car? Was it that the team was washed up and this proved it? Was it just a rash of really bad luck? Even Richard was wondering what it would take to get the deal to work.

Then came Michigan. At the Michigan International Speedway in

SIGNIFICATA

- Indianapolis Motorspeedway hosts the first Brickyard 400 and becomes an immediate fixture on the Winston Cup schedule.

- Hard coated polycarbonate windshields are permitted and become the standard material used for both the front and back windshields.

- NASCAR now allows the use of electrically driven cooling fans for the radiator. Teams are no longer required to use belt driven cooling fans.

- Custom seats, approved by NASCAR, are the only type allowed.

- Roof flaps are added just before the Daytona 500 as the latest device to help keep the cars on the ground. The flaps are required for all tracks of one mile or longer.

- Driving a Chevy Lumina, Dale Earnhardt wins his seventh Winston Cup Championship over the course of 31 races. This ties him with Richard Petty for the record number of championships won by a single driver.

Rookie stripe on Ole 43! John Andretti brought a wide yellow rookie bumper stripe along with his considerable talent to the STP Racer. Chuck Torrance

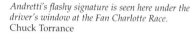

Andretti's flashy signature is seen here under the driver's window at the Fan Charlotte Race.
Chuck Torrance

Brooklyn, Wally failed to qualify the car for the fourth time. "The car was junk," he said. Wally believed it and the press printed it. Folks started thinking the Petty's equipment and team were no good. Frustration turned to nearly complete embarrassment as Dallenbach failed to qualify for the Pepsi 400, the renamed July 4th weekend classic at Daytona. To cap it all, he failed to make the race a week later in Loudon, New Hampshire. "I didn't think it could get any worse, but it keeps getting worse," said Dallenbach. Mercifully, he made the field for the second race at Pocono on July 17 and finished 16th, two laps down to the leaders. Wally qualified tenth a week later and finished eighth at Talladega. The occasional sparks of brilliance only added to the controversy over what was going on with that blue-and-red car.

The inaugural Brickyard 400 at the famous Indianapolis Motor Speedway will always be remembered as Jeff Gordon's victory. While Gordon and his Rainbow Warriors celebrated in victory lane, a yelling match spilled from the track into the garage area as things finally came to a head between Dallenbach and Petty crew chief Robbie Loomis. "The radios quit working," Petty explained. "Robbie was wanting to make some changes to try to get the radio to work. They didn't communicate in doing that. Then they both blowed up and Robbie just blowed up too much."

Team Petty is probably one of the most laid-back bunch you will ever run into. Richard's don't-get-worked-up attitude permeates the whole operation. So when team members start yelling at one another, it's big news. Obviously the team's performance had been disappointing, and the driver was sure it had to be the team. Fighting isn't tolerated in the house that Lee and Richard built. Richard talked to both Dallenbach and Loomis, and Dallenbach decided it would be best if he left the team. Watkins Glen would be his final race, after which he

and the Petty operation would part company. At that race, they ran well all day and kept the car up in the top five until a late-race incident with Rusty Wallace left Dallenbach limping home to 14th place.

The team was in 31st place in points by the time Wally left. "I'm not blaming the driver altogether. I'm not blaming the car altogether," Petty said. "The combination's not been there." The trick had become where to find it.

Richard would tell you that things happen for a reason. As things were reaching a head at Petty Enterprises, John Andretti was about to lose his ride with the financially troubled Billy Hagan team. Hagan, unable to attract a sponsor, was slowly being forced to shut down his operation. He decided that he would run only races that he had sponsorship for, which effectively put John out of a job.

Andretti's short career in stock car racing showed the potential of being able to drive anything that had wheels, just like his famous uncle Mario. An accomplished Indy car and LeMans-type racer, John simply had the misfortune of being a NASCAR

rookie with a struggling team. Hagan spoke to Richard about this talented young man when he became aware that Dallenbach's departure was imminent. Richard decided to give the young man a shot on a week to week basis.

In Andretti's first race for the team at Michigan International Raceway, the team prepared the car as usual — and added the yellow rookie stripe to the rear bumper of the STP Pontiac.

John put it on the outside of the front row.

The suspicions that the team was fielding subpar equipment which couldn't run up front evaporated like water in Death Valley. In the very place Dallenbach had called the car "junk," Andretti put it on the front row. John finished the day in 17th, but for once the team didn't have to worry about making the field.

The second Bristol race a week later had Andretti safely qualifying 23rd and finishing 30th after a crash on lap 261 put him out of the running. Darlington came next on September 4 and again, both Andretti and the team showed promise. John ran strongly throughout the race and finished 16th. "I know I drove hard because I about crashed every lap," John said after his dance with the track known as Lady in Black. He then backed it up a week later by qualifying 19th and finishing tenth at Richmond.

The next race at Dover yielded a 25th-place finish. And though he finished 21st at Martinsville, he had qualified again toward the front, starting fourth on the outside of the second row.

John's performance in the famed #43 car had proved in a few short weeks that the Pontiac Grand Prix was top-drawer equipment. For that matter, it showed that though still lacking seat time, John Andretti was a future talent who could really drive a race car. And obviously the chemistry among driver, crew, and equipment was much better with Andretti than it was with Dallenbach.

While the stats don't really show it

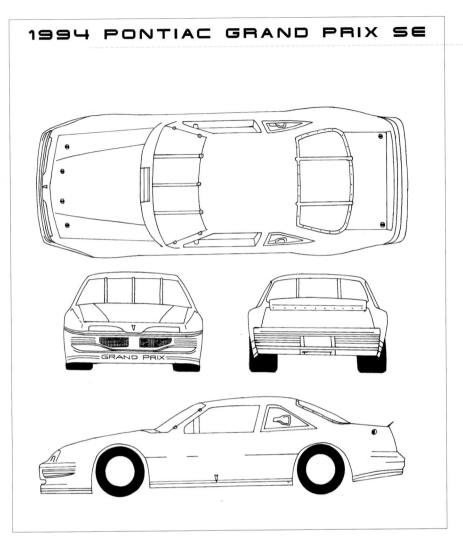

1994 PONTIAC GRAND PRIX SE

on their own, Andretti made the STP car do things Dallenbach couldn't — or at least didn't — while still logging time as a rookie. Mistakes were made a few times, but John impressed everyone enough that most Petty fans held their breath, hoping the matchup would be a permanent one.

In the last few weeks of the season he finished 21st at Martinsville, 17th at North Wilkesboro after starting third, and 24th at Charlotte. Rockingham proved to be difficult with a 25th-place finish some 26 laps down, after starting 36th in the field of 42 cars. Phoenix was no better, with a crash eliminating the car and handing Andretti his second DNF in the car. In the final race of the season at Atlanta, Andretti started ninth and finished 13th after leading the race for a while

under green. It gave Petty fans and the media a lot to cheer about. It was truly a swan song too, for John had already made up his mind to move to the new Kranefuss/Haas team.

At least the last weeks of the season with Andretti at the wheel had vindicated Robbie Loomis and the rest of the Petty team and pit crew. It vindicated the quality of the equipment being prepared by Dale Inman and the staff in the shops at Level Cross. There was room for improvement, but the team obviously still possessed the right stuff. It even made Pontiac look good for the first time since Rusty Wallace won ten victories driving a Grand Prix in 1993. Even though there was disappointment when Andretti left, there was one thing for certain: the boys from Level Cross still knew how to build a mighty good race car.

Bobby Hamilton puts the STP team back up front

Vindicaton

Bobby heads out for practice at Watkins Glen.
Jim Kupstas

It would have been easy to dismiss Petty Enterprise's rally at the end of the 1994 season as a flash in the pan or a quirk. But the dramatic way the team turned around seemed to indicate that a good chemistry between the driver, crew, and owner was as important as a good motor and chassis set-up. The encouraging closing half of the '94 season turned the STP team into a team on a mission, out to prove that the blue-and-red cars could still race with the best of them — in fact, even beat them. The flashes of brilliance fans saw weren't flashes in the pan at all — they were the signs of a team being welded together, and everyone was convinced that more sparks could fly.

The first problem, however, was to find a new driver to replace John Andretti. When Andretti decided to move on to the Kranefuss/Haas operation, Richard asked the team for input on the kind of driver who would work best with the team. Robbie Loomis said it best: he suggested looking for a driver with the same temperament as Richard himself. The team didn't have to look far. Kyle's former teammate, the 1991 rookie of the year, Bobby Hamilton is noted for his easygoing style, similar to Richard himself. Hamilton, aware that Richard was looking for a driver, hoped that he would get the nod. An announcement was made after the end of the '94 season that Hamilton would join the STP team for the 1995 season.

Speed Weeks at Daytona is always an exciting time as the team-driver-sponsor combinations debut. Hamilton had an especially strong spotlight trained on him, with the expectations that come with driving the most famous stock car in racing. The team had set some high goals for the year as well. The obvious one was to win a race, but the balance of the goals were high compared to the previous seasons' results.

The team decided to shoot for finishing in the top ten in points, not miss a single race, keep the car up front, and stay competitive with other pit crews in getting the car in and out of the pits quickly. Naturally, a pole would be nice, but with all those Fords and the new Monte Carlo, the Grand Prix certainly seemed like a dark horse.

Hamilton's response to all this was to simply mesh with the team from the very start. He qualified 25th for the Daytona 500 and finished 18th

In Bobby Hamilton, the STP team found someone that was just like Richard. Their performance together was a breath of fresh air to fans of the #43 car. Elmer Kappell

after an unfortunate run-in with Rusty Wallace. Though not a great way to start, at least the team was able to finish the race and on the lead lap.

Bobby then qualified 17th at Rockingham for the Goodwrench 500 a week later. A good run for the team

By 1995 most teams had switched to using radiators cooled with electrically driven fans instead of fans attached to the pulley assembly on the front end of the engine. Jim Kupstas

Richard still knows how to swing a mean wrench when he has to. Note that the interior of the STP Pontiacs are now light gray and not Petty Blue. Elmer Kappell

ended on lap 259 when an engine failed. A knee-jerk reaction might have been to think that things were back to the disappointing levels of the past few years, but the entire team and crew were stronger. Hamilton proved it the very next week. At Richmond, Bobby put the STP Pontiac on the front row, being edged for the pole by Jeff Gordon. Snow and cold dominated the weekend, favoring drivers patient and easy on their equipment — skills Bobby proved he has by finishing the race in ninth place.

From Richmond, the tour headed to Hampton, Georgia, and the Atlanta Motor Speedway for the Purolator 500 on March 12. Bobby qualified again in the top ten, putting the car ninth on the grid. Jeff Gordon dominated the race and the best Hamilton could manage was a 17th-place finish, four laps down. Two weeks later at Darlington for the TranSouth Financial 400, Bobby qualified 25th but finished ninth by avoiding some on-track mishaps. "We were right in the middle of every wreck and missed them all," Hamilton said. Though he claimed he just got some good openings to avoid the wrecks, team members will tell you that his peripheral vision is among the best in the business — and a lifesaver when it comes to avoiding trouble.

On April 2, Bristol hosted the Food City 500, where Bobby qualified solidly in 17th. The climb through the field wasn't easy, and the STP driver actually went a lap down after being spun by Brett Bodine on lap 134. But Hamilton stuck with it and fought his way back onto the lead lap by passing race leader Rusty Wallace on lap 288, which put him 12th in the field. After

that bit of vindication — Wallace had referred to Bobby at Daytona as "an also-ran" — Hamilton picked off car after car until at race's end he was an impressive fourth, right behind Darrell Waltrip. It was the best oval-track finish for the team since 1988, and the real vindication was that the car was the fastest on the track.

The strength the team was showing continued the following week at North Wilkesboro, when Bobby qualified a strong fourth on the grid and finished 13th for the day. Hamilton kept the car in the top ten most of the day. Then Lake Speed hit Bobby late in the race and caused a flat tire, forcing him to nurse the car to the finish and costing the team several places in the process. Nonetheless, by race's end, the STP team was eleventh in points.

Finishing the swing through the short tracks was the race at Martinsville on April 23. Bobby finished 8th. The Winston Select 500 at Talladega followed a week later. Bobby qualified 30th for the race and moved the car from the back of the pack to finish 15th on the lead lap. The road course of Sears Point Raceway in Sonoma, California, followed on May 7. Bobby qualified 21st and then pulled his way up through the pack to finish 14th.

The tour swung back to Charlotte for the running of the Coca-Cola 600 on the Memorial Day weekend. Though qualifying only 23rd on the grid, Bobby hauled his way through the field once again to finish ninth, taking a season-high seventh place in the points in the process.

The next month or so of racing wasn't as rewarding. The mid-season stretch began with the Miller Genuine Draft 500 at Dover, where Bobby qualified 14th and finished 24th, 22 laps down. The following week Pocono hosted the UAW-GM Teamwork 500. After qualifying third and leading some early laps, the car faded to 15th. A week later, on June 18 at Brooklyn, Michigan, Bobby finished 25th due to powerplant problems during the race.

Things didn't improve back at Daytona for the Pepsi 400 on July 1, either. Starting 39th in the field, the car lasted only until lap 118 before overheating ended the day for the famous #43. The skid continued at Loudon, New Hampshire, a week and a day later for the Slick 50 300. Bobby qualified 26th and finished 16th. That moved the team down to 13th in the point standings.

The team fared no better at Pocono or Talladega, with less than stellar results at either race. But the team worked hard and turned things

The first 1995 Grand Prix as it rolled out of the Petty shops. With more nose and tail area, there was hope that the Pontiac would be as competitive as the Fords and the Chevys. Nobody expected the new Monte Carlos from Chevy to dominate the first half of the season the way they did. Richard Petty Private Collection

This overhead shot at Watkins Glen shows a number of details worth noting. The nose of the Grand Prix was extended for 1995 and made flatter. The cowl area behind the hood was painted black, the center section of which is an inlet for air to the carburetor. Also note the rear window strake and roof flaps. Jim Kupstas

Rear spoilers are split down the center and have a gap between the sections to accommodate the template used to check the shape of the car. It's then taped over as shown here. Also note how the center stripe ends just in front of the spoiler. Tim Bongard

around again at the Brickyard 400 held at the famed Indianapolis Motor Speedway. Bobby qualified second, while rain delayed the second day of qualifying and eventually the race itself. Hamilton, however, was confident. The team obviously had the car hooked up to run well if conditions remained damp and cool and Bobby gleefully hoped that the rest of practice and qualifying would be washed out, giving the STP team a big advantage. Rain delayed the race until late

in the afternoon. Although Earnhardt dominated the race, the team did finish a strong 11th while other crews struggled with handling. The STP Grand Prix itself had problems turning in traffic with other cars.

From Indy, the tour moved eight days later to Watkins Glen's famous road course. The team struggled again, starting 37th and finishing 33rd, some 30 laps down. Of the cars still running at the end of the race, it was last.

A break back into the top ten came a week later at Brooklyn, Michigan, where the team finished eighth. Hamilton, who qualified for 11th place on the grid, ran a close second behind Bobby Labonte in the closing stages of the race. However, the STP team's fuel mileage was not as good as Labonte's, and a stop for fuel dropped the car back in the field. Bobby also continued to experience what he referred to as "aero push": the car refused to turn in any kind of traffic.

Bristol and Darlington's disappointing finishes offered no consolation, but in both cases the car finished higher than it qualified. At Bristol, Bobby qualified 31st in the field but managed a 20th-place finish, 44 laps down, after a rough night. Darlington was only slightly kinder, with a 14th-place finish after beginning in the 22nd spot. In recent years a 14th-place finish had been considered par, not a bad day. Now it was a disappoint-

1995 PONTIAC GRAND PRIX SE

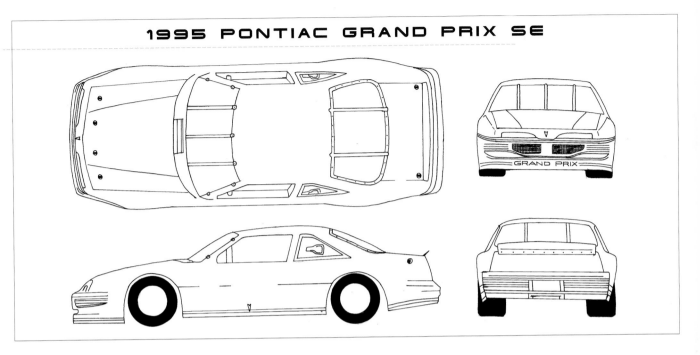

ment. The STP team had found its competitive desire again.

As if to underscore the point, the team stormed back into Richmond for the Miller Genuine Draft 400 on September 9. Bobby backed up a ninth-place qualifying effort by coming home fifth. Encouraged by this strong effort, the team arrived at Dover a week later for the MBNA 500. At first, it seemed as if the team's fortunes had reversed once again, with Bobby getting only a 32nd-place starting spot. But Hamilton again thundered through the field to lead 83 of the 500 laps around the Monster Mile.

Bobby Hamilton heads out of the garage area at Pocono. The 1995 Grand Prix was the most refined version of the car. Jerry Rutherford

While the 1995 paint scheme was simpler than in previous years, it was far from bland. This shot of the back of the car shows that the center stripe extends from the STP oval on the hood, across the roof and ends just in front of the rear spoiler, leaving the back panel solid blue. Jerry Rutherford

Jeff Gordon was the only thing that kept Hamilton from victory; Bobby finished a close second behind the DuPont driver.

The strong comeback continued at Martinsville for the Goody's 500 a week later, when Bobby showed the other side of his racing personality — patience. Cold and wet weather again curtailed practice. Hamilton started

12th on the grid, a position set by the point standings because qualifying had been washed out. During the race, conservative tire strategy kept the car competitive for longer runs. When the last caution came out, the team put only two tires on the car, and Bobby took third place at the re-start. A late pass by Terry Labonte dropped Hamilton to fourth at race's end, still good enough to give the team its third top-five finish in three races and move it back into tenth place in the points chase.

The Tyson Holly Farms 400 at North Wilkesboro was held on October 1. Again the team qualified well, putting Bobby third on the grid. After leading several times in the first half of the race, the car faded and eventually finished 16th. The tour then returned to Charlotte for the UAW-GM 500, where Bobby started ninth and finished tenth. The balance of the car was again out of whack, but the team was gradually figuring out what was causing the "aero-push." Fixed in tenth place after Charlotte, the team had a shot at finishing in the top ten if its luck held out.

Oh, for a bit of good racing luck. Petty fans held their breath and hoped for the best. Unfortunately, the last

The steep slope of the 1995 nose on the Pontiac is very evident here, especially when compared to previous years. Jim Kupstas

Even the smoothness of the windshield joining to the body is important. Molding is no longer used as seen here. Note the window clips and the straps used to secure the glass to the car. Tim Bongard

Richard gives Bobby some ideas about the handling of the car. Even though the Pontiacs had been refined for years, they still experienced a great deal of handling problems. Elmer Kappell

three races weren't what anyone could consider lucky. On October 22 at Rockingham, Bobby managed only a 30th-place finish, 21 laps down, in a disappointing and frustrating day. The STP car created a blinding cloud of collision-causing smoke as Hamilton tried to control the errant rear end of the car. Several cars meanwhile piled into one another. Ken Schrader, who was knocked out by running into the back of a slowing Mike Wallace, said it best: "I just couldn't get whoaed up in time."

Phoenix held a bit more promise. After qualifying eighth, Hamilton ran well until the car slowed suddenly and coasted into the pits with a broken distributor. After repairs, Hamilton's car was as fast as any other on the track, but the damage was already done. The result was a 31st-place finish, 19 laps in arrears.

The season-closing race was at Atlanta Motor Speedway on November 12, and again the team showed resiliency after the run of bad luck. Another excellent qualifying run put the STP Pontiac third on the grid.

As the race started, Bobby stayed right at the front, but Earnhardt wore the field out with a leading pace that bordered on monotony, and the red and blue #43 faded toward the back. Late in the race, a cut tire sent Bobby into the wall and tore up the right front corner of the car. The mishap relegated him to 25th place. The highlight of the day was Jeff Gordon capturing his first championship at the same track where he had made his Winston Cup debut in 1992 — on the same day that Richard ran his last race.

So what can be said for 1995 and the STP team? The team nearly met the lofty goals it set for itself. Its 13th place in points missed the top ten for the year by less than fifty points. Bobby, who ran more miles on the track than any other competitor, had only two DNFs for the season. He consistently qualified well and threatened

Wheels seem always to be changing. The STP team paints their wheels dark blue with a yellow pinstripe. Note the two valve stems — one for the inner liner and the other for the tire — and the small STP oval. Tim Bongard

to take a pole. Many observers believe it's a matter of time until he does. The same holds true of a win for Bobby and the team. If the team continues to mature as it has, driver and crew will eventually stand in victory lane once again. When they do, the fans are liable to tear the stands down in glee for seeing the famous number 43 back home where it belongs.

One of the features on the STP car is an adjustable Panhard Bar that can be adjusted with a socket wrench through the bright colored hole in the backglass. It is done much the same way the weight on the springs can be adjusted. Tim Bongard

The management of air into and around the cars has become so important. Note the various shapes of the ducts on or near the rear window. Tim Bongard

How a paint scheme looks on paper compared to how it actually looks on a car are two different things. A new scheme for the '96 season was first tested on an old 1995 Pontiac. Jimmy Martin/Petty Enterprises

Seeing how the real car would look gave the team a good idea of how much would be involved in preparing the special paint scheme and highlight a number of changes needed to fine-tune the final design as it would appear the following year. Jimmy Martin/Petty Enterprises

Look Ma, no fan! With the cooling fan attached to the radiator on its own bracket and separate motor, the front end of the motor looks like it's missing something. Note the single shock mounts used. Jerry Rutherford

Gas-filled shocks are what all the teams are using nowadays. The valve stem at the top of the shock allows the team to set each shock with a different gas pressure. NASCAR does not allow the changing of pressures during races. Jerry Rutherford

The STP Pontiac goes through inspection. Roof height and air dam clearance are being checked here. Note the grille work and the relative flatness of the side of the car compared to earlier years. Jerry Rutherford

The possibilities are endless

The Boys are Back

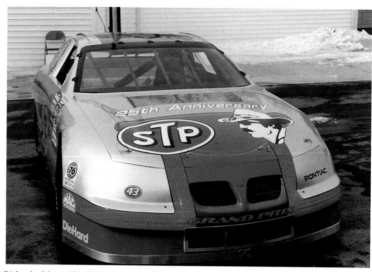

Richard celebrated his 25th season with STP as his sponsor with this special paint scheme and four other commemorative schemes throughout the season. Stan Cavanass

Y ou didn't have to be one of the faithful followers of the Petty clan to realize that something serious was going on down in those shops at Level Cross. There were warning signs throughout 1995. No one could miss the rumblings and flashes of brilliance as the team moved closer and closer to the consistency and power that would eventually put them back in victory lane once again. After coming off a strong showing in 1995, it seemed that Bobby Hamilton's racing abilities were meshing beautifully with Robbie Loomis' young crew. With a little coaxing and coaching from Dale Inman and Richard, the crew was getting stronger and more competitive. On more than one occasion Richard has said, "All these boys need to do is learn how to win. They get a taste of that first one and there will be no stoppin' them." No one doubted that the team would win again, it was simply a matter of when.

The very real prospect of seeing the famous #43 back in victory lane was a tantalizing thought for most Petty fans, but there was plenty of other exciting news and changes coming out of Level Cross.

The most obvious was the introduction of Pontiac's new Grand Prix. For years, the Grand Prix had been Winston Cup's also-ran. It always looked fast but never lived up to its potential. Even with nose extensions, tail extensions, and various forms of body doctoring, race crews frequently found themselves having to work harder at keeping their cars from being shamed into the garage area by the Chevys and Fords. Thankfully, 1995 was the last season the teams would have to race the old body style.

In the 1996 season Pontiac would be running a new version of the Grand Prix with a completely restyled body. Based on the same body as Chevrolet's potent Monte Carlo, the new Grand Prix was thought to have enough of the "right stuff" in aerodynamics, downforce, and straight-line speed to be able to duke it out with the other makes on an equal footing. In fact, Pontiac's new car was so similar to its GM sister, that some jokingly referred to it as the "Ponti-Carlo". With a much bigger tail end, larger greenhouse, and sharply sloping nose, it looked as if the Pontiac boys would be instantly more competitive and not have to worry about having to sort out their car as much.

Aside from being a great-looking race car, it didn't hurt that the Petty Winston Cup Pontiacs would be decorated in an array of STP paint schemes commemorating their 25 year associa-tion with the King and his cars. Four of Richard's more significant paint schemes from the past were used to decorate the new car. For the road courses at Watkins Glen and Sears Point, the car was painted in the plain solid blue with STP ovals that had adorned the 1972 Road Runner during Richard's first win for STP at Riverside. For the bulk of the season, fans were treated to two versions of the familiar red and blue paint scheme that adorned many of his Dodge Chargers and Chevys during the '70s. A fourth paint scheme for the new Pontiac recalled the colors that Richard's Grand Prix carried on his 200th win at the Firecracker 400 in 1984. The most spectacular scheme was the silver anniversary scheme itself. Far from tame, this special scheme had to be seen in person to be fully appreciated. The car was mostly silver with a band of Petty Blue around the bottom and a wide blue band across the top extending from the front bumper towards the rear deck lid. The Petty Blue and silver areas were separated by Rocket Red stripes — the numbers also appearing in red instead of their usual white.

The road course cars were painted just like Richard's 1972 Road Runner when he won his first race for STP at Riverside, California. The sponsor deal had been sealed just days before.
Stan Cavanass

This tail shot of the new Grand Prix shows off the huge amount of glass area and spoiler at the back of the car that helps create downforce. Stan Cavanass

The real attention getter on this paint scheme was the red and blue colors breaking up at the back end of the car giving the illusion that the paint was being ripped of the car by shear speed — even when standing still!

The commemorative schemes were a dynamic success for STP and garnered a huge amount of interest from spectators, fans, collectors and especially the media. Collector's additions of the cars were next to impossible to find and sold at a premium. Coping with five differently decorated cars was a real chore for the team, especially for Johnny Cline's body and paint department, but at one point it could have been a lot worse. During the 1995 season when Richard and STP were discussing the possible ways the 25th anniversary could be celebrated, they actually considered painting one of each paint scheme that had ever appeared on the famous #43 during the STP years. That would have been over 26 schemes!

There was more news that fueled the rumor mills and hopes of many long time Petty fans. There was another addition to King Richard's posse. Rich Bickle would drive a third #43 — but this one would be a Dodge. With the unabashed success and wild growth that NASCAR's new Super Truck series (now called the Craftsman Truck Series) was enjoying, Chrysler decided to jump in with both feet and worked out a deal that would renew the old alliance that had worked so well in years gone by. Ford and Chevy each had staked a claim in this new enterprise and to the delight of many,

so did Dodge. Without any serious factory support in 1995, Dodges consistently threatened to win as the dark horse entries. For 1996, ChryCo had upped the ante by backing a few teams — one of which was a newly formed Petty operation.

The format of the series, while similar to that of the Winston Cup Series and the Busch Grand National Series, was designed to keep costs down and keep the racing at a maximum. Races feature a break at the half way point which allow teams to do any work necessary on the trucks. This actually saves money for the teams since it requires fewer crew members than if they had to have a full contingent for yellow or green flag work like in the other two series. The engines are also restricted to a maximum compression ratio of 9.5 to 1 instead of the 14 plus to 1 that the Winston Cup mills run at. The lower compression ratios mean that the engine costs less to build, will last longer, and can be maintained for a lot less. All this translated into a racing program that could be run for right around a million dollars instead of a multi-million dollar deal that the STP Pontiac requires on the senior circuit.

Aside from those enticing reasons to get involved, there was one singular fact that proved to good to pass up. Pontiac doesn't make a pick-up truck that wouldn't be involved in the series. Richard couldn't very well run a Chevy without getting the boys at Pontiac riled from a corporate political standpoint. Worse yet might be picking a Ford, although seeing Fords again at Level Cross is somewhat hard to

imagine. But Dodge does have a pick-up and the Dodge Ram 150 was quickly becoming one of America's most popular trucks and had won numerous awards. Running a Dodge made sense at many different levels. Maurice Petty was willing to create "new" engines for the program, but the engine being used was based on the same 340 wedge that had been used with so much success almost 20 years ago. And nobody knows how to milk horsepower out of a 340 like Maurice. After all these years, he is still considered the professor of power when it comes to Chrysler engines. This program would also give the Pettys an effective R&D program in order to evaluate what potential a Dodge racing program could have. The folks at Chrysler have maintained that they weren't going to get involved in Winston Cup racing. From the Petty's point of view, good luck happens when preparation meets opportunity. If Chrysler ever changed its mind, the Pettys would be ready. That fact alone would keep Pontiac joyfully supporting the Winston Cup effort to the max in a common sense effort not to lose one of its most valuable teams.

By the end of 1995, a deal had been arranged with Dodge to become one of its two "factory-backed" teams. Richard then looked for a suitable driver, even speaking with long time friend Joe Ruttman. Ruttman was leading the points race in the truck series at the time, but he made a deal with Ford instead. The team then turned to short track master Rich

Bickle who turned out to be another of those drivers cut from the same easy going cloth as Richard. Mike Cheek, Petty's Chief Fabricator and Shop Foreman for his Winston Cup team was chosen to be the General Manager and Crew Chief of the new Ram clan. With the acquisition of shop facilities in nearby Thomasville, North Carolina, the team was ready to roll for the 1996 season.

As race cars, er..trucks go, the pick-ups feel very similar to the Winston Cup and BGN coupes. In fact, in spite of what you might think about their shape, they are more like the cars than they are unlike the cars. Throughout the course of this book, we've seen how aerodynamics have played such a key role in who's at the front and who's on the trailer heading home when the green flag drops. It would seem logical then to think that a pick-up truck dressed up in typical NASCAR racing trim would have the aerodynamic qualities of a slightly rounded brick. Worse yet, with no back glass to speak of, it would also seem logical that there wouldn't be much in the way of downforce to keep the tale end stable. A brick that wants to swap ends all the time may sound interesting, but who would want to drive something like that? Rich Bickle admitted to having similar reservations before driving one of the new trucks. "It does seem as if it shouldn't

Most folks expected the new Dodge Ram to be sponsored by STP and race in the familiar Petty Blue and STP Rocket Red paint scheme. Instead, the truck is actually sponsored by Dodge and Cummins engines. Dodge nixed the blue as a "Plymouth" color, so the pick-up is raced in Dodge's corporate red. Richard Petty Motorsports

Under the familiar looking skin of the truck is a NASCAR-style roll cage and chassis. In a manner similar to their Winston Cup cousins, the truck chassis is designed to protect the driver at all times. Chris and Brian Werkheiser

The rear corner of the chassis on the passenger side shows just how much shorter the cage is from front to back because of the size of the pick-up's cab. All the rest of the gear and arrangements are what we would expect from NASCAR. Chris and Brian Werkheiser

SIGNIFICATA

- Pontiac unveils the new Grand Prix, based on the same body as the Monte Carlo.
- Ford is allowed to reduce its roof height by 1/2 inch.

be all that stable, but the trucks really do have a lot of sticking power and downforce on the back. They really are a lot of fun to drive." Fellow Dodge driver Jimmy Hensley added, "They really don't feel all that much different from the Cup or Busch cars. The difference has as much to do with the wheel base as it does the shape." Then again, they aren't trying to run the trucks at more than 190 mph at Daytona either.

By mid-year in 1996, a full blown competition had developed between the Petty teams. The truck team had managed a trio of poles and it was

definitely a race to see who could put their car (or truck as the case might be) in the winner's circle first. Obviously, the Dodge Ram was one very potent competitor.

As for the Winston Cup boys, their effort showed strength and promise early on in the season. At Rockingham in February, Bobby was leading the race when Dale Earnhardt gave him one of Dale's patented taps that sent the STP Pontiac into the fourth-turn wall. Feeling unnecessarily robbed of their first win seemed to make the team all the more determined. Bobby's finishes grew consistently

1996 DODGE RAM PICK-UP

The race truck operation is in a facility separate from the Winston Cup operation in Level Cross. This overhead shot shows just how busy these teams had become since the series started.
Chris and Brian Werkheiser

better and stronger. A poor qualifying effort at Daytona left them with a 20th place finish at the end, but the team bounced back at Richmond by qualifying third and finishing sixth. They followed that up by starting sixth at Atlanta where they finished 16th and an eighth place finish at North Wilkesboro where they qualified fourth on the grid.

After finishing 5th in the June race at Pocono, he roared to the pole the following week at Michigan. Bobby then followed up his first pole a week later with another front row start at New Hampshire. Upon returning to Michigan, the team qualified fifth and finished 13th and then later showed its strength at Bristol by qualifying 35th and clawing its way to a 10th place finish. Bobby followed this effort up with a seventh place finish at the second Richmond race and another claw-your-way-to-the-front by starting 40th at Dover and finishing 10th. Bobby's second pole came at Martinsville in September where he finished the race with a strong third. The team wasn't just being competitive on one type of track, they were showing strength on every type of track.

The breakthrough finally came at the Dura-Lube 500 at Phoenix in late October. They not only won the race, but did it with a dominant car. For any one keeping track, a Petty Enterprises car hadn't won since October 9, 1983 at Charlotte, so it had been a long time coming.

The team finished out the season with a sixth place finish in Atlanta which also put Bobby ninth in the final Winston Cup points standing. Good qualifying efforts, solid finishes, two poles, and a treasured win — 1996 proved that the boys from Level Cross were back.

The same care and attention in making NASCAR race cars look as much like their street-going counterparts extends to the truck series as well. Here a template is used to check the profile across the front end of the Ram. Chris and Brian Werkheiser

This shot of the front end of the Grand Prix clearly illustrates how much curve there is to the body, helping direct the airflow over and around the car. Stan Cavanass

Maurice Petty and his sons run the engine shop and a good part of the truck operation. Here Maurice prepares one of his 340s for testing and break-in on the dynamometer. Chris and Brian Werkheiser

Craftsman Series Trucks, like their Winston Cup counter parts, use sheet metal to "skin" the cars (or trucks, as the case may be) over a tube sub-frame as seen here in the Ram's engine bay. Chris and Brian Werkheiser

The 25th Anniversary cars appeared at Daytona and Talladega. Note how the paint scheme breaks up towards the back of the car. Stan Cavanass

This is what one of Richard's Dodge Rams looks like before the paint is applied. The red and white paint scheme reflects Dodge's corporate colors. *Chris and Brian Werkheiser*

NASCAR's newest series is based on the ever popular American pick-up truck. Stock cars — or should we say stock trucks — have the familiar look of the street versions with some obvious changes such as ride height. *Chris and Brian Werkheiser Dodge trucks courtesy of Ilderton Dodge, High Point, NC*

Dodge has produced one of the more exciting body-styles in the North American truck market today. The racing version looks all the more impressive in its complete set of markings as shown here. *Chris and Brian Werkheiser*

To celebrate the return of Richard to the Mopar fold in 1996, Master Vans & Trucks of Ocala, FL created this special "Petty Signature Series Super Truck" based on the sharp looking Dodge 1500 Ram pick-up. *Chris and Brian Werkheiser*

Kyle returns home to form pe²

Full Circle

Sporting a colorful nose for Daytona was the newest version of the famous STP paint scheme.
Elmer Kappell

I t's funny how things come full circle. Motorsports history will record that the 1990s was the decade when multi-car teams became the rage and that many well-established Winston Cup teams cloned themselves to become two- and three-car operations in an effort to gain a competitive edge by sharing as much technology and information as possible. Teams such as Hendrick Motorsports, Robert Yates Racing, and Roush Racing set the standard by running two or three cars each. Even RCR, Richard Childress' operation, found Dale Earnhardt running with a teammate — an unthinkable notion just a few years before. For better or for worse, multi-car teams seemed to be the way to insure having a competitive car week in and week out.

As for Petty Enterprises, they had done the multi-car team deal at a time when they were the only team doing it or even capable of doing it back in the '60s and the early '80s. That all ended when Kyle had been driving for a few years and trying to field two cars became too much for both the team and the family. The Pettys know what it takes to make multi-car teams work. They were able to say with authority: "Been there. Done that." They also know what makes a multi-car effort fail. Time and hindsight had taught everyone some valuable lessons. With Maurice returning to help run the Craftsman Truck team and Dale Inman running the Winston Cup team

as the GM, the only thing that was missing was the return home of Richard's only son, Kyle.

Kyle Petty had been driving for Sabco Racing. They had recently gone the route of becoming a multi-car team. The Felix Sabates team had been Kyle's home when he was the only driver they had, piloting the #42 Mellow Yellow Pontiacs for the team. The first few years were pretty good for Kyle and Felix, with a number of wins and good finishes. The team was strong enough that they finished fifth in the Winston Cup points battle two years in a row — 1992 and 1993. This made everyone think that Kyle had finally come into his own as a driver and competitor. But something went wrong in the years that followed and no matter how hard Felix, Kyle, and the crew tried, the ensuing Winston Cup seasons could easily be described as a "fishin' hole with no fish". Finally, in October of '96 Kyle announced that after leaving Sabco, he would be starting his "own" team.

In typical Kyle style however, his idea of having his own team just put a

different twist on the currently popular multi-car team deal. His operation would be called "pe²", short for Petty Enterprises Two and would operate like a copy of the original family team. But instead of operating out of the same shops or from the same grounds, pe² took up residence in the old RaMoc shops in nearby Thomasville, North Carolina. The teams would share information and equipment without having to be in one another's hair.

For the greater family at Level Cross, Kyle creating pe² was very much a homecoming. The younger Petty even went back to using his original number, 44, and found a new sponsor with Mattel Toys and their Hot Wheels line of toy cars. The set up allowed the teams to freely exchange information when needed, without putting any real drain on either operation.

At the same time, the STP team had hopes that the '97 season would just be a continuation of the success and growth from the previous years and with a certain amount of justification. The team remained virtually unchanged from the previous season and the new

New team, new colors, new sponsor. Kyle at the wheel of his new Hot Wheels Pontiac.
Elmer Kappell

The 1997 scheme featured "Tiger Stripes" to help break up the colors on the STP
Elmer Kappell

Note how the numbers on Kyle's car always slant toward the front of the car, giving them a very
different look.
LaDon George

Pontiac Grand Prix had proven itself to be a winner and better competitor than its predecessor. While the teams were still working on refining the handling of the car, the playing field for the Pontiacs was at least level.

One of the big questions after the STP Silver Anniversary was what the 1997 paint scheme would look like. Wild or exciting schemes had become very much in vogue, using every visual trick in the book to make the cars as attractive as possible. The problem was that the classic STP scheme had used just about every variation of lines and stripes that you could possibly imagine. It was time for some fresh ideas.

Richard and STP could have gone to any number of companies that specialize in graphics in order to get the King a new set of clothes, so to speak. But instead, Richard and STP's management turned to the fans and asked them to contribute ideas for a new paint scheme and made it a contest to boot. The winner of the contest would see his scheme appear on the STP Pontiac all year long, while the finalists would have their ideas displayed together as a special art exhibit during Speedweeks.

The response was a surprise to everyone. Thousands of submissions poured in and were waded through by the judges. It also proved just how popular NASCAR's Winston Cup Series had become, with entries coming in from all 50 states in the U.S. and nine other countries. The final scheme selected was penned and painted by Lars Svensson of Sweden.

The Swede's impressive work adds a whole new dimension to the classic STP scheme. Svensson combined some of the visual highlights from some of Richard's more successful schemes with flowing lines that help accentuate the Grand Prix's, curvy body. Each scallop is further enhanced by broad white and dark blue stripes, while the nose of the car features a splash of white and yellow that makes the car appear as if it has the world's fastest flame job. In a nut shell, the winning paint scheme evokes all the dazzle of the special Silver Anniversary scheme while maintaining all the classic elements that make the famous #43 the most recognizable race car in the world and worthy of carrying on the lineage of race cars known as *The Cars of the King*.

A look at Petty transporters and car haulers over the years

Getting from Here to There

One of the more interesting stories we discovered while preparing this book was the development of the Pettys' car haulers and transporters. As one of the front-running teams, Petty Enterprises consistently found better ways of getting its race cars and equipment to the tracks and back home again.

In the early years of stock racing, drivers literally packed the family and tools into the car they were going to race and drove to the track. But as race cars began to evolve further and further from stock, they became less and less "street legal." The drive to and from the track became somewhat precarious as a result.

In his autobiography, King Richard I, Richard relates driving a lightly disguised race car across country in order to meet up with the rest of the team — in California. First he had some cutdown truck mufflers spliced onto the header pipes in a half-hearted attempt to quiet the car. Then, during a rainstorm in North Carolina, Richard had to stop and get windshield wipers — they're not standard operating equipment on a race car. By the time he reached the desert out West, he had been stopped by the authorities only once — and they let him go. Now he flashed by a sign that read "Arroyo" — a word unknown to him and most folks east of the Mississippi. It means "dry creek bed." Unfortunately, this dry creek bed had about four feet of water, which the car hit at about 100 miles an hour. "I couldn't see a thing for a few seconds," Petty wrote. "I mean, the car was completely engulfed in water, and the spray must have been visible back home." He and the car eventually dried out and continued the trip, but he'd learned that cops weren't the only road hazard he had to worry about.

Typically, in the early years, race cars were towed behind a tow car, light truck, or station wagon on twin-axle, open-bed trailers. That solved the problems with the local authorities, but it didn't help the team's need to haul more and more equipment. So by the mid-60s cars were towed behind cargo trucks. The cargo trucks could carry much more equipment, heavier tools, and more trucks.

Pictures from that time show the team's cars on trailers behind a custom-built Dodge with a double cab that had additional seating in the back for crew members. When the Pettys raced Fords in 1969, the team acquired a custom cabover Ford-powered rig for hauling. The team kept the Ford following the '69 season after reverting to the Dodge trucks.

This photo shows a few interesting points. First, the trucks in the background show what everybody else was using at the time. Secondly, the car ramp the Olds Cutlass is on rolled in and out on the rollers and last, the rear doors continued the paint scheme on the inside of the doors. Richard Petty Private Collection

Plymouth provided the Petty team with an extended cab cargo truck that was outfitted as a rolling shop by the team. Here they unload a Hemi engine while another one sits on a pallet on the ground. Bill Coulter

Things remained this way for a while, but running a race car on an open trailer behind a fairly large truck can become a soggy proposition, even in a light rain shower.

Around the time that the STP sponsorship began in the early '70s,

The problem with cargo trucks and trailers was how to protect the car — especially in rain storms. A Torino is being towed on a trailer behind the team's truck in 1969. Chuck Torrence

It wouldn't do to have a Plymouth truck hauling a Ford race car around, so Ford provided the Pettys with a Ford cargo truck to do all the hauling duties. Chuck Torrence

A Dodge tractor was the first tractor used to pull the customized fully-enclosed lowboy that carried the team's tools and car. Bill Coulter

When the old Dodge finally gave out, the team secured a Kenworth cabover to tow the hauler. Note that it, like the Dodge, has only one rear axle. Richard Petty Private Collection

Richard decided to enclose a lowboy heavy equipment trailer, so the team could tow the car with all the equipment and car safely sheltered in an enclosed trailer. Reed Trailer created a trailer that set a standard from which others were developed. "It was a real handful to drive, let me tell you," says Jimmy Martin, now the public relations manager for Petty Enterprises. During those years, Jimmy was a crew member who occasionally drove the rig to a number of races. "We had a Dodge T1000 tractor to pull the thing with. It was the last of the tractors that Dodge made before they stopped producing the big trucks. A few years after we had the trailer built, we put an air-ride suspension under it and it made driving it a whole lot easier. But prior to that, man, you could have your hands full," Martin says with a smile and a chuckle. Initially, the trailer was painted white and dark blue with STP logos on it.

The old Dodge was put in storage when it started showing signs of age,

and the team acquired several tractors to tow the modified lowboy. In due course the team used an Autocar and various Kenworth cabovers.

By 1982, teams had started to use modified moving-van trailers as the basis for their custom-built car haulers. Richard and Kyle used a specially painted trailer and Kenworth Aerodyne tractor provided by Saunder's Leasing System. This car hauler is famous for its paint scheme featuring the likenesses of Kyle and Richard.

By 1983 Kyle's operation was sponsored by 7-Eleven. The repainted trailer was towed behind a white Kenworth cabover tractor.

The trailers continued to develop, and the tractors kept changing as well. After a stint using Kenworth tractors, the team received some White/Volvo tractors from GM.

By the time the Fan Appreciation Tour began in 1992, the team was using custom-built trailers from Featherlite. An arrangement with

Navistar gave the team some beautiful International 8300 tractors to haul equipment from place to place. That combination is still being used today, with new components added from time to time. The trailer used during the Fan Appreciation Tour is now used by Richard's Busch Grand National team; the trailer used through the 1995 season will tour the country as part of a promotional arrangement with Navistar. And like the new Pontiac the team has for 1996, everyone will keep on truckin' it around in style in a brand-new Featherlite trailer.

The Petty organization is truly sold on the Navistar equipment they have. In addition to the tractor used to pull the race hauler, they also have a number of other trucks to help with duties around the shop. One of the most unusual of these vehicles is a fully enclosed roll-back show car hauler. Navistar provided the dual cab and chassis, while Jerr-Dan custom built the lift bed and enclosures. The truck is basically a standard roll-back that can winch the car onto the bed and secure it for travel. The bed is then fully enclosed with a box body to protect the car from the elements. The truck is as much a showstopper as the car it hauls!

The next step up was to a modified moving van, provided by Saunders Leasing System. The tractor has grown to a Kenworth Aerodyne sleeper cab as well. Richard Petty Private Collection

One of the more unusual trucks in the Petty Enterprises fleet is this enclosed rollback tow truck used to haul the showcars around the country. Tim Bongard

When the roll back is in the travel position, you might never suspect how the truck actually works. Aside from being easier to handle than a duely pick-up and trailer, the Petty rig gets as much attention as the show cars themselves. Tim Bongard

In recent years, the team has graduated to bigger tractors and larger trailers as purpose-built car haulers have become commonplace. This was the set-up at the beginning of the 1990s, before the Fan Appreciation Tour. Since then the team has gone through two more Featherlight Trailers. Richard Petty Private Collection

This rear angle shot of the trailer parked at the Level Cross shops shows off some interesting details. The car in front is a Dodge kit car designed to run on short tracks. Richard Petty Private Collection

The standard Jerr-Dan roll back bed was enclosed to protect the car as it travels. The car is winched up onto the bed just as it would be on a tow truck. The oversized cab is designed to accommodate the driver on the long cross-country trips that can be expected on the show car circuit. Tim Bongard

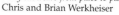

This three-quarter angle shot from the rear clearly shows the unusual configuration of the enclosed rollback truck that is used to transport the Petty showcars from place to place. Chris and Brian Werkheiser

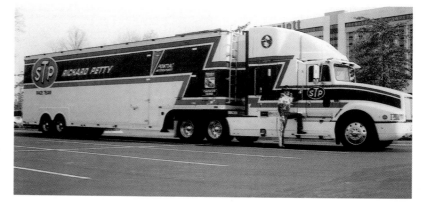

Model
Building
Section

Model by Jerry Rutherford

How to build a decent model without injury

Basic Building Techniques

Models by Mike Madlinger

Models by Bill Coulter

Building a good model of your favorite Petty race car is not that difficult. Whether you're a novice or an experienced model builder, a few basic building techniques can go a long way toward helping you achieve your goal.

First, you need a place to work, a place where you're not constantly in other people's way. It's always nice if you can dedicate a place to work: your workshop, your den, an extra bedroom, or a clean corner of the basement. Some modelers are content with "setting up shop" at the kitchen table or on a convenient folding table. A comfortable chair and good lighting are also essential.

Most basic model building can take place in any of these situations. When it comes to spray painting, however, a well-ventilated area is a must. If the weather conditions are good, you can try spray painting your model outdoors. If you must spray primer and paint indoors, stay away from the forced-air furnace or any open flame. Work near a window that can be opened for ventilation when you're finished. And be sure to wear a spray mask that covers both the nose and mouth so you don't breathe in all those fumes.

Once you have selected the Petty model you want to build and set up your work site, you will need some tools to work with. Your first investment should be a good number 11

hobby knife. It is the one tool you will likely have in your hand most often while building. A word of caution here. Hobby knife blades are extremely sharp and must be handled with great care to avoid a painful cut.

Along with the hobby knife you will need to add a jeweler's file, emery board, tweezers, sprue cutters, two grades of automotive-type wet/dry sand paper (preferably a medium grade like 320 and a fine grade like 600 will do), a small tube of automotive body filler, masking tape, and glue. **(Photo #1)**

There are a wide variety and many types of glues that are used in model car building. **(Photo #2)** The most basic is styrene tube glue. It's good for the

novice but be cautioned that it dries very slowly and gets stringy with age. Liquid glues are excellent for attaching styrene parts to each other, but they will not allow you to bond to other types of materials. Super glues are great because they are fast drying and will bond any types of materials together. However, they are a bit tricky to use because they do not always form a strong bond and become ineffective quickly due to their short shelf life. And since super glue bonds virtually any materials, it is very easy to stick your fingers together if you're not very careful!

Building a model in the style commonly referred to as "out-of-the-box", you'll first need to check the contents of the kit box against the instruction sheet. **(Photo #3)** This is always a good idea for two reasons. First, you want to be assured that all the parts it takes to build the model are indeed in the box before you actually start building. Secondly, checking out the parts

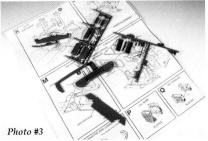

Photo #1

Photo #2

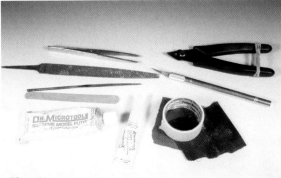

Photo #3

against the instructions familiarizes you with how the manufacturer intends the model to be put together.

Remove the parts carefully from the sprue trees with a sprue cutter. **(Photo #4)** This is especially good advice when removing plated and clear parts. If the part is removed improperly, a nick in the edge of a bumper or section of window glass is nearly impossible to repair.

Carefully glue together the pieces that make up assemblies like the engine and transmission, roll cage, and suspension components. **(Photo #5)** If you've chosen to use regular styrene glue, make certain the pieces hold firmly together until the glue has dried by wrapping a short piece of masking tape around the assembly. A household clothespin or rubber bands will also secure the pieces. Set the assemblies aside and allow sufficient time for the glue to harden. Use super glue sparingly and avoid getting it on your fingers, work surfaces, and unwanted areas of the model, such as the plated and clear parts.

As assemblies are taking shape, clean up any excess flashing or remnants of the little tags where parts were attached to the sprue. Use a file, emery board, or sandpaper. Pay special attention to removing mold lines. Use body putty to fill sink marks on the body shell, ejector pin marks on

parts like the chassis, and fill seams where the engine halves meet. **(Photo #6)** Apply putty sparingly in thin coats, especially if you have a large or deep area to fill. Once thoroughly dry, the putty can be sanded to blend in with surrounding areas.

When you have completed the initial stage of the preparation and assembly, you are ready to apply paint to various parts of the model. Some items can be painted with bottle paints and good quality artist's brushes. In most cases a number 1, 0, and 000 brush will cover all applications. **(Photo #7)**

Prime everything that is to be painted, including small pieces you will likely brush paint. Priming is especially important if the color of the plastic parts contrasts with the final color you want. Using a piece of stiff card stock or cardboard, tape the individual parts in evenly spaced rows with loops of masking tape. **(Photo #8)** This step makes it quite easy to account for all parts that need primer and to ensure that they all get a thorough, even coating. Use a primer suited to styrene plastics, such as Testor's Flat Gray Primer.

Once you have primed all the small parts and assemblies, rearrange the primed parts into groups of parts by the intended color. All the parts that are to be painted black, white, red, silver, yellow or whatever color can now be grouped together in the same fashion as when the original primer was applied.

Assemblies like the engine, front and rear suspension, and the wheels will require separate detail painting, but these parts can still be group painted when application of the basic colors is necessary. Paint the engine and transmission assembly with a gun-metal paint color first. When thoroughly dry, mask off the engine from the transmission. Then simply spray paint the transmission an aluminum paint color.

The famous Petty Blue paint color was used on many of Richard Petty's race cars. It was only in recent years that the interior, roll cage, and chassis on the 43 Pontiacs have carried the standard Dove Gray color.

If you are building one of Richard's STP-sponsored race cars, Tru-Match paints makes an excellent line of colors not only designed for use on plastic models but specifically formulated to match the real race car paints. **(Photo #9)** It's a good idea to stay with one line of paint on a project like this. Use the Tru-Match primer on the body shell, chassis, and roll cage, continuing with number 43 Blue and so on.

After the parts have been primed, wet-sand the larger ones such as the body shell and hood with 600 grit paper to ensure good paint adhesion and optimum surface smoothness. **(Photo #10)** By using small amounts of water with a little soap while sanding, ergo wet-sanding, you actually keep the sandpaper from clogging and make the work go faster. Once finished, wash the parts thoroughly and allow them to air dry before proceeding.

Attach the parts to be painted to either a paint stand or a fixture fash-

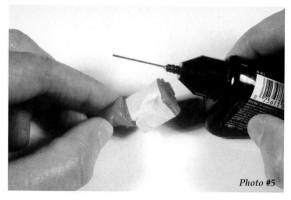

Photo #5

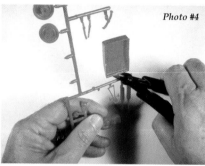

Photo #4

Photo #6

ioned from a metal coat hanger. **(Photo #11)** Make sure to shake each paint can thoroughly before spraying. Practice spraying on some scrap pieces to get the feel of the paint flow and pattern of coverage before you get serious on your model. Work deliberately when spraying your model, moving from end-to-end and side-to-side to ensure an even and thorough coat. Keep the can about eight to ten inches from the model surface.

Allow the final color coat time to dry thoroughly. A good rule of thumb for enamels is a week to ten days. Place the painted model body in a warm, dry, and dust-free environment for the duration.

The next step is to mask the body shell for applying the fluorescent red. Use a thin striping tape to establish a clean edge separating the two colors. **(Photo #12)** Cover the rest of the body with masking tape and masking

Photo #7

materials. First cover the exposed blue with flat white undercoat. Then begin slowly spraying on the number 43 Red color. Make sure to apply even coats and do not get the paint on too heavy.

Once painting is completed, it's time to cover the body shell with those colorful decals that make Petty race cars so exciting to look at. When applying water-slide decals, be patient and take your time. To do the job you'll need a small pair of sharp scissors, a flat tray-type container to hold water, and some soft facial tissues.

Using the scissors, carefully cut out and trim each decal to be applied to the model's surface. **(Photo #13)** Place the trimmed decal into the tray of water. Allow the decal to float in the water for a minute or so, checking occasionally to see if the decal film will slide around freely on the backing paper. Apply a bit of water to the area on the model where the decal will go. Remove the decal from the tray, keeping the decal film on the backing paper. Then slowly slide the film off the paper onto the surface of the model. Once it's in place, carefully press the decal with a damp (but not wet) tissue to remove the excess moisture. Allow the decal a few minutes to dry completely. At this point, proceeding cautiously, use a dry

tissue to lightly buff the decal to get out any air bubbles and remove water marks and fingerprints.

Final assembly should take place according to the printed instruction sheet. Install the roll cage, driver's seat, dashboard steering wheel, and shift lever in the interior. Glue the engine and the remainder of the drive train in place. Then attach the assembled wheels and tires to the chassis. Before placing the body in position over the chassis there are a few things to do first.

When installing chrome and clear parts like the front and rear window glass, remember that super glues fog or haze chrome plated or clear parts because of their chemical composition. Choose a two-part epoxy or white craft glue instead. **(Photo #14)** Either type of bonding agent allows some flexibility when positioning parts. The white glue dries especially clear, and any excess glue can easily be wiped away with a damp tissue.

Again, patience and perseverance will pay dividends when you take your time and follow these basic model building techniques. Of course, creating a nice-looking model of your favorite Petty race car is the ultimate goal, but you should have increased your modeling skills while having some fun and enjoying the experience too!

Photo #8

Photo #9

Photo #10

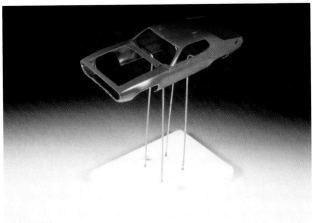

Photo #11

Photo #13

Photo #12

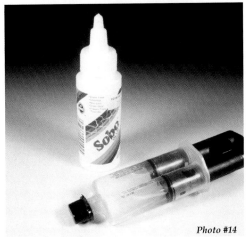

Photo #14

Beyond finger paints and house painting

Basic
Painting
Techniques

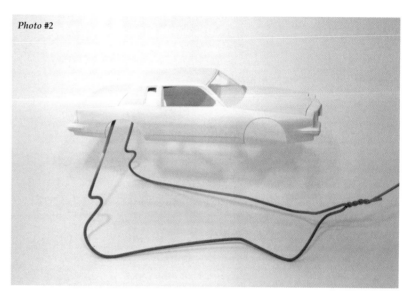

Photo #2

First, the bad news. Painting a model, especially a model race car, is more difficult than buying a bottle of soda or finding a stock car race on TV on a Sunday afternoon. It takes a bit more thought, preparation, and common sense to come up with a good paint job. Now the good news. If you can pour that bottle of soda without spilling it and build a sandwich for yourself during that stock car race, you have demonstrated enough aptitude and dexterity to paint like a pro — no kidding!

Painting is not all that hard, but most modelers treat painting as if it's either some sort of impossible task or as a necessary evil they couldn't care less about. The middle line between these two extremes, an easy one to follow, won't exponentially increase the amount of time it takes you to build a model. Stick with these hints and tips we are going to show you, and we will have you building model cars that will impress the socks off everyone.

TIP #1 — Take your time. Unlike racing, painting is not a speed-based activity. Give yourself time to do it and the paint time to dry. We are constantly shocked at how modelers try to rush through painting as if rushing will deliver the same results that patient application can. Realize that if your parts aren't properly prepared for painting, the paint will make them look worse, not better. Also realize that simple things can make the dif-

ference. Take time to completely stir **(photo #1)** or shake the paint you are using. A few quick shakes of the wrist is not enough to mix most hobby paints well enough to make them cover. Take time to do the job right. In the end it will actually save you time.

TIP #2 — Find the best way to hold the parts you are painting so that they can be handled without being damaged. Whether you are painting a small part or a large body or chassis, you need some kind of device to paint the whole part and let it dry without being touched. Several body holders now available let you paint a body shell without painting yourself in the process. Even an old bent coat hanger taped to the inside of the shell makes an excellent holding device. **(Photo #2)** It has the added

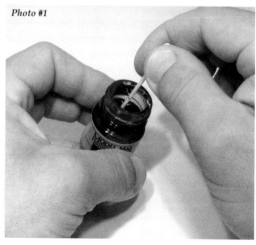

Photo #1

advantage of allowing you the option of hanging the model from some convenient pipe or hook as it dries. **(Photo #3)**

Lazy susans, or turntables, are inexpensive plastic items available at any large grocery store or department store. You can put your model or

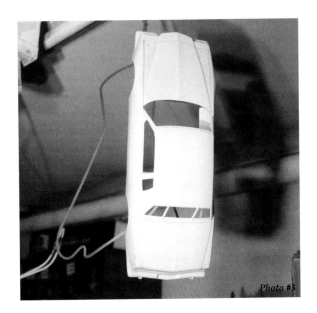

Photo #3

holding device on the tray and turn it while you are painting.

Masking tape is also a must, not only for masking, but for taping pieces to sticks and other holding devices. Sticks and clothespins come in handy for holding parts as they are painted. For example, you can jam a sharpened stick into either end of a typical engine-transmission assembly to hold it while it is painted, either by hand or with a spray can. **(Photo #4)** A wide stirring stick covered with a long loop of masking tape **(Photo #5)** is great for holding wheel rims, seats, steering wheels, and other small parts while they are spray painted. Nearly every part has some spot you can hold it with while you brush it or spray it. It simply takes a little thinking about it to figure out the best way.

TIP #3 — Be sure you have eliminated all those things that make plastic parts look like plastic parts, such as seam lines, punch marks, glue seams, and other similar flaws. Don't expect your paint to hide the basics you've neglected. Small seam lines showing through paint can make your model look like a toy rather than a quality replica. Take the time to remove those seams and marks by carefully sanding, filing, or scraping them away with a hobby knife. A brass suede brush is an excellent tool for cleaning seams off items like coil springs; 0000 steel wool quickly removes the thin

seams found on the outside of most model car body shells. Learn to look for the stuff that shouldn't be there and take the time to get rid of it. Also learn to use your sense of touch to find things that your eyes may have missed. If you can feel it, it's guaranteed you'll see it later when all the paint is on it.

TIP #4 — Learn to use both a brush and spray paints and learn when to use either one. Both are tools and learning the right time to use the right tool will make you a master painter. What do we mean by this? Well, a large item such as a body shell or a chassis plate is usually best painted using a spray can or an airbrush (a miniature spray gun). Small parts can be painted by hand — although if they are to be one color, spray painting them can sometimes speed things along. The key here is how detailed is the painting going to be. If you are trying to paint a small alternator, or oil filter, it might be best to use a small brush carefully to add the various colors needed, instead of spray painting the entire thing into one massive glob. Consider too that sometimes it's best to use a primer under your colors. It may mean spray painting the small part with a flat white primer and then hand painting the various colors after the primer dries — which leads us to the next tip.

TIP #5 — Always use a light-

colored primer under bright or light colors to ensure even paint coverage — even when hand painting. The federal ban on lead paints removed an ingredient that helped lighter-colored paints cover darker colors. Even dark colors sometimes don't cover well anymore, and the solution isn't to glop on two or three heavy coats. By the time that mess dries, you won't be able to tell an engine block from a glob of slag. The solution is to use a flat white or light gray primer on colored plastics. These can usually be sprayed on in a thin coat. Once they are dry, the final colors will usually cover in one coat. Primers also give the gloss colors something to hang on to, making coverage on the first coat almost a sure thing.

TIP #6 — The key to brush painting is the thickness of the paint and the quality of the brush, not the steadiness of the hand! Forget whatever you have ever heard about needing steady hands for great brush painting. While steady paws certainly can't hurt, they aren't what really makes for great painting. Remember that painting is moving the brush. So what if you are shaking a little? Learn to work with your body's own vibrations by using the right brush and good paint. Take a deep breath, relax, and then work slowly.

The problem with most hobbyists is that they buy model brushes priced

Photo #4

Photo #5

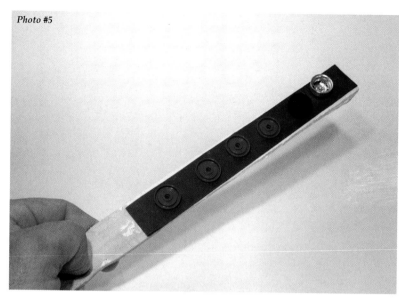

under a buck and better suited for painting small houses than for detail painting models. Buy a good quality red sable brush with long bristles. **(Photo #6)** The paint will flow better off this type of brush. Remember that how well the brush holds its point when wet counts more than its size. **(Photo #7)** Trying to paint details with a brush that won't hold a point when it's wet is like trying to thread a needle with a piece of rope: it isn't precise enough to do the job. Ditch the junk brushes, get a couple of good ones, and take good care of them.

The paint itself needs the right consistency too. First, mix your paint well, using something like a small stick to stir the paint. Don't just shake the bottle. Stirring is the only way to get the pigments, emulsifiers, and carriers to blend so that the paint will flow and dry. Paint that isn't mixed well can stay damp or sticky for a long, long time.

Once the paint is mixed, use a toothpick to put a drop of paint on your fingertip or a piece of card stock. If the drop sits there like a small jelly bean, or thin strings come off it as it is applied, the paint is too thick. If it flows all over the place so that you can see the paper or your fingerprint through the paint, it's too thin. Either remix the paint (a sure sign you may

have cheated on earlier steps) or allow the paint to stand open awhile so it can thicken. Good flowing paint is in between these two extremes.

Finally, try to add the colors to parts. Start with the lightest color first and progress to the darkest. Though this isn't always possible, it will save you lots of extra touch-up work whenever it is.

TIP #7 — The key to spray painting is learning to get a feel for how much paint is going on at any one time. Too little paint will give you poor coverage or a rough finish; too much paint can result in runs and sags. The trick is to get the coats on as smooth, wet layers.

To learn how to spray paint, try painting an empty coffee can flawlessly **(Photo #8)**. It can be a challenge to someone without much experience to use a spray can or airbrush.

There are two schools of thought on applying spray paint. The most popular is "spray sweeps." Point your spray can or airbrush just wide of your target and then slowly move across the surface in a nice level sweep. Don't stop spraying until you are off the surface. Repeat the process in overlapping sweeps until the entire subject has been covered.

The other technique, a little easier for beginners, will eventually create problems. It's sometimes called the

"bug killer" technique. Carefully spritz the subject with little bursts from the spray can, almost dusting the subject with a light coat of paint. Though easier for kids to adapt to, "bug killing" doesn't leave an even final wet coat that will dry to a high gloss. This technique is better suited for applying primer and other light base coats.

Make sure your paint is properly mixed before attempting to spray paint. Shake the spray can awhile before starting to paint. Three quick shakes of the rattle isn't going to do it. Most manufacturers recommend shaking the paint for at least a minute after you begin to hear the rattle. Simply remember that you can't shake a can of spray paint too much — but you can shake it too little, and it will show. How much to thin airbrush paint is almost a matter of personal preference. Most folks start at a 50 percent paint to 50 percent thinner mixture and then adjust from there.

A key once again is painting that coffee can. If you are getting good results with your airbrush on the can, then you will have no problems with your models. But regardless of what you are using, always be sure to test the spray on something other than your model. Spray the paper, a piece of cardboard, or some piece of scrap,

Photo #6

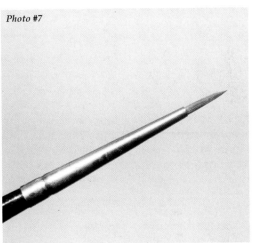

Photo #7

Photo #8

but never attempt to spray anything out of a can or airbrush until you have tested it on something worthless first.

TIP #8 — Always spray paint over a primer. Primer paints are designed to give the final color coats something to hang on to. They also tend to be neutral colors such as gray, creme, or white, so that the final color coat isn't altered by what is underneath. Primers will make light-colored paints "bounce" more and make them appear more brilliant — which leads us to the last tip.

TIP #9 — Always use flat white paint or primer as an undercoat for any fluorescent or neon color. Fluorescent or neon colors tend to be translucent, or allow you to see what is under them. In order to make them appear as bright as they are intended to be, first put down a white base coat of paint for these colors to overlie. Understand that these colors don't hide anything, so your base coat has to be perfect for the color coat to be right.

Finally, most fluorescent colors tend to dry flat or without any gloss. You will need to overspray them with a clear gloss to get them to look right. Without the clear gloss coat, you can spray a fluorescent color until the cows come home and never get it to come out glossy.

Doing those fancy paint schemes

Masking

Multi-colored paint schemes are one of the things that often make folks think that building a beautiful model is beyond them. The idea of neatly applying the paint and getting it to where it is supposed to be is usually a puzzle that lots of modelers give up on — and much too soon, to boot!

Masking and creating those multi-colored paint schemes is easy. There isn't anything complex or hard about it at all. It simply takes following a few rules and knowing a couple of really good tricks. Even the first-time modeler runs a good chance of getting this right if he follows these steps carefully, takes his time, and does his best to do a neat job. And, as in most things in life, practice makes perfect. Keep trying your newfound tricks and techniques, and you will discover that you will get better and better at it as time goes by.

A few basic reminders

Masking is simply an efficient way to cover up portions of your model so that they can be painted without damaging other layers and colors on the model. We recommend that you use either masking tape, or better yet, masking foil. Masking tape can be found anywhere that you buy tape or any kind of paint. It's good for all types of masking jobs. It can easily be used on models.

The problem with masking tape is its thickness. Paint tends to collect at

the edge of whatever masking material you use and form a ridge when the paint dries and the masking tape is removed. The edge may look sharp, but it becomes visible when you try to apply decals over it. Applying the decals over the ridge is difficult.

Some modelers use cellophane tape or clear transparent tape as "masking agents" instead of masking tape. Though both tend to be thinner, their adhesive is difficult to remove from the model without damaging the paint. They also don't conform well to the tight corners that you occasionally must mask when building a model. This type of tape has a way of lifting or puckering up, allowing the newly applied paint to creep under the tape and create a big mess.

Masking foil, a recent development designed specifically for modelers, is available from Detail Master. It is designed to do the things masking tape does, but with a sharper and thinner edge. When masking foil is removed, it leaves a much smaller edge because it's so much thinner than masking tape.

In the step-by-step guide that follows, we have used a combination of masking tape and foil. If you can't find any of the masking foil at your local hobby shop, you can substitute masking tape and follow the same instructions.

Three of the most common mistakes made when masking can be easily avoided. The first is not applying

the edge of the masking material firmly enough to create a good seal. Think of sealing the masking tape as if you were trying to seal a bowl with plastic wrap. By draping the wrap over the top of the bowl and not sealing it properly, you risk having the contents spill out. It takes extra effort to make sure that the entire bowl is wrapped so nothing leaks out. In masking, it's the same deal: you don't want anything leaking under the masking.

Masking tape requires a bit of rubbing the edge in order to seal it properly. Masking foil requires less pressure; other types of masking agents, like clear transparent tape, require more. Be sure to rub down the edges before you paint.

The second most common mistake is applying the masking to the model in a less-than-clean environment. Make sure that you and your work area are free of dust, debris, and other junk that can get into your paint. In other words, if you have sanded, built, filed, or glued recently, be sure to clean off yourself and your workbench before you even think of putting your first piece of tape on your model.

The third most common mistake is rushing the job. If you pull your masking agents off too soon, you risk damaging the fresh paint with fingerprints, dents, and scrapes in the paint. On the other hand, you can tear off earlier layers of paint or damage them if you apply the masking agent on top

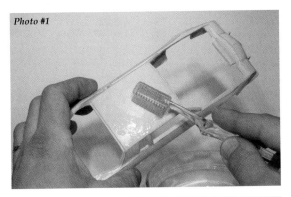

Photo #1

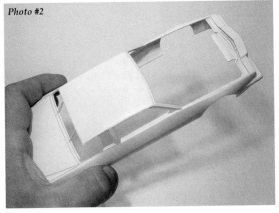

Photo #2

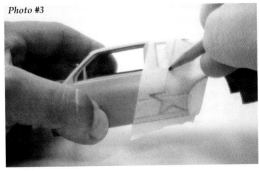

Photo #3

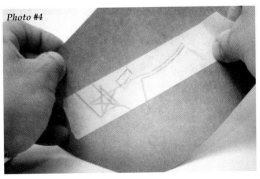

Photo #4

your first coat of primer. Be sure to allow the model to air dry or use a hair dryer to dry the model. Avoid wiping the model with anything — it will put lint or dust back on the model. **(Photo #1)**

Step 2 — Apply a primer coat to both the inside and outside of the model, best done in two steps. Check the model for any flaws in the paint or in the bodywork and make any repairs necessary. Use the lightest color primer possible, white or very light gray being the preferred colors. **(Photo #2)**

Step 3 — Spray paint the interior of the car with the appropriate interior color. Petty race cars have traditionally been Petty Blue on the inside since the mid '60s. However, in recent years the cars have light gray interiors with many of the suspension parts painted in equipment blue. The chassis are delivered to Petty Enterprises in the light gray color. When the car needs refurbishing for the first time, the team had been repainting the chassis Petty Blue. As of late, they have switched over to maintaining the chassis in the light gray color because it's easier on the eyes and easier to maintain.

Step 4 — Cut out the decals that separate the colors on your car and trace them onto a piece of paper or card stock. You can even use tracing paper if necessary and then glue the paper to some card stock. Then cut the template out with a good pair of scissors.

Step 4A — Sometimes you have to use the body as your guide, as in the case of Bobby Allison's Miller American Buick LaSabre. Apply a strip of masking tape over the car. Use a pencil to note any distinctive body

of those layers when they are completely dried and cured. Remember that most paints dry to the touch quickly — in the matter of a few hours, actually. But even then, they are still soft below the surface, easily marred if any kind of pressure is applied over them. The key is allowing the paint time to dry sufficiently so that you don't do any damage. Twenty-four hours is a good drying time for most hobby enamels while automotive paints should be dry enough to remove the masking in as few as three or four hours.

Think it through

Remember that it's far easier to think your painting through instead of trying to un-paint a model. It's imperative that you plan your color scheme carefully and then the order in which you are going to apply the paint. If you apply a multi-color paint scheme, you have to decide which color to apply first and then where the actual dividing lines between the colors go. As we mentioned in the previous chapter, fluorescent colors have to be applied over a light-colored base coat — preferably white. They also

don't mask well, so it's preferable to apply these bright colors last.

The worst mistake you can make is to eyeball where the dividing lines should go. The separation lines between colors are often dictated by the decals provided in the kit or from an aftermarket supplier, or by some major body details. Carefully read your instruction sheets and note where the separation lines should go.

If the pattern is complicated — as in the 1987 Miller American Buick LeSabre of Bobby Allison, the 1995 Interstate Batteries Monte Carlo, or Richard and Kyle's STP Buick Regals from 1981 — it's best to use a pattern to keep the paint scheme even and symmetrical. The pattern or template can be as simple as a piece of index card or a file folder. By tracing the pattern needed on the card stock (using decals as your guide), you create a reversible template you can use on either side of the car. Take a look at the step-by-step below to see the specifics of this technique and the rest of what's involved in masking a multi-colored paint scheme.

Step 1 — Wash your model with warm, soapy water before applying

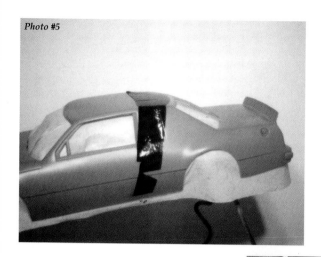
Photo #5

Photo #6

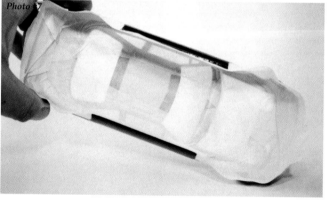
Photo #7

reference points such as window openings or wheel well openings. Then sketch in the required design. In this case, the star was part of the complex design. **(Photo #3)**

Step 4B — Remove the tape from the body and apply the tape to some card stock. Then use a ruler to "square up" the star and the overall template. **(Photo #4)** Cut the template out using a good pair of scissors.

Step 5 — Use this template to lightly trace the pattern onto the car until all your separation lines are sketched in. Use a very soft pencil such as a #1 1/2 or #2 to do the job. Harder pencils will dig into the soft primer. **(Photo #5)**

Step 6 — When satisfied that you have the pattern right on the car, decide what color you will apply first. As a rule of thumb, apply lightest colors first and work up to the darkest colors last. The exception always is to apply fluorescent colors last in order to avoid masking over the delicate neon colors. In the case of Petty cars, that means you apply the Petty Blue first, so you mask off the areas that will be Rocket Red.

Step 7 — Using thin strips of masking foil, outline the areas that will later be painted Rocket Red. **(Photo #6)** Rub over the edges lightly with a cotton swab. Since the masking foil is thinner than masking tape, it will leave less of a ridge and paint buildup at the edges.

Step 8 — Use masking tape to fill in the areas not covered by the masking foil.

Step 9 — Mask off the inside of the car, being sure to cover all the windows and other openings. Add a skirt to the bottom of the car from the inside as shown in order to keep overspray from getting up into the car. **(Photo #7)**

Step 10 — Tape the shell to an old paint can, coat hanger, or commercially available paint stand to hold the body shell while painting. An old lazy susan turntable also makes painting easier without having to touch the model. **(Photo #8)**

Step 11 — Spray paint the model with your first color, in this case Petty Blue. Allow the model to dry for a while — at least until the paint is dry to the touch — before removing any masking.

Step 12 — Carefully remove the masking starting with the inside of the model. Then remove all the masking tape first and work out toward the separation lines. **(Photo #9)**

Step 13 — Remove any small pieces of masking that get stuck with a small flat set of tweezers or tongs. If you are using such a tool, use extreme care so that you don't dig into the paint or primer. With all the masking removed, set the model aside and allow the paint at the separating lines time to dry.

Step 14 — Inspect the model for any flaws and correct them before going on. Then wash the model once again, drying it as you did in Step #1.

Step 15 — Mask over the previously painted areas with masking film on the edges again.

Step 16 — Fill in the open areas again with masking tape and mask the interior of the car again as well.

Step 17 — Spray paint the car with the final color to be applied, in this case the Rocket Red.

Photo #8

Photo #9

Photo #10

Step 18 — Remove the masking from the car as you did before and allow the edges of this latest layer of paint to dry. **(Photo #10)**

Step 19 — If needed, scuff sand the edges where the two colors meet with 3400 grit sanding film or 600 grit emery cloth.

Step 20 — Put the model back on the paint stand and apply a coat or two of clear over the entire model. **(Photo #11)** This will make the finish more uniform and will give the fluorescent colors the gloss they need before applying any decals. That's next, so turn to the next chapter and see how it's done.

Photo #11

Decaling

If painting doesn't intimidate a modeler, then decaling often does. Many folks have problems putting decals on models — but once again, it's simply a matter of following a few easy rules and learning a couple of tricks that make this task a very enjoyable and satisfying one.

Waterslide decals aren't supposed to hide mistakes in building. If your model has been poorly assembled, don't count on a spiffy decal job to make it look better. Usually, it's the other way around: though good decals can help even out the separation between colors or even hide a small blemish, they will not solve a rough or uneven paint job. In fact, decals will have a hard time sticking to a model with a poor paint job.

The best surface for decals is a smooth finish — and the smoother, the better. And though many decals are now printed on backing film that tends to disappear, often the film is much bigger than the printed image, which can cause application problems. Most of all, decals often need help in "snuggling" down on the various contours a body can have. A decal job looks really good when it accentuates the paint, looks as if it's painted on, and leaves nothing sticking up from the model.

Preparation is the key

Making the decals on your model look as good as those on real race cars

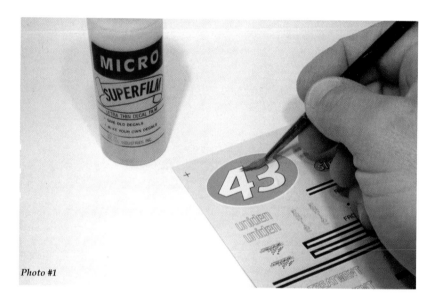

Photo #1

is easy to do, but it takes a little extra preparation.

First, understand that decals slide onto your model when you apply them. Your paint finish has to be really smooth in order to make decals work right. Think of the paint job on your model as if it's your driveway in front of your home. If your driveway is newly paved or paved and sealed, then sliding stuff on and off it (like snow, for instance) is easy. But if it's rough, like a gravel or stone driveway, shoveling that snow will be a real bear. Think about laying a giant decal over a stone driveway. Right away you can see where you are going to run into trouble. Now think about laying a big decal on a sheet of glass. Get the picture? Make sure your paint job

is smooth before you start to decal. If it's really rough and bumpy, try rubbing the paint job out a little with a fine grade of sanding film or emery cloth or with some polishing compound and water, such as DuPont #7 Polishing Compound.

Another solution is to rub the finish out a little and then add another coat of clear to the model. The clear could fill in a lot of the rough spots and help level things off, but do so only sparingly. Don't expect a heavy coat of clear to solve a multitude of sins.

Second, understand that not all decals are ready to go right off the sheet, especially if the model has been sitting around for some time. Many Richard Petty models out there that some folks will want to build are now

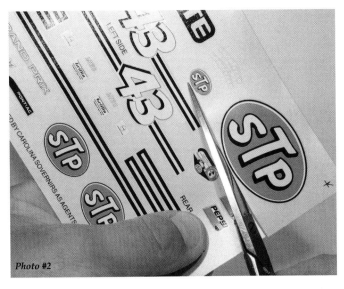

Photo #2

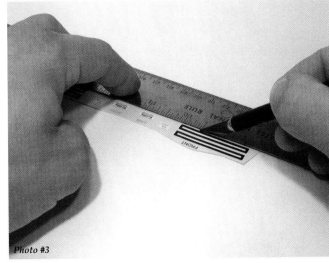

Photo #3

considered antiques. But before you drop the decals in the drink, be sure to coat them with some Micro Super Film. This product is designed to keep decals from breaking apart due to age or dryness. Super Film is brushed on over decals with a soft sable brush **(photo #1)**. Even if you think you glopped it on, it dries clear and in a very thin layer. By using it, you will bind old decals back together and keep the edges of the image from fraying when the decal is properly trimmed.

When the Super Film dries, cut out the major shapes of the decals with a pair of scissors. Don't attempt to trim the decals at this point; just break the sheet into workable pieces **(photo #2)**.

The next step is trimming the decals as close to the image as possible. This is a lot easier to do than it sounds, especially if you try these two tricks. The first trick is to use a metal straight-edge ruler and a sharp hobby knife for trimming any straight lines such as trim stripes, logo boxes, etc. **(photo #3)**. By using a ruler, you can get right up to the edge of the image and get rid of all that extra "carrier film" that makes a model decal look like a model decal instead of the real thing. An 18-inch ruler with a strip of cork on the back of it works well. It keeps the ruler from slipping as the cuts are made. The second trick is to

use a pair of good, small scissors for close detail cutting, especially curves **(photo #4)** and small decals such as sponsor decals. Again, the idea is to get rid of as much carrier film as possible and make the decals appear much more like the real vinyl stickers on the cars.

The next step is to set yourself up with a clean work area. You'll need paper towels, a bowl or coffee cup with warm water in it, a soft brush, and a pair of tweezers or tongs. Be sure too that your work area has decent lighting and a fair amount of elbow room. Because stock cars typically have decals on all sides of the car — and frequently in layers — don't expect to decal the entire car in one sitting. You can easily run into problems by accidentally repositioning freshly applied decals on one side of the car while you are applying decals to the other. Work carefully and slowly so you don't undo your own work.

To apply the decals, select one you want to apply and drop it into the water after you have trimmed it as well as you can. Most decals will curl up as they hit the water, but as they sit for a few moments and absorb some

of the water they will start to relax and uncurl. When they do, use your tweezers to fish the decal — backing paper and all — from the water. Place it on a piece of paper towel and allow it to relax a bit more **(photo #5)**. This will allow the glue to soften enough for the decal to slide cleanly off the backing paper.

As the decal relaxes, use the soft brush to brush some water onto the area of the model where the decal will be applied. This water will act as a lubricant as you slide the decal onto the model and position the decal. Then pick up the decal and backing paper and slide the decal into place on the model. Use the brush to move the decal around whenever you can **(photo #6)**. If you have to touch the decal with your fingers, be sure to wet them first. This will keep the decal from sticking to your fingers and keep you from tearing the decal. The idea here is to float the decal into position.

Now use a small piece of paper towel to pat the decal down and draw off the excess water **(photo #7)**. If the decal moves in the process, nudge it back to where it belongs. If it won't budge, just add a little more water

Photo #4

Photo #5

using the brush to re-float the decal and get it back where it belongs. Wick off the excess water and pat the decal down again. Repeat the process until all your decals are in place.

There are just a few other things to keep in mind. If you are doing stripes that wrap around the car, such as those on many of Petty's recent cars, begin in one corner or convenient spot and apply the decals first until they are all in place. Like wallpapering a room with a pattern, there is nothing more frustrating than coming around the last corner to discover that the pattern doesn't match up where it should. Try to start at a spot where you know things will later line up, such as one side of the car. And if you have to re-float a decal after it's been on for a little while, do so gently and with a lot of patience and water. It can be done.

Apply the sponsor decals last. Usually very small, they can get lost easily. They frequently don't match photos of the car exactly, so you may have to use a little artistic license and apply them where they fit the best.

When all the decaling is done, most experienced modelers will coat the decals with decal-setting solution. Several brands are available, some stronger than others, but they all soften the decals and get them to snuggle down over door lines or

other engraved details. Though not required, especially with the newer aftermarket decals that are available, a setting solution can help a decal stick better to the model.

If you are satisfied with how the decals look, you may want to protect them by adding another coat of clear paint over them. Check the type of

Photo #6

paint you are using to see if it is compatible with your brand of decals. Do this by applying some clear paint over a spare decal. You'll know. It's best to keep this protective coat as light as possible. Then polish and wax your model to your heart's content. No doubt, it'll be a winner!

Photo #7

Basic Detailing

Photo #1

Once you feel comfortable with your basic building ability, it's time to add a few basic detailing techniques to your model-building skills. This isn't a major leap forward as much as it's the next logical step in increasing your modeling prowess.

Many of the following tips will quickly become an accepted part of the way you normally go about building a model. Some detailing must take place with the building of the model. Other detailing is best accomplished after various building steps are completed.

The Engine

Beyond painting the engine and transmission the proper colors, adding fundamental systems like spark plug wires, battery cables, top and bottom radiator hoses, and oil cooling lines requires planning. In most cases it's a good idea to pre-drill spark plug holes in valve covers — only on hemi-powered cars, like this replica of Richard's 1964 Daytona winner. **(Photo #1)** Use .050 inch diameter bit in a pin vise or a Dremel Mini-Mite portable drill.

Don't forget the coil, which requires a wire of its own. Probably the easiest way to prepare the distributor cap to hold all nine ignition wires is to drill out the center large enough to insert the whole bundle. Once the cap is glued in place, it's hard to tell without a magnifying glass how this was accomplished.

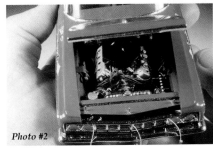

Photo #2

Using Detail Master coated wire for spark plug wire detail, drape it sufficiently to look realistic when it is run from the distributor to each spark plug hole.

Next, add the proper oil-cooling lines from the engine pan to the reservoir and then on to the oil cooler located behind the right side of the grille. You will likely need to install the engine/transmission into the engine compartment after the initial wiring but before the cooling lines are placed in their final positions.

Installing battery cables is fairly simple. The ground wire should be attached to the front of the engine block; the lead wire should be run to a hole in the firewall. Again, planning will help. Adding these details is best done after the battery has been installed in the engine compartment. **(Photo #2)**

The Chassis

Detailing a chassis can be as simple or as complex as you desire and is very much a matter of the individual modeler's taste.

Photo #3

You can choose to use various shades of dark gray and metallic colors of bottle paint on front and rear suspension parts to give the finished parts a more realistic look, rather than painting everything the same color. **(Photo #3)**

Header dump pipes can be fashioned from either aluminum or plastic tubing. Use 5/32 to 3/16 inch diameter tubing. If using plastic tubing, you need a heat source like a candle or a low-wattage light bulb to warm the walls of the tubing so it can be bent to the proper shape. Once you're satisfied with the length and bend of the tubing, ream out the interior wall of the tubing with a number 11 hobby knife blade to thin it for a more realistic appearance.

Photo #4

Photo #5

Photo #6

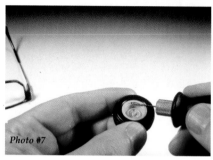

Photo #7

Here's a simple method to plumb the rear end pump and cooler: use various sizes of chrome craft braid found at most well-stocked craft shops. Run the cooling lines through the chassis floor into the inside rear of the interior so they intersect the cooling fan. **(Photo #4)**

The Wheels and Tires

Selecting the correct tires for the period is important. For a mid-'60s stock car like the Petty '64 Plymouth, use a narrow-treaded Goodyear tire. Though many of the cars, including Petty's, used Firestone and Goodyear tires during practice, Goodyears were mounted on the car during the Daytona 500.

To make any race car tire look used, simply rotate the tires one at a time around your index finger while scuffing the treaded surface with coarse sandpaper. Sanding away just a little tread surface achieves that "I've been racing a few laps" look. **(Photo #5)**

Painting the "Goodyear" lettering on the sidewall of the tire is easy using a flat acrylic white model paint. **(Photo #6)** Sign painters' "One Shot" lettering paint also works well. Use a "000" brush and a dab of paint, working slowly. If you get too much white paint down between the individual letters, simply clean your brush and use some flat black to touch up your mistakes.

Make realistic-looking valve stems by drilling a small-diameter hole in each wheel near the edge of the rim. **(Photo #7)** Once the hole is drilled, a short wire is then glued in place. When the glue dries, paint the stem flat black and then hit the end of the valve stem with a touch of silver paint for the look of a cap.

The tried-and-true way of making a realistic-looking wheel weight is to place a dab of white craft glue along the edge of the wheel rim and allow it to dry. Since racing wheels and tires sometimes have more than a single balance weight, you may wish to repeat the process at another point on the wheel rim.

Once the craft glue is dry, paint the remaining shape, using a gun-metal color of bottle paint applied with a small brush. Then use a dash of silver paint in the center of your new "wheel weight" to represent the clip that attaches it to the edge of the rim.

The Interior

Many times interior detail goes unnoticed, especially in a '60s super-speedway race car with closed side windows. However, it's still a good idea to add extra detail for those with the eyesight to see such things.

Instrument panel gauges' faces really come to life if you first paint them with flat black bottle paint. Once the flat black dries, carefully "pick out" the raised letters and numerals with silver paint and an extra-fine-tipped brush. **(Photo #8)** Don't forget to paint the pointer needle on each gauge with red paint to make it stand out against the background.

You can make simple and effective seat belts and shoulder harnesses using strips of 1/8-inch wide masking tape. Using regular masking tape, remove a piece from the roll and lay it out flat on a hard surface that's safe to use for cutting. With a straight edge and a hobby knife, make repeated parallel cuts approximately 1/8 inch apart. Cut some lengths about an inch long and place them in position on the driver's seat — both the lower cushion and the seat back. **(Photo #9)** When you're satisfied with the position and length of each piece, brush paint them with flat black bottle paint. When they are dry, use a small brush with silver bottle paint to "suggest" the buckles and adjustment hardware. Again, if you've been a bit generous with the silver paint, touch up the area around the belt hardware with a brush and some flat black bottle paint until you're satisfied with the way things look.

The Body

You can enhance exterior detail using Bare Metal chrome foil. It's easy to use, though you may want to practice with it to get the feel of how it is best applied and trimmed out. Cut

Photo #8

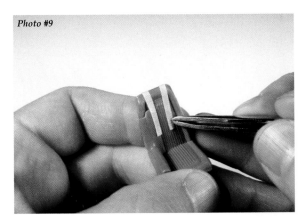

Photo #9

Photo #10

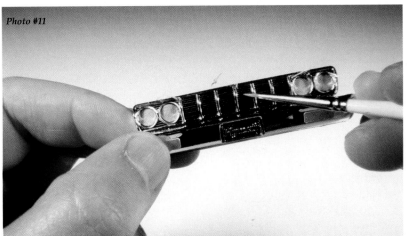

Photo #11

Photo #12

strips of the foil and apply them to the trim around the edges of the front, side, and rear windows. Carefully rub the foil down, making sure it gets tucked into and around all the areas and shapes it's applied to. Once you're satisfied with how it's positioned, trim the excess with a hobby knife (and a fresh no. 11 blade). Then burnish the foil into its final place with a facial tissue. **(Photo #10)**

Achieve added realism by applying a thin flat black "wash" to recessed areas like the grille mesh. Simply thin a small amount of flat black until it's the consistency of water. Using a no. 1 brush, apply generous amounts to the grille area. **(Photo #11)** Before the wash dries, gently wipe the high spots with your finger and a facial tissue, making sure to leave the solution in the recessed areas.

Working hood pins might look like a major project, but they are not difficult to make. First, make a support to mount the pins, as was done on this '64 Petty Plymouth. Once the panel is glued in place, close the hood and determine where to locate the pin post holes. Using a .060 inch diameter bit, drill the holes in the proper place on both the hood and rear deck. Make sure the holes drilled through the hood also protrude through the support panel.

At this point, cut sewing needles to length so that the eyelet on each rests just above the surface of the hood and rear deck. Glue the base of the needles where they enter the support panel. Once the glue dries, cut off the excess length of each

sewing needle on the underside of the support panel.

Then find a small-diameter, uncoated wire that will easily pass through the needle eyelet. From the uncoated wire, form hood-pin retainer clips like those shown in the diagram. Test fit the clips by sliding them into their respective needle eyelets, just like those on a full-size race car. **(Photo #12)** Finally, using short lengths of silver sewing thread, glue one end of each piece of

thread to each clip. Then drill holes in the grille below each hood and glue the loose end of the thread into each new hole. Repeat the process for the pins in the rear deck.

These basic building techniques are only the beginning. Your model-building efforts can be carried today as far as you are willing to dream. But remember the realities of any worthy pastime: get those basic skills down pat!

Resin Conversions

An intriguing aspect of model building has been the growth of an aftermarket that supplies extra parts and kits you can't obtain from the regular plastic model manufacturers. This "cottage industry" is made up of dozens of little companies frequently run out of basements and garages as part-time businesses, although some of the more successful ones have made the transition to full-time operations.

A huge part of this aftermarket is companies that specialize in resin conversion parts or body shells. "Resin" is an inclusive term that can mean polyester resin, polymer resin, polyurethane resin — in short, epoxies that cure into a hard, plastic-like substance without requiring expensive injection-molding machines or molds to create the various parts being offered. These castings, usually creme or tan in color, can cost anywhere from $10 for a nose-and-bumper conversion kit to $40 for a complete body with several other detail parts.

Though the prices of resin kits may seem shocking compared to those of a regular kit, the items usually aren't even offered by the conventional model companies. For example, if you

are building a complete collection of Richard Petty's race cars over the years, there are many cars that are not offered by the model manufacturers. The Pontiac Grand Prix 2+2 has never been manufactured as a plastic kit. Neither has the 1978 Dodge Magnum. For that matter, the 1995 Pontiac Grand Prix will probably never see the light of day as a regular kit, either. The only way you will ever see either of these cars is as a resin body or a conversion kit that alters existing kits. If you really want the kit, $40 isn't a lot of money when resin is the only game in town.

Resin in many ways acts like styrene, the plastic used in most model kits. It's soft and pliable like styrene, and it can be sanded, filed, painted, and modified much the same

way styrene can be. In fact, if you do it right, you won't be able to tell a styrene kit from a resin one once it's painted and finished. There are some differences, however, and you need to be aware of them. Because of the cost of most resin products, mistakes are all the more costly, so please pay attention to these words of advice.

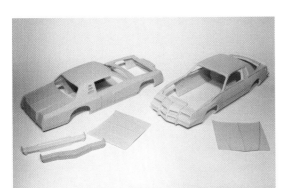

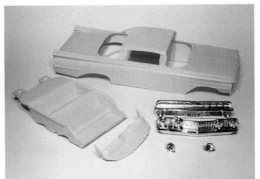

Resin kits can be simple shells or complete reproductions. Although expensive, it may be the only way to get a model of that rare or unusual car.

Working with resin

The first thing you will probably notice about a resin body or part is that it usually has more flash and requires much more clean-up and preparation than a styrene kit will. Excess resin in the windows or wheel wells is par for the course. It's all part of the way these items are molded.

Resin can be sanded, cut, sawed, and filed just like styrene, but you may discover that it seems to be both softer and harder than its injection-molded counterpart. Overall, resin tends to be softer, but what makes it seem harder at the same time is that it's more brittle and tends to chunk during some types of machining. Never try to "adz" or scrape resin with a hobby knife. The knife will more than likely skip and catch in the quirky compound, leaving all sorts of nasty gashes and marks. Always use a finer sandpaper than you would on styrene and sand ever so slowly, frequently checking your progress. Be sure to use a sanding block whenever possible to keep from sanding depressions into the resin, especially if you are sanding putty, fillers, or dried super glue. Those compounds tend to be much harder than resin. You can easily sand too much of the surrounding resin away while trying to sand the fillers unless you use a sanding block.

You will discover that regular plastic glues don't work for long on resin. If you do get the parts to stick together initially, they will fall apart with little or no provocation later on. The glues that do work are cyanoacrylates (commonly known as super glue, crazy

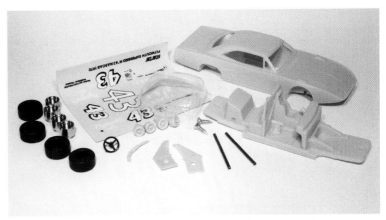

Small scale resin models have also been popular in recent years. These kits are usually from overseas manufacturers and can be more expensive than their larger domestic counterparts.

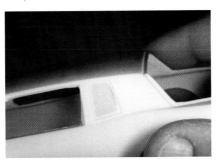

Flash is a common problem on resin casting and needs to be addressed carefully. Mistakes can be costly.

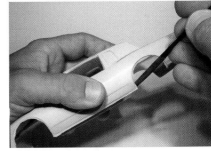

A file can help remove much of the heavy casting flash you may find, but be careful not to overdo it.

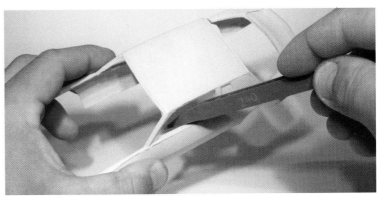

An emery board or sanding stick is a handy tool for doing the fine sanding needed to finish cleaning any remaining flash.

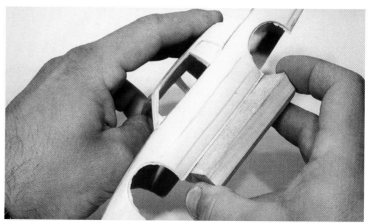

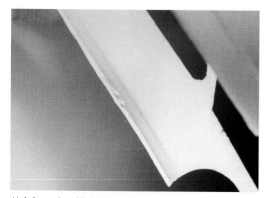

Air holes are best filled with gap-filling superglue. Once dry, use a sanding stick or sanding block to smooth the area.

A sanding block is a useful tool that will help keep edges flat and true.

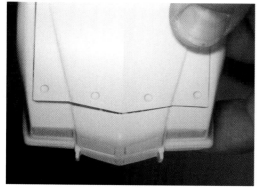

Occasionally the parts in a kit won't match very well. In situations like the one shown, it's best to fill the gaps with strips of sheet plastic and sand the parts to their proper shape.

Grille openings often need help. It's best to carefully hand file the grille opening by first drilling a hole in the center of the grille.

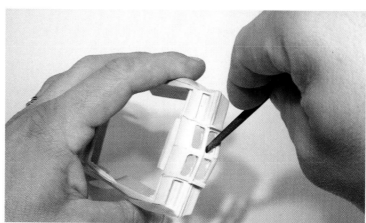

Use a round rasp to quickly rough out the opening, but use care when doing so. Finish the opening with a fine jeweler's file, working carefully as you go.

glue, or instant bond glue) and five-minute epoxy. White glue is especially good for bonding clear parts, such as windows, to the finished model.

Primer is an absolute necessity when using resin parts or bodies. Paint doesn't stick well to resin, at least not as well as it does to styrene. Resin surfaces also tend to have release agents, such as silicone, that have to be completely washed off the model before any paint will adhere. The best advice to new modelers is to scuff sand the finished body with a very fine sanding film or sandpaper, and then wash the model thoroughly with warm water and soap, scrubbing lightly with an old toothbrush. Consider using a lacquer-based primer as well. Floquil has a metal figure primer and a white primer for use under its lacquer-based railroad paint. It works well under enamel, with more

"bite" than enamel primer. Using it on resin thus avoids some of the problems you run into with enamel.

As a final word of advice if you are using a complete resin body on a regular plastic chassis: be sure to check the fit of the body on the chassis before you do any serious painting or decaling. Occasionally you will find

that the bodies are cast a little thick; they need to be adjusted before they fit or sit on the chassis properly. You may also have to add some attachment points to the inside of the body to make it fit.

That's all you need to know. Resin parts and bodies will double the number of modeling subjects you can build.

Advanced Techniques

Most of us will live our model-building lives content to build models from kits offered by the model manufacturers. Perhaps we'll even modify kits with resin conversion parts or a new resin body. But on occasion, there will be cars that even the resin casters haven't attempted yet — and that's where advanced model building techniques come into play.

Randy Derr is an acknowledged master of building unusual models that incorporate gobs of "scratch-building" or alterations that change a model to something entirely different.

Randy built the model in question, a replica of the Pontiac Grand Prix prototype, as an entry in the very first Circle Track model contest. He really wanted to have a viable entry, and after toying around with the idea of building "The NASCAR Stock Car of the Future, circa 2000," he settled on something less radical. He knew that Pontiac was getting ready to introduce the new Grand Prix in spring

1988, and that the division would probably unveil its racing version at the 1988 Daytona 500. He would build a car of the future, but not so far into the future. After contacting a friend at Pontiac who just happened to be working on racing projects, Randy was offered a stack of 8x10 color prints of a prototype of the new car done up as if it were Richard Petty's car. He gladly accepted and set to work.

Armed with these photos and body panel measurements taken from an early pilot vehicle, Randy began to create Richard's new ride for 1988. Starting with the Hardee's Oldsmobile kit by Monogram, he began modifying the body to the Grand Prix shape. The Pontiac was several inches narrower and shorter than the Olds, so he sectioned the

roof, hood, and trunk for the proper dimensions. If you look carefully, you can see the section lines faintly in the first photos of the model, before any primer was applied. Randy used the photos of the prototype and scaled the various dimensions needed from them. The "A," "B," and "C" pillars were also modified to give the correct angles of the new car. He "roughed" in window openings and smoothed the sides of the body. Then he milled the accent line at the beltline into the model using a ball-end cutter on a Dremel Mototool.

The seemingly most difficult part to reproduce was the shapely front air dam and fascia. Randy made the front fascia using a "layer technique" that involves dividing the fascia into several layers vertically and then cutting each layer from sheet plastic of the

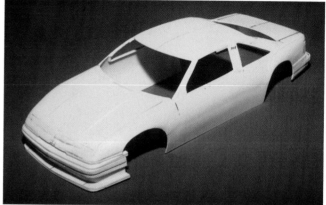

A front end view of the model as it was being "roughed out" into its basic shape. Note that Randy doesn't use much filler to do his shaping, but uses sheet plastic to do the job.

proper thickness. These layers are then stacked like a loaf of bread stood on end and the edges of each layer smoothed into the next. Randy then added the grille surround using a separate piece of sheet plastic and blended it in too.

After finalizing and correcting the outside contours, Randy ground out the inside of the fascia using a Dremel tool to give it the correct thickness. You can see the layers in the first photos of the unprimed model.

During this phase of the building, Randy took several photos of the model and compared them to the photos of the full-size car. He found that if he looked only at the model, his eye would unconsciously correct flaws in contours and proportions. On the other hand, if he looked at photos of the model, the flaws stood right out. "Must be something about 2-D versus 3-D," Randy mused.

Once he completed the body, finishing the rest of the model was fairly straightforward. The rear end of the chassis had to be shortened somewhat to fit under the new body, but that was about it. Randy added posable front wheels, as well as trunk and fuel cell details. The engine compartment was also fully wired, plumbed, and detailed. The model was painted using Martin Seymour Basin Street Blue acrylic enamel automotive paint and Testors Fluorescent Red model paint.

The markings came primarily from the Monogram Petty Pontiac kit that was out at the time, except for the

A view from the tail shows how each detail was penciled in. Note how the sheet plastic is stacked under the nose to create the complex shape of the front air dam.

Pencil marks helped to keep everything symmetrical and guided Randy when adding other details later on.

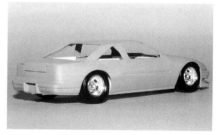

Once construction had been refined and completed, the model received a coat of primer and was rechecked to ensure that it had the proper shape.

large STP logo on the hood and number meatball on the roof. Randy painted the red ovals onto a blank decal sheet and then applied the letters or numbers.

Randy finished the model in time for the contest, and he received a runner-up award for his efforts. At the time the model was completed, the Monogram kit of the new Grand Prix was still months away, so the model always attracted attention at the contests and shows. Of course that all came to an end when the Monogram kit was finally released, but it was fun while it lasted.

Is such an effort within the reach of most modelers? Well, with some experience gained by building models out of the box and some practice working with sheet plastic, most modelers can learn the techniques necessary to do this kind of radical modeling. No doubt it isn't easy, but it can yield some stunning and unique results.

Not only did the shape of the car have to be correct, but it needed to sit properly on the chassis. Scratchbuilding requires a lot of test fitting.

When all the basic construction was complete, the model received a beautiful two-tone paint job copied from the prototype photos.

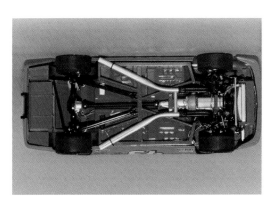

Getting the right shape would be enough for some modelers, but not Randy Derr. His Pontiac had an engine bay complete with all the plumbing and...

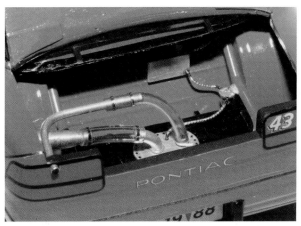

...an opening rear deck lid to display the fully detailed truck with all the fuel cell plumbing in place.

Even the underside got the full detailing treatment. The model is truly a work of art.

Randy used a set of photos like this one of the prototype car under development to help him replicate Pontiac's then brand new incarnation of the Grand Prix.

Can't get enough of a good thing

Petty Collections

Len Carsner started his collection with a pair of 1993 Pontiacs. The #44 car in the foreground represents the car as it was raced by Rick Wilson in Richard's first year as a car owner.

Human beings by nature are "pack rats," accumulating this or that which holds some special interest for them. Whether a person collects postage stamps, coins, matchbooks, china figurines, or clothing buttons, the human need to amass "stuff" is lumped into a catch-all category called "hobbies."

Collecting scale model automobiles is one of those time-honored hobbies. Whether it's plastic promotional cars, metal car banks, or model car kits, the theme is the same: we collectors just can't seem to get enough of whatever it is we collect!

A model car collector differs greatly from a model car builder, who forms a collection of specific built models with a particular theme in mind. The collector must invest his or her money and provide space to display or store the prized bounty.

By contrast, the model car builder invests not only money but another precious commodity — time! The collector learns the ins and outs of his chosen hobby; the model builder must not only know his subject but must also develop marketable building skills — for when you build a model you have put something of yourself into the finished product. And if you do show the product publicly you open yourself up to scrutiny and the unavoidable judgment of others, fellow hobbyist or not. Collecting commercially produced model cars doesn't demand the same degree of

Len's #43 represents the Pontiac as Richard drove it at Indianapolis Motor Speedway in a few ceremonial hot laps during NASCAR's first official test there.

A few of co-author Bill Coulter's Petty models. Each model in a collection tends to have its own history.

risk to one's ego as creating a replica of a famous race car — especially race cars as well-known as those with the number 43 emblazoned on them.

Many of us have a collection of Richard Petty model cars painted, assembled, and detailed by our own hands. Richard Petty model car collections can be small, moderate, or large. Even a small or moderate-size model collection can depict many "three-dimensional moments in time" from the King's illustrious career.

Leonard Carsner of Piqua, Ohio, is a long-time Richard Petty fan and a

long-time model car builder. He began building models with his father when he was a youngster. For Len, living in the Midwest, NASCAR Winston Cup racing seemed a long way off until television brought it into our living rooms in the late '70s.

For Len, Richard Petty's final race at Atlanta, Georgia, in November 1992 brought mixed emotions. Sparked by the idea of a Petty STP Pontiac in the Indianapolis Motor Speedway Museum (a little over two hours from where Len lives) and Richard Petty hot lapping the Brickyard in his own

Coulter's model of the 1964 Daytona 500 winner.

The Belvedere has a fully detailed engine compartment.

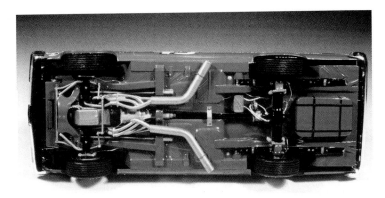

The underside of the model has also been fully detailed.

race car, Len Carsner began a Petty collection. Two cars of significance — the "hot lap" STP Pontiac and the 1993 STP Pontiac driven by Rick Wilson, the first Petty race car with the King as the owner but not driver — were his first subjects.

Car 43 is based on the Monogram 1/24 scale Pontiac Grand Prix kit with an updated resin '93-'94 body shell made by SouthernScale Replicas in Spartanburg, South Carolina. The 44 STP Pontiac is also based on the Monogram kit. Both cars are painted using Tru-Match spray cans and use Jaxx yellow tampo-printed tires. Slixx decals were used for the major body markings: numbers 9243/1001 (43) and 9344/1011 (44). Blue Ridge Decals sheet number BR-401 supplied the instrument faces and seat belts. Scale Model Speedway window nets were used on both cars.

Of course, a Petty model collection could start anywhere in any era. But if you're looking for an excellent starting point, the vehicles picked by Len Carsner couldn't be better.

Co-author, Bill Coulter's collection of Richard Petty-built models currently stands at seven and, as they say, "counting." This collection currently comprises two 1964 Plymouths, a 1965 Barracuda drag car, a 1970 Superbird, a 1971 Plymouth, a 1972 STP Dodge (so far the only two-tone Petty model in the collection), and a 1972 Dodge Dart "Kit Car." Like any unique grouping of items, each has its own story.

Why two 1964 Petty Plymouths? The first '64 Plymouth, built in the late '60s when his only direct exposure to NASCAR Grand National racing was through magazines and TV, used what little information he could

uncover — much of it based on his best guess.

Coulter read a story in one of the racing publications at the time about the fierce battle late in the '64 season between Richard and Ford driver Fred Lorenzen. He decided his model would represent the look of the Petty cars he saw in these articles. Over the years he often wished he had modeled the car Richard drove to victory at Daytona that year.

Many years later Bill was asked to produce an article for a modeling magazine featuring a favorite Petty car. He decided to build that Daytona-winning Plymouth and apply any new information and of course, improved building skills he had developed in the interim.

His second '64 Petty Plymouth took shape, and in many ways it is a vast improvement over the first one.

Coulter's Barracuda is not a model of any particular version, but rather a representation of Richard's 1965 drag car.

The Cuda's engine bay is stuffed with a detailed model of the Plymouth's famous Hemi.

The Plymouth Superbird looked fast even while standing still and Bill's model captures the feel of the real thing.

Coulter's collection includes a 1972 Dodge Charger (foreground) and a 1971 Plymouth Road Runner (background).

He had discovered additional information that showed him ways to improve over his first effort.

Both '64 Plymouths were built from the Jo-Han GC-964 kit with scratchbuilding modifications. The first model was painted with Chrysler Equipment Blue lacquer from an aerosol can. The second car was painted with 1971-73 Plymouth Basin Street Blue acrylic enamel through an airbrush. The markings are a combination of Cady Design sheet number 631 and dry transfer lettering.

The 1965 Barracuda drag car in Coulter's collection was built for a show theme for an NNL (Nameless National Luminaries) gathering at Toledo, Ohio, some ten years ago. The

theme that year was "a day at the drags." Many friends, knowing he was partial to Petty race cars, figured he wouldn't have anything to bring to the show. To their surprise, a Petty drag car was on display for the show theme!

The 'Cuda was built from scrap box parts he accumulated over the years from '65 Barracuda kits and other models. The model shows no particular period but rather tries to capture the overall look from that "boycotted" season of drag racing.

The grille came from an AMT '65 Valiant Signet snap kit. The engine is from Jo-Han's 1968 Plymouth Fury Kit. Paint is again Basin Street Blue applied with an airbrush. The mark-

ings are from various Petty kit decal sheets and some lettering is hand-painted.

Coulter's Superbird, built during 1972, is based on pieces from the Jo-Han kit. The interior is from an AMT Chevelle. The roll cage was taken from an MPC Firebird kit. The chassis is heavily modified from the kit pieces with the addition of the entire front snout from an MPC early-'70s NASCAR stocker. The rear suspension is various scrapbox pieces utilizing the rear axle and leaf springs from an MPC 1970 Charger kit.

Basin Street Blue acrylic enamel paint is decorated with decals from the MPC Petty Plymouth kit number 1701. The 1/25 scale Richard Petty behind the wheel (with a wet shop cloth in his mouth) is heavily modified from an early 1960s Ulrich kit of a man in street clothes.

The 1971 Plymouth in Bill's collection is really his first attempt to build a Petty race car from a street-stock annual kit. He heavily gutted the stock interior and modified a roll cage from the Jo-Han '64 to fit in the car. Bill stripped the chassis of anything not essential to building a race car and filled in many areas of the chassis floor with sheet plastic and body filler.

This model was actually the first one in the collection painted with BSB acrylic enamel. The markings are a mixture of items from the Jo-Han '64

Bill's Dart "Kit Car" was used by AMT as a prototype for their kit of the same car.

with the Pepsi logos hand painted on clear decal film.

The Petty/STP Dodge Charger model shown here was built between the June and August NASCAR races at Michigan International Raceway in 1972. Actually there were two models built in that two month period; the first one was given to Richard Petty at the August race at MIS. Because no model kit manufacturer at the time produced an STP Charger kit, Coulter built the models using two MPC '71 Petty Plymouths for the running gear with body shells from two MPC '71 Baker Dodge kits.

Finding the markings for these two STP Chargers was tricky, especially the large STP logos. Fortunately, after a bit of investigation, Bill found a radio control race car manufacturer offering a 1/10 scale decal sheet with an array of large STP logos.

Because the fluorescent red used on the Petty race car is nearly impossible to capture on film, Bill only had his visual memory of the color to guide him. In trying to match the special red paint he used Testors Fluorescent Red over flat white. The final hue of the color was tinted slightly with a light coat of transparent red and then clear coated.

Richard Petty looked the model over thoroughly for a few moments after receiving it. He commented that it was the first of its kind he had

received. And then he blurted out something about how fast Bill got this thing done!

Coulter's 1972 Dart "Kit Car" is unique because he did not build the model from the AMT kit of the same description. The model was built at the request of AMT for the hobby industry trade show held in Chicago in 1975 in anticipation of the release of their kit.

He built the prototype model using parts from the MPC Bill Schrewsbury LA Dart wheel stander kit; the MPC Ramchargers Dart funny car kit; a 1971 MPC Duster chassis; and various scrap box parts for interior, engine, wheels, and tires. After the Chicago and New York hobby trade shows of 1975 AMT

asked if Bill would like the model returned for his Petty collection. Of course, they didn't have to ask twice. As Bill's collection shows, every model has a story of its own. That's what makes each collection unique.

When it comes to really large collections of built models of Richard Petty race cars, few compare to the amazing display created by Rick Sailer of Salt Lake City, Utah. Rick has managed to chronicle nearly every year of Petty's storied 33 years in racing with what can truly be described as a "labor of love."

Rick Sailer has never been to Level Cross, North Carolina, and he has never met Richard Petty, but Rick has always been a Petty fan nonetheless. Rick, an industrial designer of ultra-contemporary furniture, trained for his occupation at the Parsons School of Design in New York and Paris. He's worked on Madison Avenue, played guitar in a rock-and-roll band, and tried his hand at acting. But above all he's a dedicated model car builder.

Rick started to get serious about his Petty model collection just three years ago. (He already had a model of Petty's '64 Plymouth he'd built in the 1960s, so you could say his Petty collection consisted of one car for 30 years.) Since making the decision to build a Petty collection, Rick has added 24 more cars — all in just the last 36 months.

Rick Sailer's collection is a true passionate effort and contains detailed models of 25 of Richard's cars.

This Magnum is one of Rick's latest additions to his vast collection.

Often times a modeler will need to use something other than a race car kit to build the models he or she needs for their collections.

Some of the cars, such as the '62, '63 and '64, come from Jo-Han street-stock plastic kits. Other Petty models built by Rick started life as street-stock releases, such as the '71-'72 Plymouth Satellite from Monogram Models and the 1973 Dodge from an MPC kit.

Rick modified the 1959 Plymouth from an R and R Vacuum Craft hard-top resin body into a Plaza. The same is true of the 1961 Fury built from an All-American Models resin kit. Other Sailer models in resin include the '65 R&R Plymouth, '77 Chevy Monte Carlo and '78 Dodge Magnum, as well as the 1986 Pontiac Grand Prix 2+2 from Mad Dog Models.

The 1960 Petty Plymouth is the only one in Rick's collection fashioned from an original acetate dealer promotional model. His STP/Petty Caprice came from the rare Ertl kit, which featured a cast-metal body.

There are a couple of unusual pieces in Sailer's Petty collection. The model built to commemorate Richard's final ride and the Fan Appreciation Tour is the battle damaged version in which Petty finished the last laps at Atlanta in 1992.

Another unusual piece is the original '66-'67 Plymouth, which Rick crafted from cardboard and wood filler. The model has since been replaced in the collection with a new version built from the recently released Revell '67 GTX kit.

The newest addition to the Sailer Petty Collection is a handsome rendition of Richard's first race car, the hand-me-down 1957 Oldsmobile convertible. This model is built from a

fine resin kit manufactured by Ric Petty's SouthernScale Replicas. (Believe it or not, Ric Petty says he's not a relative of the slightly more famous Petty family.)

Rick Sailer utilizes most of the kit or aftermarket decals to build his Petty models. Sometimes, though, he does resort to creating markings by hand. Recently he was in desperate need of Air Lift shock absorber decals and couldn't find any. Undaunted, Rick drew the shapes by hand and lettered them with dry transfer. Once he reduced the artwork to the size needed, Rick painted the color areas, cut out the new markings, and glued them to the race car model. Likewise, the Forward Look markings on the hood of the '60 and '61 Plymouths are handmade. The varying sizes of letters forming the word "Plymouth" were painstakingly hand-cut from a sheet of adhe-

sive-backed "Form-a-line" film. Each piece was then meticulously positioned to form the letters.

Rick Sailer readily points out that his collection contains only 25 built models. According to Rick, "A Petty model collection is never done. And anyway, what fun would a collection be if it was totally finished?" Fortunately, Rick Sailer is busy at work as you read these words, adding another Petty model to his collection.

Collecting Richard Petty models is one thing, but putting a part of yourself into every piece in your collection sets the model car builder apart from the crowd. Remember one important point: to create a Petty model collection you can be moderately skilled or even a novice. You don't have to be a professional model builder to have a notable display. But above all, remember to have fun. Enjoyment is what all this time and effort is all about.

Where to get the good stuff

Petty Kit Summary

"My luck was good in 1964 — everywhere. We built a big, new brick house over near Daddy's. After (the kids) were tucked away (at night), I built model cars. Can you imagine that? I built big cars all day, and little ones at night. But it was relaxing for me."

Richard Petty from **King Richard I**

Virtually every major American model car kit manufacturer at one time or another produced something bearing that most famous of race car numbers — 43!

Most of the Petty models that once were found from drug emporiums to hobby shops are now out of production. Manufacturers such as the original AMT (Aluminum Model Toys) and MPC (Model Products Corporation), Jo-Han Models (now the property of Seville, Inc.), Ertl Company (current owners of AMT and MPC tooling), and most recently Monogram Models, Inc., have tried their hands at replicating a multitude of Petty model kits.

Case-hardened steel tooling for injection-molded plastic kits costs anywhere from $150,000 to $250,000. A manufacturer that makes the commitment to produce a particular model kit expects to sell hundreds of thousands of units — generally the case with any plastic kit bearing the name of Richard Petty. Though many of the following kits are out of production, some were produced for many years and in considerable quantities.

Presented next is a listing of plastic kits in various scales, a comment or two about the kit, and its current status.

PLASTIC KITS

Jo-Han 1964 Plymouth Sport Fury 1/25 scale No. C-164

This kit is what is commonly referred to as an "annual." Annual kits, as the name implies, represent the yearly body-style changes that occur on new cars. These kits, understandably, are (and were) issued just once each model year.

This item represents an era when manufacturers loaded the kit box with an array of building options. Though this kit is not a dedicated Petty model, it does contain decals, roll cage, racing seat, dashboard and steering wheel, racing wheels and tires, and racing equipment for the engine and drivetrain. This kit is out of production.

Jo-Han 1964 Petty Plymouth 1/25 scale No. GC 964

Jo-Han Models revamped its '64 Plymouth Sport Fury annual molds to produce this version, which was first released in the late 1960s in a flat box that featured the option of building either a Petty racer or a Golden Commandos funny car. Later the funny-car option was deleted from the kit in favor of the Petty version. This later version was re-released numer-

ous times in various colors of plastic, including one called "Petty Blue." This kit is currently out of production.

Jo-Han 1965 Plymouth Fury III 1/25 scale No. C 1565

Just like the previous model kit No. C-164, this kit is also an annual. The available Petty option for this kit is more fiction than fact: Richard Petty never drove a '65 Fury in NASCAR competition. The kit manufacturer was in a quandary at the time. First, Plymouth had just reintroduced a full-size car line, the 1965 Fury. Of course Richard Petty was driving the intermediate-size car, the Belvedere. Second, Richard Petty was sitting out the 1965 NASCAR Grand National season because of the hemi engine controversy. Third, the only engine option in this kit is the hemi in question. Yes, you can build a Petty model

from this kit, but what would be the point? This kit is out of production.

Jo-Han 1969 Road Runner 1/25 scale No. GC2200

The original-issue kit was primarily an annual street-stock kit that contained parts and decals to build a No. 43 version. Richard Petty didn't decide to race Fords in 1969 until late in 1968. Jo-Han Models, with no time to make the change, therefore offered a model of a car Petty never raced. This kit is currently out of production.

Jo-Han 1970 Superbird 1/25 scale No. GC1470/1970

This kit, like the '69 Road Runner, was originally an annual release with optional parts to build a Petty race car. This kit was also re-released many times with some molded in a color called "Petty Blue." This kit is currently out of production.

MPC 1972 Road Runner oval track race car 1/25 scale No. 1701

This kit was the first issue of a new NASCAR series by MPC in 1972. It was a dedicated race car model kit with no street-stock parts. The unique feature of this kit was its adjustable wheelbase chassis. The concept was used as the basis for many other MPC

NASCAR kits, including other Petty race cars. In 1995 Ertl announced the reissue of this much-sought-after kit, only to find there wasn't enough of the tooling intact to produce it. This kit is out of production.

AMT 1972 Dodge Dart short track racer 1/25 scale No. T229

This kit, released by AMT about 1975, was part of a series of three Mopar short-track stock car kits. This model depicts the version of the Chrysler Kit Car, which was built to NASCAR late-model sportsman specifications. The other versions of this model kit are of the short-track variation. This is the only kit produced of a Petty late-model short-track car. For the most part the tooling for this kit still exists. This kit is out of production.

AMT 1972 Dart and Petty race car hauler 1/25 scale No. T569

This Petty race-team model kit included the previously mentioned Dodge Dart, to which a Ford truck was added to haul the race car. Because the Pettys were heavily aligned with Chrysler at the time, they did not want a kit produced that featured a competitor's make of vehicle. This kit was canceled shortly after production was begun. Production

figures on this kit are sketchy at best. There may have been as few as 20,000 or as many as 60,000 issued. A rare kit, it is out of production.

MPC 1973 Charger oval track race car 1/25 scale No.1708

This kit used the chassis and running gear from the Petty Road Runner but featured a 1973 Charger body shell, reflecting Richard's change to that make in the middle of the 1972 season. This out of production kit has suffered the same fate as the '72 Plymouth Road Runner.

MPC 1974 Charger oval track race car 1/16 scale No. 3053

This kit, without a doubt the most technically accurate stock car model ever produced, features a clear plastic body shell. Just reading the instruction booklet will help you better understand how full-size Mopar race cars were built at the time. With the interest in "The Dukes of Hazard" TV

show, the original tooling was modified to produce a new kit that featured a 1969 Charger 500 body shell. This kit is out of production.

MPC 1974 Charger oval track race car 1/25 scale No. 1713

This kit, an update to the '74 Charger kit, was released in early 1977. It featured a huge one-piece decal section for the STP red portion of the two-tone paint scheme. Because it was manufactured from part of the original tooling used in the '72 Petty Plymouth and '73 Petty Dodge, reissuing this kit is probably not possible. This kit is out of production.

Ertl 1980 Caprice 1/25 scale No.8105

This kit featured a cast-metal body shell and hood with the remaining parts of the kit injection molded in polystyrene plastic. The decals were not the usual water-slide type but the peel-off-and-stick-on type. This kit, obviously aimed at the less-skilled modeler, will today probably interest only the serious collector. This kit is out of production.

Monogram 1984 Pontiac 1/24 scale No. 2722

This kit, molded in "Petty Blue" styrene plastic, is similar to Richard's 200th victory car. Using this kit and

Slixx Decals sheet No. 1984-43, you can build a faithful reproduction of that famous race car. This kit was molded in a color of plastic called "Petty Blue." The full-size original Petty Pontiac is on permanent display in the Smithsonian in Washington, D.C. The original kit is out of production.

AMT/Ertl 1984 Pontiac 1/25 scale No. 8044

This simplified model was originally produced as a snap kit. The finished model has an acceptable appearance but the kit lacks the attention to detail and sophistication of the Monogram product. For example, the kit had no opening hood, and consequently there is no engine. This kit, molded in a color of plastic called "Petty Blue," is out of production.

AMT/Ertl 1985 Pontiac 1/16 scale No. 6741

These Ertl-produced large scale stock car kits were the first such attempt since MPC's Petty Charger model kits. There were two Thunderbirds and two Pontiacs in the series. Of course the Pontiacs were Kyle's and Richard's Grand Prix. The models were not up to the standards of the earlier MPC effort. This kit is out of production.

AMT/Ertl 1990 Pontiac 1/25 scale No.6728

This was the first of a new series of 1/25 scale plastic kits produced by Ertl in 1990 to compete directly with Monogram's stock car model kits. This kit, molded in gray styrene, had excellent detail and featured an opening truck. This kit is out of production.

AMT/Ertl 1991 Pontiac 1/32 scale No.8709

This is a simplified version of the larger 1/25 scale AMT/Ertl Pontiac kit. No glue is required for assembly because this is a snap-type kit. Thankfully, the decals are of the water-slide variety.

Monogram Models The Racing Pettys Combo 1/24 scale No. 6389

This is a 1995 release from Monogram Models. The kit will build either Kyle's or Richard's '81 STP Buick and the No. 42 and No. 43 STP Pontiacs the Pettys raced as teammates in 1982. The Buick Regal and Pontiac Grand Prix, which come from existing tooling, are molded in a color of plastic called "Petty Blue."

RESIN KITS

The following listing covers the abundant Petty model kits produced in 1/43 scale. Unlike injection-molded plastic kits, resin kits are available for a short time and in drastically smaller quantities. The tooling for a resin kit probably costs less than $10,000. The manufacturer will generally make no more than 300 to 500 examples before stopping production and moving on to another subject. Most of the kits below are cast in resin, an epoxy mate rial that works much like plastic. Any exceptions to that material are noted.

Starter 1964 Petty Plymouth 1/43 scale No. Ply007

This simplified kit builds a reasonable likeness of Richard Petty's '64 car, but it is not an exact replica of the Daytona winner. This kit is out of production.

Starter 1966-67 Plymouth 1/43 scale No. Ply008

Richard Petty won the Daytona 500 for the second time in 1966. He won the NASCAR championship for the second time in 1967. This resin kit is the only model of those race cars. This kit is out of production.

Starter 1969 Talladega 1/43 scale No. For026

This resin kit is the only dedicated model of the car Petty drove through most of the 1969 season, when he was with Ford. The model is of the Talladega. It will not create the standard Torino used to win Riverside that year. This kit is out of production.

Starter 1970 Superbird 1/43 scale No. Ply003

This kit creates an excellent representation of the Petty "winged warrior" from the 1970 NASCAR Grand National season. This kit is out of production.

Starter 1971 Plymouth 1/43 scale No. Ply009

This small-scale kit builds the car Richard Petty drove to victory in the '71 Daytona 500. This is also the Plymouth Richard drove to the 1971 NASCAR Championship. This kit is out of production.

Starter 1972 STP Plymouth 1/43 scale No. Ply010

This is a resin kit of the first Petty Plymouth to carry the now-familiar two-tone paint scheme of STP red and Petty blue. This kit is out of production.

Starter 1974-75 Charger 1/43 scale No. Dod006

This Starter model is an excellent kit of Petty's championship car from 1974 and 1975. This kit is out of production.

John Day 1975 Petty/STP Charger (no kit number) oval track race car 1/43 scale

This kit, cast in white metal, was one of the first American stockers manufactured by a European kit maker. Considered crude by today's production standards, it can still be built into a handsomely finished model. This kit is out of production.

Starter 1977 Chevy Monte Carlo 1/43 scale No. Che039

Here Starter has produced an excellent representation of the first Chevrolet Richard Petty drove in Grand National competition. This kit is out of production.

Starter 1977 Oldsmobile Cutlass 1/43 scale No. Old003

Another excellent model of a Petty winner, this one is of the car used to record the 1979 Daytona 500 victory. This kit is out of production.

Starter 1978 Magnum 1/43 scale No. Dod009

The last Mopar race car Petty drove before going to a Chevy Monte Carlo in 1978 was the Dodge Magnum. He didn't have the same success he enjoyed in his faithful Chargers. This resin kit is still available.

Starter 1981 Buick Regal 1/43 scale No. Bui005

For a long time this was the only dedicated model kit of Petty's 1981 Daytona 500-winning race car. This kit is out of production.

Starter 1985 Pontiac 1/43 scale No. Pon008

This kit was the French manufacturer's first offering of a Petty race car. The primary parts are cast in resin with some photo-etched pieces, rubber tires, and excellent multi-color decals. This is out of production.

Starter 1986 Pontiac 2+2 1/43 scale No. Pon009

This kit represents Pontiac's version of the Chevy Monte Carlo aero coupe. The pointed nose and bubble-style rear window set it apart from the standard Grand Prix. It is the only model of this unique Petty race car. This kit is out of production.

Starter 1989 Pontiac 1/43 scale Pon006

This resin kit from Starter is the same style as the two previously listed models as respects the resin body and base plate, rubber tires, etc. This kit is still available.

Starter 1993 Pontiac 1/43 scale Pon007 (the No. 44 car)

The number 43 was retired for the 1993 season. Rick Wilson drove the car for Richard Petty after his retirement and used the number 44. This kit is out of production.

Starter 1994 Pontiac 1/43 scale Pon010 (the new 43 car)

Again Starter hardly missed a beat by quickly updating the '93 kit to produce the car as it appeared with Wally Dallenbach ,Jr., and John Andretti. They shared the driving duties in the 1994 Petty Pontiac, now sporting the famous number 43.

DIECAST MODELS

The availability of diecast race car miniatures in the past five years has exploded. The quality, attention to detail, and price ranges from less than a dollar to more than $100. No attempt is made here to try listing everything. What are listed next are some of the more interesting Petty models.

Franklin Mint 1977 Petty/STP Oldsmobile 1/24 scale 1979

This is a model of the type of car Petty drove to victory in the Daytona 500 and in which he won his seventh championship. The model remains a steady seller for the Franklin Mint. Though the model does suffer from some shortcomings, it is a handsome replica and a welcome addition to any Petty model collection.

Franklin Mint 1970 Superbird 1/24 scale

This diecast Petty Superbird was recently released by the Franklin Mint. As raced, the car had the wheels painted dark blue instead of chrome plated. The front spoiler mounted below the long tapered nose was omitted during production. But all things considered, this is probably the best Petty race car yet from Franklin Mint.

Ertl 1992 Pontiac 1/18 scale No.7461

This model, one of the first large scale diecast race cars produced by Ertl, remained one of the most popular. Currently out of production.

Ertl 1980 Caprice 1/64 scale No. 1679

The only small-scale model of a Petty Caprice. It is out of production, somewhat rare, and prices tend to be high.

Ertl Stock Car Set 1/64 scale No. 1941-241H

The four-car set includes Petty's 1981 Buick. The Petty Buick was also sold separately in its own blister pack.

Racing Collectibles 1992 Pontiac 1/64 No.649203051

Nicely done replica with excellent details, though the body colors may be off a bit.

Racing Champions Petty Fan Appreciation Tour '92 Pontiac No. 61992 RPT-1

There are 29 cars in this series, representing each race on the 1992 schedule. The Daytona and Atlanta models (first and last race of the season) are more sought-after by collectors.

Racing Champions 1970 Superbird 1/64 scale No. 01156A Second version of this model, imprinted "Southern Plymouth" on quarter panels, is highly sought after by collectors. Racing Champions may have produced over 750,000 of these models.

Racing Champions 1970 Superbird 1/43 scale No. 07070

The body shell on this model is molded in blue plastic. The numerals are made with a process called "Tampo printing." The contingency sponsor decals on the front fenders are "stick-ons."

Racing Champions 1991 Pontiac 1/43 scale No. 07050

The body is molded in blue and the striping is painted on using a template. The numerals are Tampo printed, while the other markings are "stick-ons."

Road Champs "Pullback" Pontiac 1/43 scale No. 3020

The "pullback" models differ from the standard models because they contain a spring-loaded mechanism attached to the rear wheels. When the model is placed on a hard surface and pulled back, the mechanism is engaged; when released, the car moves forward rapidly.

Road Champs 1992 Pontiac 1/43 scale No. 30251

The body shell is painted Petty blue and the graphics are Tampo printed. There is only a partial interior plate and the windows are "blacked-out."

Road Champs Transport 1/43 scale No. 3015

There are numerous transporters in a variety of scales. Probably the most expensive is the first Petty transporter produced by Winross valued at $250 to the early Matchbox item priced at $400.

Ertl 1981 Buick "Pullback" 1/43 scale No. 2882T

This diecast has the same mechanism as the Pontiac mentioned earlier. The unique thing about this model is that although it's a Buick, the paint scheme is from Petty's 1982 Pontiac!

SLOT CARS etc.

HO-scale slot cars have long been popular with people having limited space for a slot track layout. Racing cars have also been very popular subjects for slot cars made by Tyco. Likewise, miniature slot cars carrying the number 43 have by far been the most popular subject for slot car manufacturers. The following are just a few examples of Petty HO slot cars.

Tyco 1970 Plymouth Superbird

One of the first Petty race cars done up as a slot car. This model is still available.

Tyco 1974 Dodge Charger

Though its colors may not be exactly correct, it is still a nice replica.

Tyco 1977 Oldsmobile

One of the few replicas in any scale of the car that carried Petty to his sixth Daytona 500 victory and seventh championship.

Tyco 1981 Buick

Until recently this little gem was the only replica of Petty's winning car from the 1981 Daytona 500.

DECALS, DECALS, DECALS!

Many times one aftermarket item makes the difference between building a replica of your favorite Petty car and only dreaming about it. That one thing is a water-slide decal. Fortunately, over the years when there wasn't a complete kit available of one of Richard's racers, a decal sheet could be found, and with a plastic hobby kit for the right body, chassis, engine, wheels and tires, the model was built.

Listed next are some of the more commonly available water-slide decal sheets that have been popular with model builders. As noted some items are out of production.

Fred Cady Design
P.O. Box 576
Mount Prospect, Illinois 60056
No. 117 '70 Petty Enterprises, No.'s 40 and 41 (builds Pete Hamilton's Superbird)

No. 607 '88 Pontiac STP and Petty general sheet, No.'s 42 and 43 (two sheets)

No. 622 '69 Ford, East Tennesssee Ford, No. 43 (builds either short nose or Talladega Torino)

No. 631 '64 Plymouth Petty Enterprises, No. 41 and 43 (builds either Petty or Jr. Johnson's '64 Plymouths)

Unfortunately all of these fine decal sheets are out of production.

JNJ Hobbies
6512 Baum Drive, Suite 8
Knoxville, Tennessee 37919

No. 86-120 No. 42 and 43 only (numerical outlines printed in blue allows you to build a variety of contemporary Petty race cars)

No. 88-145 STP Ovals only (these ovals can be used on just about any Petty car starting with 1972)

No. 89-188 No. 43 East Tennessee Motors '69 Ford (builds either Petty's standard Torino or Talladega)

These three decal sheets should still be available.

SLIXX DECALS
13075 Springdale St., Suite 456
Westminister, California 92683

No. 9243-1001 Petty Fan Appreciation Tour (builds Petty's final year behind the wheel of a Pontiac)

No. 8443-1009 Petty's 200th Win, '84 Grand Prix (Use the Grand Prix from the Monogram Racing Petty kit to build this famous Petty race car.)

No. 9344-1011 STP Pontiac No. 44, Rick Wilson

No. 6743-1019 Petty's '67 Plymouth, 27 wins and 10 in a row (Build this famous Petty racer when you start with Revell's '67 Plymouth GTX kit.)

No. 9443-1020 STP Pontiac, Wally Dallenbach (You will need a Southern Scale resin body to build this '94 Petty race car.)

All these Petty decals are currently available.

As you can see, it take very little imagination to mix and match to build a number of other Petty race cars using many of these decals listed. With the continued popularity of Richard Petty, don't be too surprised to see many more number 43 decal sheets produced in the future.